GROWING UP IN NEW GUINEA

>>>>>>>>>>>>>>> <<<<<<<<<<<<<<<

A Comparative Study of
Primitive Education

By

MARGARET MEAD

With a New Preface by the Author
for the 1975 Edition

MORROW QUILL PAPERBACKS
NEW YORK

TO REO FORTUNE

PREFACE FOR THE 1975 EDITION

This was my second book, and the first anthropological study of young children's growth in a primitive society. In Samoa, where I had studied adolescent girls, I found that I needed to study pre-adolescents in order to understand adolescents. So I decided to push my studies still further down to include small children also, as they grew to manhood and womanhood in a primitive South Sea society. This was my first experience of a preliterate society where no one could read or write and active warfare had stopped only a decade before. It was also the first field work that Reo Fortune and I did together. We were married just before going to Manus. He was astonished to find how much more open and frank the Manus were compared to the Dobuans he had studied; I was astonished that they were so much more energetic and materialistic than the Samoans.

The lagoon-dwelling people welcomed us as possible participants in their economic life who would save them the trouble of long canoe voyages in search of the newly introduced European goods. We learned to understand the details of their lives because anthropological training had equipped us to do so—to learn a primitive language rapidly, to take the stream of events which passed before our eyes and structure it in an understandable way. But the experience of the people we were studying was too far from our own for them to understand us or what we were trying to do. We came away with notebooks filled, a pile of photographs, vivid memories of a life lived in twenty-four-hour contact with the inhabitants of the noisy fishing village in the midst of which our house stood. When we left they beat the death gong rhythm, for they did not expect ever to see us again.

I wrote this book while I was preparing for another trip to New Guinea, hopeful that in the future I would receive some news of the people, especially the children whom I had known so well. Occasionally a ship would touch Manus, and some passenger would write me a note. But it seemed to be a finished episode. I had caught the people at a moment in time, after warfare had vanished, before the missions had reached them, and I knew that before long the winds of change, blowing inexorably from the west, would change their lives forever. Meanwhile, here they are, just as I knew them, and as I wrote about them, fixed within the pages of a book, as paintings of earlier ages are fixed in frescoes in Crete or paintings on Grecian vases—timeless and part of our human experience.

A book like this has to be understood in the context of the period in which it was written, what the author had learned and hoped to learn, as well as the position of the people who were studied in the process of changing from a primitive people to members of the modern world. In the late 1920s we did not have any of the methods that we have today for preserving records of human behavior. We had no tapes, no films, no video, no projective tests. I had no models, although there were two delightful accounts written by amateurs of American Indian and African child life. But I did have a lot of questions.

My questions centered around two themes: if, as Freud, Piaget and Levy Bruhl maintained, adult savages (as we called primitive peoples then) were like civilized children, what were primitive children like? This sounds like an obvious question, but no one had asked it. There was an assumption that somehow primitives—child and adult—could be thought of together, while for our own children, the most meticulous attempts to trace their psycho-social development were in order. So I set out to find out what a set of primitive children were like; how did they learn to be adults; was their thinking the same as that of all children everywhere, as psychologists were postulating—animistic, filled with beliefs in magic and mythical beings, unreceptive to reality?

The second problem in which I was already interested, but which I didn't realize would become a focus of my research, was whether societies could be changed by changing the way children were brought up. In the 1920s the findings of psychoanalysis and the utopian hopes of a better society met in ideas of progressive education whereby children were to go to schools where learning would be a pleasure instead of an onerous burden; where cooperation was to be substituted for competition; marks would be eliminated and children would meet their adult teachers in free and easy interchange. From such a change in type of schooling, preceded by greater permissiveness in the care of infants and young children, it was believed that we could produce societies which were less competitive, less exploitive, less given to war and oppression than our own.

World War I was still vivid in our minds, as was the way in which the United States had first promoted the dream of a more peaceful world through the League of Nations, and then betrayed that dream. It was a period of affluence and inflation on the one hand, and of withdrawal from economic and political concerns on the other. My generation, who had graduated from college within the previous ten years, was more concerned with individuals than with social movements, with the potentialities of the human spirit than with the organization of agriculture, the dangers of unemployment, the unwieldy nature of cities, or the consequences of mechanization. All this was to come just a few years later, as the Great Depression settled on the United States and its ramifications spread around the world.

But in 1928, when I set out for Manus, we were still talking about a car in every garage and a chicken in every pot. Meanwhile, as young anthropologists, as writers and artists (and there were only a very few of us who realized what was happening), we were deeply concerned with the wholesale destruction of the culture of the few surviving primitive societies. Our own hopes for a better world were intertwined, as they are today, with the belief that if children could be reared differently, part of our problem could be solved.

In many ways it was a period not unlike the early 1970s. An emphasis on the whole personality of the child, seen as an individual, contrasted with the *behaviorism* of the period— which would now be called *behavior modification*—under which children were submitted to strict regimes in which the physical expression of affection was severely rationed. There were arguments about the relative virtues of permissiveness —characterized by the story of the child who left a progressive school for a traditional one and proclaimed happily that in her new school: "If you want to be good you can, and if you don't want to fight, you don't have to." There were arguments then and now about how much the absence of the commuting father from the home deprived the children growing up in the suburbs. Then, as we are doing today, there were many arguments about a work ethic which stressed material possessions and material success at the expense of human relations and the arts. Then, as today, there were those who advocated a more permissive attitude toward the building of human character.

It was from an atmosphere of affluence, materialism and competition, characterized as the doctrine of "dog eat dog" or "any boy can be President," that I set out on the field trip of which this book is one record. A few weeks after we returned from Manus, in the autumn of 1929, the bank failures began and the stock market crashed. My father, an economist whose prophecies I trusted, warned: "Sister, you have just ten years to the next war!" My response was to make up my mind to spend as much of those ten years as possible in the Pacific, rescuing as much as I could of the priceless knowledge which was still preserved there. A world war then, while a terrible prospect, did not pose the threats that the beginning of World War II brought to humankind, and the possibility of total destruction of all living beings was still a poetic and science fiction nightmare. But the wave of modernization, coupled with the missionary zeal of Euro-American society, was sweeping fast over the world; it was possible that with the preoccupations of another war, and more widespread destruction in the Pacific, there would be nothing left.

So Reo Fortune and I worked as fast as possible. I was fortunate to have an appointment as Assistant Curator at The American Museum of Natural History, where writing up my research was expected as part of my regular duties. Reo Fortune had a fellowship at Columbia University. I worked on this book and he worked on his book on Manus religion during the day, and we read what we had written to one another in the evening. The complimentariness of our shared knowledge also kept a lively flow of information going back and forth during the day by telephone. His feeling that the way in which children were reared made very little difference to what they became in the end, since the society always won, was stronger than mine and accounts somewhat for the emphasis in this book. I did not yet have a clear idea of how the way in which children were reared shaped their characters and their expression of social institutions they shared with many other people, to which they gave a different twist, as the various immigrant groups who arrived in the United States shaped and altered the separate European traditions within which this country was colonized.

But I was already a trained observer. The observations contained in this book, set as they were in a much simpler and more incomplete theoretical understanding of what is today called the study of Culture and Personality, have stood up in the light of later research in Manus, in other parts of the world, and of developing theories. This is the way the Manus were in 1928–29. Neither they nor any other people in the world will ever be the same again. By living themselves and by welcoming—although without comprehending their goals—two white strangers, representatives of the penetrating groups of another race and a far different culture, the Manus people of Peri Village in 1928 contributed tremendously to our knowledge of human beings and thus to our knowledge of ourselves and later generations.

Today, in a far more dangerous world than that of 1929, and under the shadow of an impending new World War, we are facing a restatement of the problems that confronted us at the beginning of the Great Depression. We have the same advocates today of free untrammeled competition, the operation of the market system, the education of human beings to work incessantly and unceasingly all their lives for deferred rewards, under the lash of a strict and unforgiving conscience. And we also have today the controversy over whether we can change the nature of society by bringing children up differently. Will institutions like Headstart, located in the midst of urban slums, rescue the children from following the models of despairing deprivation which they see in the adults all around them, or is something more needed?

Today, as when I wrote this book, we are seeking ways to release the potentialities of children, to regain some of the easy communication with our own bodies which the Manus achieved for their own children with a creativity which neither we nor the Manus have known how to preserve. Today, as then, we are wondering about the relative virtues of puritanically driven acquisitiveness and a standard of living higher than the world has ever known for the fortunate in developed and developing countries, and a misery of unfulfilled expectations greater than the world has ever known for the billion and a half less fortunate.

While I was writing about the Manus, the now defunct

Saturday Evening Post asked me to write an article comparing the life of Manus adolescents and our own. I wrote an article discussing the way the Manus experience of a halcyon childhood, throughout which an expectation of unremitting effort in adult life was instilled, compared with the American childhood experience and with the American view of adolescence as the best time of life, only to be followed by a less rewarding adulthood. The article was not only refused, but refused indignantly as contrary to all our values!

We now know what we did not know then about the way children are reared. As infants in the home, and later within the educational system of the wider society, child-rearing methods expose them thoroughly to the culture of their society, so that they perforce assimilate the values of that society. Moreover, just how, when and by what means these values are inculcated makes a great deal of difference. Whether children will later accept the values of the society with vigorous approval, dull conformity, quiet desperation, despair or potential rebelliousness is closely related to how they are reared and how phases of freedom and restriction follow each other.

We know a great deal that we did not know then of how the swaddling of infants fits into the way Russian children first experience life and the way Russian parents later look upon children. We know how Japanese infancy, during which there is great expression of warmth and permissiveness toward aggression, is followed by strict and exacting school years, and how violent behavior can break through this discipline. We know how the association in the United States between mischief and rebellion against schools contrasts with the association of school discipline and political responsibility in the Soviet Union.

When this book was written, we did not know any of these matters, so crucial to any attempt to make real changes in any society, so significant in periods of rapid social change, so essential to our understanding of relationships among different nation states. But it is upon studies like this that we were able to build later studies which assumed significance during World War II and are assuming significance today. Because it is a record of a vanished way of life, because it provided one basis for later studies of cultural character, because the issues it raises are issues that are as alive today as they were then, I am glad that this new edition is being issued.

Since World War II, I have made six return trips to Manus, which has now entered the modern world.

MARGARET MEAD
The American Museum of Natural History,
New York
April, 1975

LIST OF REFERENCES

Fortune, R. F. (1935) *Manus Religion*. Lincoln: University of Nebraska Press, 1965.

Mead, Margaret. (1928) *Coming of Age in Samoa*. Morrow Paperback Editions, New York, N.Y.

————. (1964) *Continuities in Cultural Evolution*. New Haven: Yale University Press, 1968.

————. "Kinship in the Admiralty Islands," *Anthropological Papers of The American Museum of Natural History*, 34, Pt. 2 (1934), pp. 183–358.

————. *Margaret Mead's New Guinea Journal*. Produced by Craig Gilbert for National Educational Television. 90 minutes, 16 mm, sound, color. Distributed by National Educational Television Film Service, Indiana University Audio-Visual Center, Bloomington, Indiana, 1968.

————. *New Lives for Old*. New York: William Morrow and Company, 1956, 1966.

————. *New Lives for Old*. Horizons of Science Series, Vol. 1, No. 6. Educational Testing Service, Princeton, New Jersey. 20 minutes, 16 mm, sound, color. Distributed by Indiana University, Audio-Visual Center, Bloomington, Indiana, 1960.

Schwartz, Theodore. "The Paliau Movement in the Admiralty Islands, 1946–1954," *Anthropological Papers of The American Museum of Natural History*, 49, Pt. 2 (1962), pp. 207–422.

ACKNOWLEDGMENTS

I MADE this study as a fellow of the Social Science Research Council and I wish to acknowledge my great indebtedness to the generosity of the Board of Fellowships of that body. For the training which prepared me to undertake this inquiry I have to thank Professor Franz Boas and Dr. Ruth F. Benedict. I owe a debt of gratitude to Professor A. R. Radcliffe-Brown of the University of Sydney who most kindly sponsored my field trip with the Australian research and governmental interests and also gave me much advice and help.

I have to thank my husband, Reo Fortune, for assistance in the formulation of my problem, for long months of co-operative effort in the field, for much of the ethnographic and textual material which underlies this study and for patient criticism of my results.

I am indebted to the Department of Home and Territories of the Commonwealth of Australia and to the Administration of the Mandated Territory of New Guinea for furthering my research whenever possible; most particularly I have to thank His Honour Judge J. M. Phillips and Mr. E. P. W. Chinnery, Government Anthropologist. For hospitality and courteous assistance I would also thank Mr. J. Kramer and Mr. and Mrs. Burrows of Lorengau; Mr. F. W. Mantle and Mr. and Mrs. Frank MacDonnel, Mrs. C. P. Parkinson of Sumsum and Mr. and Mrs. James Twycross of Rabaul.

For the opportunity to work up my material I am indebted to the American Museum of Natural History, and for assistance in the long and laborious task of manuscript preparation and revision I have to thank Dr. Benedict, Miss Eichelberger, Mrs. Stapelfeldt and Miss Josephson.

CONTENTS

PART ONE
GROWING UP IN MANUS SOCIETY

PART TWO
REFLECTIONS ON THE EDUCATIONAL PROBLEMS OF TO-DAY IN THE LIGHT OF MANUS EXPERIENCE

CONTENTS

Appendices

PART ONE

GROWING UP IN MANUS SOCIETY

I

INTRODUCTION

THE way in which each human infant is transformed
into the finished adult, into the complicated individual
version of his city and his century is one of the most fascinating studies open to the curious minded. Whether
one wishes to trace the devious paths by which the un-
formed baby which was oneself developed personality,
to prophesy the future of some child still in pinafores,
to direct a school, or to philosophise about the future of
the United States—the same problem is continually in
the foreground of thought. How much of the child's
equipment does it bring with it at birth? How much
of its development follows regular laws? How much
or how little and in what ways is it dependent upon
early training, upon the personality of its parents, its
teachers, its playmates, the age into which it is born? Is
the framework of human nature so rigid that it will
break if submitted to too severe tests? To what limits
will it flexibly accommodate itself? Is it possible to re-
write the conflict between youth and age so that it is less
acute or more fertile of good results? Such questions
are implicit in almost every social decision—in the

mother's decision to feed the baby with a spoon rather than force it to drink from a hated bottle, in the appropriation of a million dollars to build a new manual training high school, in the propaganda plans of the Anti-Saloon League or of the Communist party. Yet it is a subject about which we know little, towards which we are just developing methods of approach.

But when human history took the turn which is symbolised in the story of the confusion of tongues and the dispersion of peoples after the Tower of Babel, the student of human nature was guaranteed one kind of laboratory. In all parts of the world, in the densest jungle and on the small islands of the sea, groups of people, differing in language and customs from their neighbours, were working out experiments in what could be done with human nature. The restless fancy of many men was drawing in diverse ways upon their historical backgrounds, inventing new tools, new forms of government, new and different phrasings of the problem of good and evil, new views of man's place in the universe. By one people the possibilities of rank with all its attendant artificialities and conventions were being tested, by a second the social consequences of large scale human sacrifice, while a third tested the results of a loose unpatterned democracy. While one people tried out the limits of ceremonial licentiousness, another exacted season-long or year-long continence from all its members. Where one people made their dead their gods, another chose to ignore the dead and rely instead upon a philosophy of life which viewed man as grass that grows up in the morning and is cut down forever at nightfall.

Within the generous lines laid down by the early patterns of thought and behaviour which seem to form our common human inheritance, countless generations of men have experimented with the possibilities of the human spirit. It only remained for those of inquiring mind, alive to the value of these hoary experiments, to read the answers written down in the ways of life of different peoples. Unfortunately we have been prodigal and blind in our use of these priceless records. We have permitted the only account of an experiment which it has taken thousands of years to make and which we are powerless to repeat, to be obliterated by fire-arms, or alcohol, evangelism or tuberculosis. One primitive people after another has vanished and left no trace.

If a long line of devoted biologists had been breed-ing guinea pigs or fruit flies for a hundred years and recording the results, and some careless vandal burnt the painstaking record and killed the survivors, we would cry out in anger at the loss to science. Yet, when history, without any such set purpose, has presented us with the results of not a hundred years' experiment on guinea pigs, but a thousand years' experiment on human beings, we permit the records to be extinguished with-out a protest.

Although most of these fragile cultures which owed their perpetuation not to written records but to the memories of a few hundred human beings are lost to us, a few remain. Isolated on small Pacific islands, in dense African jungles or Asiatic wastes, it is still pos-- sible to find untouched societies which have chosen so- lutions of life's problems different from our own, which can give us precious evidence on the malleability of human nature.

Such an untouched people are the brown sea-dwell- ing Manus of the Admiralty Islands, north of New Guinea.* In their vaulted, thatched houses set on stilts in the olive green waters of the wide lagoon, their lives are lived very much as they have been lived for un- known centuries. No missionary has come to teach them an unknown faith, no trader has torn their lands from them and reduced them to penury. Those white men's diseases which have reached them have been few enough in number to be fitted into their own theory of disease as a punishment for evil done. They buy iron and cloth and beads from the distant traders; they' have learned to smoke the white man's tobacco, to use his money, to take an occasional dispute into the Dis- trict Officer's Court. Since 1912 war has been prac- tically abolished, an enforced reformation welcome to a trading, voyaging people. Their young men go away to work for two or three years in the plantations of the white man, but come back little changed to their own villages. It is essentially a primitive society without written records, without economic dependence upon white culture, preserving its own canons, its own way of life.

* See Appendix II, "Ethnographic Notes on the Manus Tribe."

INTRODUCTION

The manner in which human babies born into these water-dwelling communities, gradually absorb the traditions, the prohibitions, the values of their elders and become in turn the active perpetuators of Manus culture is a record rich in its implications for education. Our own society is so complex, so elaborate, that the most serious student can, at best, only hope to examine a part of the educational process. While he concentrates upon the method in which a child solves one set of problems, he must of necessity neglect the others. But in a simple society, without division of labour, without written records, without a large population, the whole tradition is narrowed down to the memory capacities of a few individuals. With the aid of writing and an analytic point of view, it is possible for the investigator to master in a few months most of the tradition which it takes the native years to learn.

From this vantage point of a thorough knowledge of the cultural background, it is then possible to study the educational process, to suggest solutions to educational problems which we would never be willing to study by experimentation upon our own children. But Manus has made the experiment for us; we have only to read the answer.

I made this study of Manus education to prove no thesis, to support no preconceived theories. Many of the results came as a surprise to me.* This description of the way a simple people, dwelling in the shallow

* See Appendix I, "The Ethnological Approach to Social Psychology."

[5]

lagoons of a distant south sea island, prepare their children for life, is presented to the reader as a picture of human education in miniature. Its relevance to modern educational interest is first just that it is such a simplified record in which all the elements can be readily grasped and understood, where a complex process which we are accustomed to think of as written upon too large a canvas to be taken in at a glance, can be seen as through a painter's diminishing glass. Furthermore in Manus certain tendencies in discipline or accorded license, certain parental attitudes, can be seen carried to more drastic lengths than has yet occurred within our own society. And finally these Manus people are interesting to us because the aims and methods of Manus society, although primitive, are not unlike the aims and methods which may be found in our own immediate history.

We shall see how remarkably successful the Manus people are in instilling into the smallest child a respect for property; how equally remarkable is the physical adjustment which very young children are taught to make. The firm discipline combined with the unflagging solicitude which lie back of these two conspicuous Manus triumphs, contradict equally the theory that a child should be protected and sheltered and the theory that he should be thrown into the waters of experience to "sink or swim." The Manus world, slight frameworks of narrow boards above the changing tides of the lagoon, is too precarious a place for costly mistakes. The successful fashion in which each baby is efficiently adapted to its dangerous way of life is relevant to the problems which parents here must face as our mode of life becomes increasingly charged with possibilities of accident.

Perhaps equally illuminating are the Manus mistakes, for their efficiency in training dexterous little athletes and imbuing them with a thorough respect for property is counterbalanced by their failure in other forms of discipline. The children are allowed to give their emotions free play; they are taught to bridle neither their tongues nor their tempers. They are taught no respect for their parents; they are given no pride in their tradition. The absence of any training which fits them to accept graciously the burden of their tradition, to assume proudly the rôle of adults, is conspicuous. They are permitted to frolic in their ideal playground without responsibilities and without according either thanks or honour to those whose unremitting labour makes their long years of play possible.

Those who believe that all children are naturally creative, inherently imaginative, that they need only be given freedom to evolve rich and charming ways of life for themselves, will find in the behaviour of Manus children no confirmation of their faith. Here are all the children of a community, freed from all labour, given only the most rudimentary schooling by a society which concerns itself only with physical proficiency, respect for property and the observance of a few tabus. They are healthy children; a fifty per cer infant death rate accomplishes that. Only the mos' survive. They are intelligent children; there are only three or four dull children among them. They have perfect bodily co-ordination; their senses are sharp, their perceptions are quick and accurate. The parent and child relationship is such that feelings of inferiority and insecurity hardly exist. And this group of children are allowed to play all day long, but, alas for the theorists, their play is like that of young puppies or kittens. Unaided by the rich hints for play which children of other societies take from the admired adult traditions, they have a dull, uninteresting child life, romping good humouredly until they are tired, then lying inert and breathless until rested sufficiently to romp again.

The family picture in Manus is also strange and revealing, with the father taking the principal rôle, the father the tender solicitous indulgent guardian, while the mother takes second place in the child's affection. Accustomed as we are to the family in which the father is the stern and distant dictator, the mother the child's advocate and protector, it is provocative to find a society in which father and mother have exchanged parts. The psychiatrists have laboured the difficulties under which a male child grows up if his father plays patriarch and his mother madonna. Manus illustrates the creative part which a loving tender father may play in shaping positively his son's personality. It suggests that the solution of the family complex may lie not in the parents assuming no rôles, as some enthusiasts suggest, but 'n their playing different ones.

INTRODUCTION

Besides these special points in Manus educational practice, there is also a curious analogy between Manus society and America. Like America, Manus has not yet turned from the primary business of making a living to the less immediate interest of the conduct of life as an art. As in America, work is respected and industry and economic success is the measure of the man. The dreamer who turns aside from fishing and trading and so makes a poor showing at the next feast, is despised as a weakling. Artists they have none, but like Americans, they, richer than their neighbours, buy their neighbours' handiwork. To the arts of leisure, conversation, story telling, music and dancing, friendship and love making, they give scant recognition. Conversation is purposeful, story telling is abbreviated and very slightly stylised, singing is for moments of boredom, dancing is to celebrate financial arrangements, friendship is for trade, and love making, in any elaborate sense, is practically unknown. The ideal Manus man has no leisure; he is ever up and about his business turning five strings of shell money into ten.

With this emphasis upon work, upon the accumulation of more and more property, the cementing of firmer trade alliances, the building of bigger canoes and bigger houses, goes a congruent attitude towards morality. As they admire industry, so do they esteem probity in business dealings. Their hatred of debt, their uneasiness beneath undischarged economic obligations is painful. Diplomacy and tact are but slightly valued; obstreperous truthfulness is the greater virtue.

[9]

The double standard permitted very cruel prostitution in earlier days; the most rigorous demands are still made upon the virtue of Manus women. Finally their religion is genuinely ethical; it is a spiritualistic cult of the recently dead ancestors who supervise jealously their descendants' economic and sexual lives, blessing those who abstain from sin and who labour to grow wealthy, visiting sickness and misfortune on violators of the sexual code and on those who neglect to invest the family capital wisely. In many ways, the Manus ideal is very similar to our historical Puritan ideal, demanding from men industry, prudence, thrift and abstinence from worldly pleasures, with the promise that God will prosper the virtuous man.

In this stern workaday world of the adult, the children are not asked to play any part. Instead they are given years of unhampered freedom by parents whom they often bully and despise for their munificence. We often present our children with this same picture. We who live in a society where it is the children who wear the silk while the mothers labour in calico, may find something of interest in the development of these primitive young people in a world that is so often like a weird caricature of our own, a world whose currency is shells and dogs' teeth, which makes its investments in marriages instead of corporations and conducts its overseas trade in outrigger canoes, but where property, morality and security for the next generation are the main concerns of its inhabitants.

This account is the result of six months' concentrated

and uninterrupted field work. From a thatched house
on piles, built in the centre of the Manus village of
Peri, I learned the native language, the children's
games, the intricacies of social organisation, economic
custom and religious belief and practice which formed
the social framework within which the child grows up.
In my large living room, on the wide verandahs, on the
tiny islet adjoining the houses, in the surrounding
lagoon, the children played all day and I watched them,
now from the midst of a play group, now from behind
the concealment of the thatched walls. I rode in their
canoes, attended their feasts, watched in the house of
mourning and sat severely still while the mediums con-
versed with the spirits of the dead. I observed the
children when no grown-up people were present, and
I watched their behaviour towards their parents.
Within a social setting which I learned to know inti-
mately enough not to offend against the hundreds of
name tabus, I watched the Manus baby, the Manus
child, the Manus adolescent, in an attempt to understand the way in which each of these was becoming a
Manus adult.

II

I

TO the Manus native the world is a great platter, curving upwards on all sides, from his flat lagoon village where the pile houses stand like long-legged birds, placid and unstirred by the changing tides. One long edge of the platter is the mainland, rising from its fringe of mangrove swamps in fold after fold of steep, red clay. The mainland is approached across a half mile of lagoon, where the canoe leaves a path in the thicket of scum-coated sea growth, and is entered by slowly climbing the narrow tortuous beds of the small rivers which wind stagnant courses through the dark forbidding swamps. On the mainland live the Usiai, the men of the bush, whom the Manus people meet daily at set hours near the river mouths. Here the Manus fishermen, the landless rulers of the lagoons and reefs, bargain with the Usiai for taro, sago, yams, wood for housebuilding, betel nut for refreshments, logs for the hulls of their great outrigger canoes,—buying with their fish all the other necessities of life from the timid, spindly-legged bush people. Here also the people of Peri come to work the few sago patches which they long ago traded or stole from the Usiai; here the children come for a fresh water swim, and the women to gather firewood and draw water. The swamps are infested with sulky Usiai, hostile demons and fresh water monsters. Because of them the Manus dislike both the rivers and the land and take pains never to look into the still waters lest part of their soul stuff remain there.

At the other edge of the platter is the reef, beyond which lies the open sea and the islands of their own archipelago, where they sail to trade for cocoanuts, oil, carved wooden bowls and carved bedsteads. Beyond, still higher up the sea wall, lies Rabaul, the capital of the white man's government of the Territory of New Guinea, and far up on the rim of the world lies Sydney, the farthest point of their knowledge. Stretching away to right and left along the base of the platter lie other villages of the Manus people, standing in serried ranks in brown lagoons, and far away at each end of the platter lies the gentle slope of the high sea wall which canoes must climb if they would sail upon it.

Around the stout house piles, the tides run, now baring the floor of the lagoon until part of the village is left high and dry in the mud, now swelling with a soft insistence nearly to the floor slats of the houses. Here and there, around the village borders, are small abrupt islands, without level land, and unfit for cultivation. Here the women spread out leaves to dry for weaving, the children scramble precariously from rock to rock. Bleaching on the farther islands lie the white bones of the dead.

This small world of water dwellings, where men who

are of one kin build their houses side by side, and scat-
ter sago on the edge of the little island which they have
inherited from their fathers, shelters not only the living
but also the spirits of the dead. These live protected
from the inclemency of wind and rain beneath the house
thatch. Disowned by their descendants, they flutter
restlessly about the borders of the small islets of coral
rubble which stand in the centre of the village and
do duty as village greens, places of meeting and
festivity.

Within the village bounds, the children play. At low
tide they range in straggling groups about the shallows,
spearing minnows or pelting each other with seaweed.
When the water rises the smaller ones are driven up
upon the little islets or into the houses, but the taller
still wade about sailing toy boats, until the rising tide
drives them into their small canoes to race gaily upon
the surface of the water. Within the village the sharks
of the open sea do not venture, nor are the children in
danger from the crocodiles of the mainland. The paint
with which their fathers decorate their faces for a voyage into the open seas as a protection against malicious
spirits is not needed here. Naked, except for belts or
armlets of beads or necklaces of dogs' teeth, they play
all day at fishing, swimming, boating, mastering the arts
upon which their landless fathers have built their secure
position as the dominant people of the archipelago.
Up the sides of the universe lie dangers, but here in the
watery bottom, the children play, safe beneath the eyes
of their spirit ancestors.

[14]

II

In the centre of a long house are gathered a group of women. Two of them are cooking sago and cocoanut in shallow broken pieces of earthenware pottery, another is making beadwork. One old woman, a widow by her rope belt and black rubber-like breast bands, is shredding leaves and plaiting them into new grass skirts to add to those which hang in a long row from above her head. The thatched roof is black from the thick wood smoke, rising incessantly from the fires which are never allowed to go out. On swinging shelves over the fires, fish are smoking. A month-old baby lies on a leaf mat, several other small children play about, now nursing at their mothers' breasts, now crawling away, now returning to cry for more milk. It is dark and hot in the house. The only breath of air comes up through the slats in the floor and from trap door entrances at the far ends of the house. The women have laid aside their long drab cotton cloaks, which they must always wear in public to hide their faces from their male relatives-in-law. Beads of sweat glisten on their shiny shaven heads, sign of the wedded estate. Their grass skirts, which are only two tails worn one before and one behind, leaving the thighs bare, are wilted and work-bedraggled.

One woman starts to gather up her beads: "Come, Alupwa," she says to her three-year-old daughter.

"I don't want to." The fat little girl wriggles and pouts.

[15]

"Yes, come, I must go home now. I have stayed here long enough making bead-work. Come."

"I don't want to."

"Yes, come, father will be home from market and hungry after fishing all night."

"I won't." Alupwa purses her lips into ugly defiance.

"But come daughter of mine, we must go home now."

"I won't."

"If thou dost not come now, I must return for thee and what if in the meantime, my sister-in-law, the wife of my husband's brother, should take the canoe? Thou wouldst cry and who would fetch thee home?"

"Father!" retorted the child impudently.

"Father will scold me if thou art not home. He likes it not when thou stayest for a long while with my kinsfolk," replies the mother, glancing up at the skull bowl, where the grandfather's skull hangs from the ceiling.

"Never mind!" The child jerks away from her mother's attempt to detain her and turning, slaps her mother roundly in the face. Every one laughs merrily.

Her mother's sister adds: "Alupwa, thou shouldst go home now with thy mother," whereupon the child slaps her also. The mother gives up the argument and begins working on her beads again, while Alupwa prances to the front of the house and returns with a small green fruit from which the older children make tops. This she begins to eat with a sly glance at her mother.

"Don't eat that, Alupwa, it is bad." Alupwa denantly sets her teeth into the rind. "Don't eat it. Dost not hear me?" Her mother takes hold of the child's hand and tries to wrest it away from her. Alupwa immediately begins to shriek furiously. The mother lets go of her hand with a hopeless shrug and the child puts the fruit to her lips again. But one of the older women intervenes.

"It is bad that she should eat that thing. It will make her sick."

"Well, then do thou take it from her. If I do she will hate me." The older woman grasps the wrist of the screaming child and wrenches the fruit from her.

"Daughter of Kea!" At the sound of her husband's voice, the mother springs to her feet, gathering up her cloak. The other women hastily seize their cloaks against their brother-in-law's possible entrance into the house. But Alupwa, tears forgotten, scampers out to the trap door, climbs down the ladder to the veranda, out along the outrigger poles to the canoe platform, and along the sharp gunwale to nestle happily against her father's leg. His hand plays affectionately with her hair as he scowls up at his wife who is sullenly descending the ladder.

III

It is night in Peri. From the windowless houses with their barred entrances, no house fires shine out into the village. Now and then a shower of incandescent ashes falls into the sea, betraying that folk are still awake within the silent houses. Under a house, at the other end of the village, a dark figure is visible

[17]

against the light cast by a fan-shaped torch of palm leaves. It is a man who is searing the hull of his water-worn canoe with fire. Out in the shallows near the pounding reef, can be seen the scattered bamboo torches of fishermen. A canoe passes down the central water-way, and stops, without a sound, under the verandah of a house. The occupant of the canoe stands, upright, leaning on his long punt, listening. From the interior of the house comes the sound of low sibilant, indrawn whistlings. The owner of the house is holding a séance and through the whistles of the spirit, who is in pos-session of the mouth of the medium, he communicates with the spirits of the dead. The whistling ceases, and a woman's voice exclaims: "Ah, Pokus is here and thou mayst question him."

The listener recognises the name of Pokus, although the voice of his mortal mother, the medium, is strained and disguised. His lips form the words: "Wife of Pokanas is conducting the séance."

The owner of the house speaks, quickly, in a voice of command: "Thou, Pokus, tell me. Why is my child sick? All day he is sick. Is it because I sold those pots which I should have kept for my daughter's dowry? Speak, thou, tell me."

Again the whistling. Then the woman's voice drow-sily. "He says he does not know."

"Then let him go and ask Selanbelot, my father's brother, whose skull I have given room under my roof. Let him ask him why my child is sick."

Again whistling. Then the woman's voice, softly: "He says he will go and ask him."

From the next house comes the sharp angry wail of a child. The floor creaks above the listener's head and the medium says in her ordinary voice, "Thou, Pokanas. Wake up. The child is crying. Dost thou sleep? Listen, the child is crying, go quickly."

A heavy man climbs down the ladder and perceiving the man in the canoe: "Who is it? Thou, Saot?"

"Take me quickly in thy canoe. The child has wakened and is frightened." As the young man punts the father across to his child, the whistling begins again.

IV

Against the piles at the back of his veranda a man lounges wearily. After a whole night's fishing and the morning at the market he is very sleepy. His hair is combed stiffly back from his head in a pompadour. Around his throat is a string of dogs' teeth. From his distended ear lobes dangle little notched rings of coconut shell, and through the pierced septum of his nose is passed a long slender crescent of pearl shell. His G-string of trade cloth is held fast by a woven belt, patterned in yellow and brown. On his upper arms are wide woven armlets coated with black, rubber-like gum; in these are stuck the pieces of the rib bones of his dead father. On the rough floor boards lies a small grass bag, from which projects a polished gourd on which intricate designs have been burned. In the mouth of the gourd is thrust a wooden spatula, the end carved to represent a crocodile eating a man. The carved head extends in staring unconcern from the crocodile's ornate jaws. The lounger stirs and draws from the bag the lime gourd, a cluster of bright green betel nuts and a bunch of pepper leaves. He puts a betel nut in his mouth, leisurely rolls a pepper leaf into a long funnel, bites off the end, and dipping the spatula into the powdered lime, adds a bit of lime to the mixture which he is already chewing vigorously.

The platform shakes as a canoe collides with one of the piles. The man begins hastily gathering up the pepper leaves and betel nut to hide them from a possible visitor. But he is not quick enough. A small head appears above the edge of the verandah and his six-year-old son, Popoli, climbs up dripping. The child's hair is long and strands of it are caked together with red mud; before they can be cut off, his father must give a large feast. The child has spied the treasure and hanging onto the edge of the verandah he whines out in the tone which all Manus natives use when begging betel nut: "A little betel?" The father throws him a nut. He tears the skin off with his teeth and bites it greedily.

"Another," the child's voice rises to a higher pitch. The father throws him a second nut, which the child grasps firmly in his wet little fist, without acknowledgment. "Some pepper leaf?"

The father frowns. "I have very little, Popoli."

"Some pepper leaf." The father tears off a piece of a leaf and throws it to him.

The child scowls at the small piece. "This is too little. More! More! More!" His voice rises to a howl of rage.

"I have but a little, Popoli. I go not to market until the morrow. I go this afternoon to Patusi and I want some for my voyaging." The father resolutely begins to stuff the leaves farther into the bag, and as he does so, his knife slips out of the bag and falls through a crack into the sea.

"Wilt get it, Popoli?"

But the child only glares furiously. "No. I won't, thou, thou stingy one, thou hidest thy pepper leaf from me." And the child dives off the verandah and swims away, leaving his father to climb down and rescue the knife himself.

v

On a shaded verandah a group of children are playing cat's cradle.

"Molung is going to die," remarks one little girl, looking up from her half-completed string figure.

"Who says so?" demands a small boy, leaning over to light his cigarette at a glowing bit of wood which lies on the floor.

"My mother. Molung has a snake in her belly."

The other children pay no attention to this announcement, but one four-year-old adds after a moment's reflection, "She had a baby in her belly."

"Yes, but the baby came out. It lives in the back of our house. My grandmother looks out for it." "If

[21]

Molung dies, you can keep the baby," says the small boy. "Listen!"

From the house across the water a high piercing wail of many voices sounds, all crying in chorus, "My mother, my mother, my mother, oh, what can be the matter?"

"Is she dead yet?" asks the small boy, wriggling to the edge of the verandah. Nobody answers him. "Look." From the rear of the house of illness, a large canoe slides away, laden high with cooking pots. An old woman, gaunt of face, and with head uncovered in her haste, punts the canoe along the waterway.

"That's Ndrantche, the mother of Molung," remarks the first little girl.

"Look, there goes Ndrantche with a canoe full of pots," shout the children.

Two women come to the door of the house and look out. "Oho," says one. "She's getting the pots away so that when all the mourners come, the pots won't be broken."

"When will Molung die?" asks little Itong, and "Come for a swim," she adds, diving off the verandah without waiting for an answer.

III

THE Manus baby is accustomed to water from the first years of his life. Lying on the slatted floor he watches the sunlight gleam on the surface of the lagoon as the changing tide passes and repasses beneath the house. When he is nine or ten months old his mother or father will often sit in the cool of the evening on the little verandah, and his eyes grow used to the sight of the passing canoes and the village set in the sea. When he is about a year old, he has learned to grasp his mother firmly about the throat, so that he can ride in safety, poised on the back of her neck. She has carried him up and down the long house, dodged under low-hanging shelves, and climbed up and down the rickety ladders which lead from house floor down to the landing verandah. The decisive, angry gesture with which he was reseated on his mother's neck whenever his grip tended to slacken has taught him to be alert and sure-handed. At last it is safe for his mother to take him out in a canoe, to punt or paddle the canoe herself while the baby clings to her neck. If a sudden wind roughens the lagoon or her punt catches in a rock, the canoe may swerve and precipitate mother and baby into the sea. The water is cold and dark, acrid in taste and blindingly salt; the descent into its depths is sudden, but the training within the house holds good. The baby does not loosen his grip while his mother rights the canoe and climbs out of the water.

Occasionally the child's introduction to the water comes at an even earlier age. The house floor is made of sections of slats, put together after the fashion of Venetian blinds. These break and bend and slip out of place until great gaps sometimes appear. The unwary child of a shiftless father may crawl over one of these gaps and slip through into the cold, repellent water beneath. But the mother is never far away; her attention is never wholly diverted from the child. She is out the door, down the ladder, and into the sea in a twinkling; the baby is gathered safely into her arms and warmed and reassured by the fire. Although children frequently slip through the floor, I heard of no cases of drowning and later familiarity with the water seems to obliterate all traces of the shock, for there are no water phobias in evidence. In spite of an early ducking, the sea beckons as insistently to a Manus child as green lawns beckon to our children, tempting them forth to exploration and discovery.

For the first few months after he has begun to accompany his mother about the village the baby rides quietly on her neck or sits in the bow of the canoe while his mother punts in the stern some ten feet away. The child sits quietly, schooled by the hazards to which he has been earlier exposed. There are no straps, no baby harnesses to detain him in his place. At the same time, if he should tumble overboard, there would be no tragedy. The fall into the water is painless. The mother or father is there to pick him up. Babies under two and a half or three are never trusted with older children or even with young people. The parents demand a speedy physical adjustment from the child, but they expose him to no unnecessary risks. He is never allowed to stray beyond the limits of safety and watchful adult care.

So the child confronts duckings, falls, dousings of cold water, or entanglements in slimy seaweed, but he never meets with the type of accident which will make him distrust the fundamental safety of his world. Although he himself may not yet have mastered the physical technique necessary for perfect comfort in the water, his parents have. A lifetime of dwelling on the water has made them perfectly at home there. They are sure-footed, clear eyed, quick handed. A baby is never dropped; his mother never lets him slip from her arms or carelessly bumps his head against door post or shelf. All her life she has balanced upon the inch-wide edges of canoe gunwales, gauged accurately the distance between house posts where she must moor her canoe without ramming the outrigger, lifted huge fragile water pots from shifting canoe platforms up rickety ladders. In the physical care of the child she makes no clumsy blunders. Her every move is a reassurance to the child, counteracting any doubts which he may have accumulated in the course of his own less sure-footed progress. So thoroughly do Manus children trust their parents that a child will leap from any height into an adult's outstretched arms, leap blindly and with complete confidence of being safely caught.

Side by side with the parent's watchfulness and care goes the demand that the child himself should make as much effort, acquire as much physical dexterity as possible. Every gain a child makes is noted, and the child is inexorably held to his past record. There are no cases of children who toddle a few steps, fall, bruise their noses, and refuse to take another step for three months. The rigorous way of life demands that the children be self-sufficient as early as possible. Until a child has learned to handle his own body, he is not safe in the house, in a canoe, or on the small islands. His mother or aunt is a slave, unable to leave him for a minute, never free of watching his wandering steps. So every new proficiency is encouraged and insisted upon. Whole groups of busy men and women cluster about the baby's first step, but there is no such delightful audience to bemoan his first fall. He is set upon his feet gently but firmly and told to try again. The only way in which he can keep the interest of his admiring audience *is* to try again. So self-pity is stifled and another step is attempted.

As soon as the baby can toddle uncertainly, he is put down into the water at low tide when parts of the lagoon are high and others only a few inches under water. Here the baby sits and plays in the water or takes a few hesitating steps in the yielding spongy mud. The mother does not leave his side, nor does she leave him there long enough to weary him. As he grows older, he is allowed to wade about at low tide. His elders keep a sharp lookout that he does not stray into deep water until he is old enough to swim. But the supervision is unobtrusive. Mother is always there if the child gets into difficulties, but he is not nagged and plagued with continual "don'ts." His whole play world is so arranged that he is permitted to make small mistakes from which he may learn better judgment and greater circumspection, but he is never allowed to make mistakes which are serious enough to permanently frighten him or inhibit his activity. He is a tight-rope walker, learning feats which we would count outrageously difficult for little children, but his tight-rope is stretched above a net of expert parental solicitude. If we are horrified to see a baby sitting all alone in the end of a canoe with nothing to prevent his clambering overboard into the water, the Manus would be equally horrified at the American mother who has to warn a ten-year-old child to keep his fingers from under a rocking chair, or not to lean out of the side of the car. Equally repellent to them would be our notion of getting children used to the water by giving them compulsory duckings. The picture of an adult voluntarily subjecting the child to a painful situation, using his superior strength to bully the child into accepting the water, would fill them with righteous indignation. Expecting children to swim at three, to climb about like young monkeys even before that age, may look to us like forcing them; really it is simply a quiet insistence upon their exerting every particle of energy and strength which they possess.

Swimming is not taught: the small waders imitate their slightly older brothers and sisters, and after floundering about in waist-deep water begin to strike out for themselves. Sure-footedness on land and swimming come almost together, so that the charm which is recited over a newly delivered woman says, "May you not have another child until this one can walk and swim." As soon as the children can swim a little, in a rough and tumble overhand stroke which has no style but great speed, they are given small canoes of their own. These little canoes are five or six feet long, most of them without outriggers, mere hollow troughs, difficult to steer and easy to upset. In the company of children a year or so older, the young initiates play all day in shallow water, paddling, punting, racing, making tandems of their small craft, upsetting their canoes, bailing them out again, shrieking with delight and high spirits. The hottest sun does not drive them indoors; the fiercest rain only changes the appearance of their playground into a new and strange delight. Over half their waking hours are spent in the water, joyously learning to be at home in their water world.

Now that they have learned to swim a little, they climb freely about the large canoes, diving off the bow, climbing in again at the stern, or clambering out over the outrigger to swim along with one hand on the flexible outrigger float. The parents are never in such a hurry that they have to forbid this useful play.

The next step in water proficiency is reached when the child begins to punt a large canoe. Early in the morning the village is alive with canoes in which the elders sit sedately on the centre platforms while small children of three punt the canoes which are three or four times as long as the children are tall. At first glance this procession looks like either the crudest sort of display of adult prestige or a particularly conspicuous form of child labour. The father sits in casual state, a man of five feet nine or ten, weighing a hundred and fifty pounds. The canoe is long and heavy, dug out of a solid log; the unwieldy outrigger makes it difficult to steer. At the end of the long craft, perched precariously on the thin gunwales, his tiny brown feet curved tensely to keep his hold, stands a small brown baby, manfully straining at the six foot punt in his hands. He is so small that he looks more like an unobtrusive stern ornament than like the pilot of the lumbering craft. Slowly, with a great display of energy but not too much actual progress, the canoe moves through the village, among other canoes similarly manned by the merest tots. But this is neither child labour nor idle prestige hunting on the part of the parents. It is part of the whole system by which a child is encouraged to do his physical best. The father is in a hurry. He has much work to do during the day. He may be setting off for overseas, or planning an important feast. The work of punting a canoe within the lagoon is second nature to him, easier than walking. But that his small child may feel important and adequate to deal with the exacting water life, the father retires to the central platform and the infant pilot mans the canoe. And here again, there are no harsh words when the child steers clumsily, only a complete lack of interest. But the first sure deft stroke which guides the canoe back to its course is greeted with approval.

The test of this kind of training is in the results. The Manus children are perfectly at home in the water. They neither fear it nor regard it as presenting special difficulties and dangers. The demands upon them have made them keen-eyed, quick-witted, and physically competent like their parents. There is not a child of five who can't swim well. A Manus child who couldn't swim would be as aberrant, as definitely subnormal as an American child of five who couldn't walk. Before I went to Manus I was puzzled by the problem of how I would be able to collect the little children in one spot. I had visions of a kind of collecting canoe which would go about every morning and gather them aboard. I need not have worried. A child was never at a loss to get from house to house, whether he went in a large canoe or a small one, or swam the distance with a knife in his teeth.

In other aspects of adapting the children to the external world the same technique is followed. Every gain, every ambitious attempt is applauded; too ambitious projects are gently pushed out of the picture; small errors are simply ignored but important ones are punished. So a child who, after having learned to walk, slips and bumps his head, is not gathered up in kind, compassionate arms while mother kisses his tears away, thus establishing a fatal connection between physical disaster and extra cuddling. Instead the little stumbler is berated for his clumsiness, and if he has been very stupid, slapped soundly into the bargain. Or if his misstep has occurred in a canoe or on the verandah, the exasperated and disgusted adult may simply dump him contemptuously into the water to meditate upon his ineptness. The next time the child slips, he will not glance anxiously for an audience for his agony, as so many of our children do; he will nervously hope that no one has noticed his *faux pas*. This attitude, severe and unsympathetic as it appears on the surface, makes children develop perfect motor co-ordination. The child with slighter original proficiency cannot be distinguished among the fourteen-year-olds except in special pursuits like spear throwing, where a few will excel in skill. But in the everyday activities of swimming, paddling, punting, climbing, there is a general high level of excellence. And clumsiness, physical uncertainty and lack of poise, is unknown among adults. The Manus are alive to individual differences in skill or knowledge and quick to brand the stupid, the slow learner, the man or woman with poor memory. But they have no word for clumsiness. The child's lesser proficiency is simply described as "not understanding *yet*." That he should not understand the art of handling his body, his canoes well, very presently, is unthinkable.

In many societies children's walking means more

trouble for the adults. Once able to walk, the children are a constant menace to property, breaking dishes, spilling the soup, tearing books, tangling the thread. But in Manus where property is sacred and one wails for lost property as for the dead, respect for property is taught children from their earliest years. Before they can walk they are rebuked and chastised for touching anything which does not belong to them. It was sometimes very tiresome to listen to the monotonous reiteration of some mother to her baby as it toddled about among our new and strange possessions: "That isn't yours. Put it down. That belongs to Piyap. That belongs to Piyap. That belongs to Piyap. Put it down." But we reaped the reward of this endless vigilance: all our possessions, fascinating red and yellow cans of food, photographic material, books, were safe from the two- and three-year-olds who would have been untamed vandals in a forest of loot in most societies. As in the attitude towards physical prowess, there is no attempt to make it easy for the child, to demand less than the child is capable of giving. Nothing is put out of the child's reach. The mother spreads her tiny brightly coloured beads out on a mat, or in a shallow bowl, right on the floor within the reach of the crawling baby and the baby is taught not to touch them. Where even the dogs are so well trained that fish can be laid on the floor and left there for an hour without danger there are no excuses made for the tiny human beings. A good baby is a baby which never touches anything; a good child is one who never touches anything and never asks for anything not its own. These are the only important items of ethical behaviour demanded of children. And as their physical trustworthiness makes it safe to leave children alone, so their well-schooled attitudes towards property make it safe to leave a crowd of romping children in a houseful of property. No pots will be disturbed, no smoked fish purloined from the hanging shelves, no string of shell money severed in a tug of war and sent into the sea. The slightest breakage is punished without mercy. Once a canoe from another village anchored near one of the small islands. Three little eight-year-old girls climbed on the deserted canoe and knocked a pot into the sea, where it struck a stone and broke. All night the village rang with drum calls and angry speeches, accusing, deprecating, apologising for the damage done and denouncing the careless children. The fathers made speeches of angry shame and described how roundly they had beaten the young criminals. The children's companions, far from admiring a daring crime, drew away from them in haughty disapproval and mocked them in chorus.

Any breakage, any carelessness, is punished. The parents do not condone the broken pot which was already cracked and then wax suddenly furious when a good pot is broken, after the fashion of American parents who let the child tear the almanac and the telephone book and then wonder at its grieved astonishment when it is slapped for tearing up the family Bible. The tail of a fish, the extra bit of taro, the half rotten betel nut, cannot be appropriated with any more impunity than can the bowl of feast food. In checking thefts, the same inexorableness is found. There was one little girl of twelve named Mentun who was said to be a thief and sometimes taunted with the fact by other children. Why? Because she had been seen to pick up objects floating in the water, a bit of food, a floating banana, which obviously must have fallen out of one of the half a dozen houses near by. To appropriate such booty without first making a round of the possible owners, was to steal. And Mentun would have to exercise the greatest circumspection for months if she were not to be blamed for every disappearance of property in the years to come. I never ceased to wonder at the children who, after picking up pieces of coveted paper off the veranda or the islet near our house, always brought them to me with the question, "Piyap, is this good or bad?" before carrying away the crumbled scraps.

The departments of knowledge which small children are expected to master are spoken of as "understanding the house," "understanding the fire," "understanding the canoe," and "understanding the sea."

"Understanding the house" includes care in walking over the uncertain floors, the ability to climb up the ladder or notched post from the verandah to the house floor, remembering to remove a slat of the floor for spitting or urinating, or discarding rubbish into the sea, respecting any property lying on the floor, not climbing on shelves nor on parts of the house which would give beneath weight, not bringing mud and rubbish into the house.

The fire is kept in one or all of the four fireplaces ranged two along each side wall, towards the centre of the house. The fireplace is made of a thick bed of fine wood ash on a base of heavy mats edged by stout logs of hard wood. It is about three feet square. In the centre are three or four boulders which serve as supports for the cooking pots. Cooking is done with small wood, but the fire is kept up by heavier logs. Neat piles of firewood, suspended on low shelves, flank the fireplaces. Swung low over the fire are the smoking shelves where the fish are preserved. Understanding of the fire means an understanding that the fire will burn the skin, or thatch, or light wood, or straw, that a smouldering cinder will flare if blown upon, that such cinders, if removed from the fireplace, must be carried with the greatest care and without slipping or bringing them in contact with other objects, that water will quench fire. "Understanding the fire" does not include making fire with the fire plough, an art learned much later when boys are twelve or thirteen. (Fire is never made by women, although they may assist by sheltering the kindling dust between their hands.)

Understanding canoe and sea come just a little later than the understanding of house and fire, which form part of the child's environment from birth. A child's knowledge of a canoe is considered adequate if he can balance himself, feet planted on the two narrow rims, and punt the canoe with accuracy, paddle well enough to steer through a mild gale, run the canoe accurately under a house without jamming the outrigger, extricate a canoe from a flotilla of canoes crowded closely about a house platform or the edge of an islet, and bail out a canoe by a deft backward and forward movement which dips the bow and stern alternately. It does not include any sailing knowledge. Understanding of the sea includes swimming, diving, swimming under water, and a knowledge of how to get water out of the nose and throat by leaning the head forward and striking the back of the neck. Children of between five and six have mastered these four necessary departments.

Children are taught to talk through the men's and older boys' love of playing with children. There is no belief that it is necessary to give a child formal teaching, rather chance adult play devices are enlisted. One of these is the delight in repetition. Melanesian languages very frequently use repetition to give an intensity to speech. To go far is expressed by "go go go," to be very large by "big big big." So an ordinary anecdote runs: "So the man went went went. After a while it was dark dark night. So he stopped stopped stopped stopped stopped. In the morning he awoke. His throat was dry dry dry. He looked looked for water. But he found none. Then his belly was angry angry, etc." Although strictly speaking these repetitions should all have a function in expressing duration or intensity, very often the mere habit of repetition runs away with the narrator and soon he will be saying, "Now he met a woman. Her name was Sain Sain

Sain," or even repeating a preposition or particle. A crowd also has a tendency to pick up a phrase and repeat it or turn it into a low monotonous song. This is particularly true if one chances to utter a phrase in a singsong tone, to call it out in another key from the surrounding conversation, or even to mutter to oneself. The most casual and accustomed phrases, like, "I do not understand," or "Where is my canoe?" will be taken up in this way and transformed into a chant which the group will repeat with complete self-satisfaction for several minutes thereafter. Tricks of pronunciation and accent are picked up and imitated in the same way.

This random affection for repetitiousness makes an excellent atmosphere in which the child acquires facility in speech. There is no adult boredom with the few faulty words of babyhood. Instead these very groping words form an excellent excuse for indulging their own passion for repetition. So the baby says "me," and the adult says "me." The baby says "me" and the adult says "me," on and on in the same tone of voice. I have counted sixty repetitions of the same monosyllabic word, either a true word or a nonsense syllable. And at the end of the sixtieth repetition, neither baby nor adult was bored. The child with a repertoire of ten words associates one word like *me* or *house* with the particular adult who engaged in this game, and will shout at his uncle or aunt as he passes in a canoe, "me," or "house," hopefully. Nor is he disappointed: the obliging adult, as pleased as the child, will call back "me" or "house" until the canoe is out of earshot. Little girls are usually addressed as *"Ina,"* little boys as *"Ina"* or *"Papu"* by adults and the child replies "Ina" or "Papu," establishing two reciprocals which are not included in the formal kinship system.

What is true of speech is equally true of gesture. Adults play games of imitative gesture with children until the child develops a habit of imitation which seems at first glance to be practically compulsive. This is specially true of facial expression, yawning, closed eyes, or puckered lips. The children carried over this habit of repeating expression in their response to a pencil of mine which had a human head and bust on the end of it. The bust gave the effect of a thrown-out chest. The thin lips seem compressed, to a native, and almost every child, when first looking at the pencil, threw out the chest and compressed the lips. I also showed the children one of those dancing paper puppets which vibrate with incredible looseness when hung from a cord. Before the children used to marvel at the strange toy, their legs and arms were waving about in imitation of the puppets.

This habit of imitation is not, however, compulsive, for it is immediately arrested if made conscious. If one says to a child who has been slavishly imitating one's every move, "Do this the way I do," the child will pause, consider the matter, and more often than not refuse. It seems to be merely a habit, a natural human tendency given extraordinary play in early child-hood and preserved in the more stereotyped forms in the speech and song of adult life. It is most marked in children between one and four years of age and its early loss seems to be roughly correlated with precocity in other respects.

Adults and the older children are very much interested in the baby's learning to talk, and comment on different degrees of facility. Conversation also turns upon the relative talkativeness of different small children. "This one talks all the time. He can't do a thing without telling you that he is doing it." Or: "This one hardly ever speaks, even when he's spoken to, but his eyes are always watching." Despite the great encouragement given to articulateness, there are many untalkative children, but this seems to be a matter of temperament rather than a matter of intelligence. The quiet children when they did talk displayed as good a vocabulary as the garrulous infants, and very often showed a greater knowledge of what was going on about them.

Children encouraged to garrulity sometimes seem to carry over this habit into adult life. At least, it is a temptation to make a comparison between the child who exploits his new instrument, language, by constant comment, as: "This is my boat. Come on. Going in my boat. My boat is in the water now. Right in the water now. All in the water. Other boats in the water. Get the paddle. Yes. I get the paddle. I'll paddle. No, I won't paddle. I'll punt. This is my punting pole. My pole. Punting," etc.—and the man who cultivates an imperfect knowledge of pidgin English in the same way, and will keep up a stream of conversation like this:

"Get him hammer. All right. Fight him. Fight him. Fight him nail. Hammer he good fellow along nail. Me savee. Me savee make him. All right. Me work him now. Me work him, work him. All right. He fast now. He fast finish. Me catch him other fellow nail. Where stop hammer. He stop along ground. All right. Catch him hammer." This conversational accompaniment of activity is not found among the most intelligent men.

Repetition is a very useful medium for teaching pidgin English to the young children. Young men who have been away to work for the white man return to their villages and teach the younger boys, who in turn teach the very small boys. There is a class feeling about pidgin which prevents the women, who do not go away to work, from learning it. But it is a common spectacle to see two or three twelve-year-old boys gathered about a three- or four-year-old little boy, "schooling him." An older boy gives the cues: "I think he can." "I think he no can." "Me like good fellow kai kai (food)." "Me like kai kai fish." "One time along taro." And the child repeats the lines in his piping little voice without any grasp of their significance. But as it fits in so well with the game of repetition for repetition's sake neither teacher nor pupil tires easily, and the result is that boys of thirteen and fourteen speak perfect pidgin although they have never been out of their isolated villages. Learning pidgin is as much of a feat for native children as learning French by similar methods would be for our children. It involves learning a large new vocabulary, new idioms, the pronunciation of some unfamiliar sounds. So in this atmosphere of delight in repetition and imitation, a new language is taught painlessly by one age group to another. The general set shows not only in the willingness to teach and the enjoyment of the lessons but also in the younger child's continuous practising. As the baby practised its first Manus words with endless glee over the hundredfold repetition of one syllable, so the six-year-old goes about repeating long passages of pidgin with perfect pronunciation and cadence, but without understanding more than a tenth of what he is saying.

The girls are often present at these lessons; they hear the men speak pidgin to the boys. The men when they are angry speak in pidgin to the girls and women but with two exceptions no pidgin passes feminine lips. Women in delirium will speak excellent pidgin which the natives explain in terms of possession of the woman's mouth by the spirit of a former work boy. The other exception is even more significant—the cases where small girls, imitating their brothers, teach smaller children the language which they usually refuse to speak or to understand. The desire to imitate the formal teaching situation is stronger than the convention against betraying a knowledge of pidgin. Both of these examples are interesting as cases of learning with an almost complete lack of audible practice. They are comparable to the cases of those children whose speech habits have seemed seriously retarded and who suddenly begin speaking in complete sentences.

Other activities learned through imitation are dancing and drumming. The small girls learn to dance by standing beside their mothers and sisters at the turtle dance given to shake the dust out of the house of mourning. Occasionally a child is incited to dance at home while the mother taps on the house floor. Six- and seven-year-olds have already grasped the very simple step: feet together and a swift side jump and return to position in time to the drum beats. The men's dance is more difficult. The usual loin cloth or G-string is laid aside and a white sea shell substituted as pubic covering. The dance consists in very rapid leg and body movements which result in the greatest possible gymnastic phallic display. It is a dance of ceremonial defiance, accompanied by boasting and ceremonial insult, most frequently performed on occasions when there is a large display of wealth in a payment between two kin groups connected by marriage. Those who make the heavy payment of dogs' teeth and shell currency dance and dare the other side to collect enough oil and pigs to repay them. Those who receive the payment dance to show their defiant acceptance of the obligation which they are undertaking. The smaller children are all present at this big ceremony and watch the men's athletic exploits. Boys of four and five begin to practise, and the day that they master the art of catching the penis between the legs and then flinging it violently forward and from side to side, is a day of such pride that for weeks afterwards they perform the dance on every occasion, to the great and salacious amusement of their elders. Slightly older boys of ten and twelve make a mock shell covering out of the seed of a nut and practise in groups.

Whenever there is a dance there is an orchestra of slit drums of all sizes played by the most proficient drummers in the village. The very small boys of four and five settle themselves beside small hollow log ends or pieces of bamboo and drum away indefatigably in time with the orchestra. This period of open and unashamed imitation is followed by a period of embarrassment, so that it is impossible to persuade a boy of ten or twelve to touch a drum in public, but in the boys' house when only a few older boys are present, he will practise, making good use of the flexibility of wrist and sense of rhythm learned earlier. Girls practise less, for only one drum beat, the simple death beat, falls to their hands in later life.

The drum language the children understand but make no attempt to execute. This language consists of a series of formal phrase beginnings which mean "Come home—," or "I am now going to announce how many days it will be before I will do something," etc. The first one will be followed by the individual combination of beats which is the call of a particular household for any of its members. The second is followed by slow beats, interspersed with a formal spacing beat. Every one in the village stops work or play to count these beats, but only a knowledge of who is beating the drum and what he is planning to do in the near future make it possible to interpret the announcement. The children stop their play to hear which house call follows the formal introduction, and go back to their games if it is not their own. They seldom bother to further identify the call. If a date is announced they mechanically count the days and may stop to guess who is beating the drum. There their interest ceases. One ceremony is too like another to matter. But there are three drum calls which do interest them, the beats announcing that some one is about to die, that some one is dead, and the drum beat which means "Trouble,"—theft, or adultery. For these they will pause in their play and possibly send a small boy to inquire into the cause. The drum beat for death is so simple that children can make it and are sometimes permitted to do so in the event of the death of an unimportant person.

Singing is also learned through imitation of older children by younger children. It consists in a monotone chant of very simple sentences, more or less related to each other. A group of children will huddle together on the floor and croon these monotonous chants over and over for hours without apparent boredom or weariness. They also sing when they are chilled and miserable or when they are frightened at night.

Similarly the art of war is learned by playful imitation. The men use spears with bamboo shafts and cruel arrow shaped heads of obsidian. The children make small wooden spears, about two and a half feet in length and fasten tips of pith on them. Then pairs of small boys will stand on the little islets, each with a handful of spears, and simultaneously hurl spears at each other. Dodging is as important a skill as throwing, for the Manus used no shields and the avalanche of enemy spears could only be dodged. This is an art which requires early training for proficiency, and boys of ten and twelve are already experts with their light weapons. The older men and boys, canoe building on the islet, or paddling by, stop to cheer a good throw. Here again, the children are encouraged, never ridiculed nor mocked.

Fishing methods are also learned yearly. Older men make the small boys bows and arrows and tiny, pronged fish-spears. With these the children wander in groups about the lagoon at low tide, skirting the small rocky islands, threading their way through the rank sea undergrowth, spearing small fish for the sport of it. Their catch, except when they net a school of minnows in their spider-web nets, is not large enough to eat. This toying with fishing is pursued in a desultory fashion by children from the ages of three to fifteen. Then they will go on expeditions of their own and sometimes join the young men on excursions to the north coast after turtle, dugong, and kingfish.

Small children are also sometimes taken fishing by their fathers. Here as little more than babies they watch the procedures which they will not be asked to practise until they are grown. Sometimes in the dawn a child's wail of anger will ring through the village; he has awakened to find his father gone fishing without him. But this applies only to small boys under six or seven. Older boys prefer the society of other children and of grown youths, but shun the company of adults. Boys of fourteen and fifteen never accompany their parents about their ordinary tasks except when a boy has fallen out with his playmates. For the few days of strain which follow he will cling closely to his parents and be officiously helpful, only to desert them again as soon as friendly relations are re-established.

Little girls do very little fishing. As very tiny children they may be taken fishing by their fathers, but this is a type of fishing which they will never be required to do as grown women. Women's fishing consists of reef fishing, fishing with hand nets, with scoop baskets, and with bell shaped baskets with an opening at the top for the hand. Girls do not begin this type of fishing until near puberty.

Of the techniques of handwork small boys learn but little. They know how to whiten the sides of their canoes with seaweed juices; they know how to tie a rattan strip so that it will remain fast; they have a rudimentary knowledge of whittling, but none of carving. They can fasten on a simple outrigger float if it breaks off. They know how to scorch the sides of their canoes with torches of coconut palm leaves, and how to make rude bamboo torches for expeditions after dark. They know nothing about carpentry except what they remember from their early childhood association with their fathers.

But children have learned all the physical skill necessary as a basis for a satisfactory physical adjustment for life. They can judge distances, throw straight, catch what is thrown to them, estimate distances for jumping and diving, climb anything, balance themselves on the most narrow and precarious footholds, handle themselves with poise, skill, and serenity either on land or sea. Their bodies are trained to the adult dance steps, their eye and hand trained to shooting and spearing fish, their voices accustomed to the song rhythms, their wrists flexible for the great speed of the drum sticks, their hands trained to the paddle and the punt. By a system of training which is sure, unhesitant, unremitting in its insistence and vigilance, the baby is given the necessary physical base upon which he builds through years of imitation of older children and adults. The most onerous part of his physical education is over by the time he is three. For the rest it is play for which he is provided with every necessary equipment, a safe and pleasant playground, a jolly group of companions of all ages and both sexes. He grows up to be an adult wholly admirable from a physical standpoint, skilled, alert, fearless, resourceful in the face of emergency, reliable under strain.

But the Manus' conception of social discipline is as loose as their standards of physical training are rigid. They demand nothing beyond physical efficiency and respect for property except a proper observance of the canons of shame. Children must learn privacy in excretion almost by the time they can walk; must get by heart the conventional attitudes of shame and embarrassment. This is communicated to them not by sternness and occasional chastisement, but through the emotions of their parents. The parents' horror, physical shrinking, and repugnance is communicated to the careless child. This adult attitude is so strong that it is as easy to impregnate the child with it as it is to communicate panic. When it is realized that men are fastidious about uncovering in each other's presence and that a grown girl is taught that if she even takes off her grass skirt in the presence of another woman the spirits will punish her, some conception of the depth of this feeling can be obtained. Prudery is never sacrificed to convenience; on sea voyages many hours in duration, if the sexes are mixed the most rigid convention is observed.

Into this atmosphere of prudery and shame the children are early initiated. They are wrapped about with this hot prickling cloak until the adults feel safe from embarrassing betrayal. And here social discipline ceases. The children are taught neither obedience nor deference to their parents' wishes. A two-year-old child is permitted to flout its mother's humble request that it come home with her. At night the children are supposed to be at home at dark, but this does not mean that they go home when called. Unless hunger drives them there the parents have to go about collecting them, often by force. A prohibition against going to the other end of the village to play lasts just as long as the vigilance of the prohibitor, who has only to turn the back for the child to be off, swimming under water until out of reach.

Manus cooking is arduous and exacting. The sago

is cooked dry in a shallow pot stirred over a fire. It requires continuous stirring and is only good for about twenty minutes after being cooked. Yet the children are not expected to come home at mealtime. They run away in the morning before breakfast and come back an hour or so after, clamouring for food. Ten-year-olds will stand in the middle of the house floor and shriek monotonously until some one stops work to cook for them. A woman who has gone to the house of a relative to help with some task or to lay plans for a feast will be assaulted by her six-year-old child who will scream, pull at her, claw at her arms, kick and scratch, until she goes home to feed him.

The parents who were so firm in teaching the children their first steps have become wax in the young rebels' hands when it comes to any matter of social discipline. They eat when they like, play when they like, sleep when they see fit. They use no respect language to their parents and indeed are allowed more license in the use of obscenity than are their elders. The veriest urchin can shout defiance and contempt at the oldest man in the village. Children are never required to give up anything to parents: the choicest morsels of food are theirs by divine right. They can rally the devoted adults by a cry, bend and twist their parents to their will. They do no work. Girls, after they are eleven or twelve, perform some household tasks, boys hardly any until they are married. The community demands nothing from them except respect for property and the avoidance due to shame.

Undoubtedly this tremendous social freedom rein-
forces their physical efficiency. On a basis of motor
skill is laid a superstructure of complete self-confidence.
The child in Manus is lord of the universe, undisciplined, unchecked by any reverence or respect for his
elders, free except for the narrow thread of shame
which runs through his daily life. No other habits of
self-control or of self-sacrifice have been laid. It is
the typical psychology of the spoiled child. Manus
children demand, never give. The one little girl in the
village who, because her father was blind, had loving
service demanded of her was a gentle generous child.

But from the others nothing was asked and nothing
was given.

For the parents who are their humble servants the
children have a large proprietary feeling, an almost
infantile dependence, but little solicitude. Their egocentricity is the natural complement of the anxious pandering love of the parents, a pandering which is allowed
by the restricted ideals of the culture.

IV

A MANUS child's family is very different from the picture of American family life. True, it consists of the same people: father, mother, one or two brothers or sisters, sometimes a grandmother, less frequently a grandfather. At night the doorways are barricaded carefully and the parents insist that the children be all home at sundown except on moonlight nights. After the evening meal the children are laid on mats for sleep, or allowed to fall asleep in the elders' arms, then gently laid down. The bundles of cocoanut leaves light the dark corners of the house fitfully. At first glimpse this looks like the happy intimate family of our own preference, where strangers are excluded and the few people who love each other best are closeted together around the fire.

But a closer knowledge of Manus homes reveals many differences. Young men do not have houses of their own, but live in the backs of the houses of their older brothers or young uncles. When two such families live together the wife of the younger man must avoid the older man. She never enters his end of the house, partitioned off by hanging mats, when he is at home. The children, however, can run about freely between the two families, but the continual avoidance, the avoidance of all personal names, and the fact that the younger man is dependent upon the older, tends to strain relationships between the two little households. The Manus are prevailingly paternal, a man usually inherits from his father or brother, a wife almost always goes to live in her husband's place.

But although the family group is small, and the tie between children and parents close, the relationship between husband and wife is usually strained and cold. Father and mother seem to the child to be two disparate people both playing for him against each other. The blood ties of his parents are stronger than their relationship to each other, and there are more factors to pull them apart than there are to draw them together. A glance into some of these Peri families will illustrate the fundamental feeling tone which exists between husbands and wives.

Let us take for instance the family of Ndrosal. Ndrosal is a curly-haired, handsome waster, quick to boast and slow to perform. His first wife bore him two boys and died. His sister's husband adopted the elder; the younger stayed with him to be cared for by his new wife, a tall, straight-limbed woman from a faraway village. The new wife straightway bore him a girl which refused to thrive. Month after month the baby fretted and wailed in the little hanging cradle its father fashioned for it. While the baby was so ill it might not be taken from the house on any pretext nor might the mother leave it for more than a few minutes. Month after month she stayed in the house swinging the cradle, growing pale and wan herself. Food was not too plentiful. Ndrosal was very devoted to his elder sister, a woman of definite and unmistakable character. She was middle-aged, a woman of affairs, always busy and always needing her brother's help. When the baby became ill, she took the other child, so both of Ndrosal's little boys were in his sister's house. He loved to carry them about on his back, to lie prone and let them play over his body; or take them fishing. So he spent most of his time in his sister's house next door, and when he made a good haul of fish, most of it went into his sister's pot. His wife had no close relatives in the village, but one day a younger sister of her husband brought her some crabs. Crabbing is woman's work, so there had been no shell fish in the house for months. She cooked them eagerly, careless of the fact that one of the varieties was forbidden to all members of her husband's family. Her husband came home late, empty handed, and demanded his supper. His wife served him crabs, and in answer to his questions professed to be pretty sure that the tabu variety was not among them. Cooked, it was impossible to distinguish them. He began to eat his supper, grumbling over her short answer and lack of concern with his tabus. Almost immediately the baby started to cry. His younger sister and her husband were temporarily lodged in the back of the house. His sister went to the cradle but the baby still wailed. Ndrosal turned sternly to his wife, "Give that child thy breast." "She's nursed enough to-day. She's not hungry, only sick," the wife answered. "Nurse her, dost thou hear me, thou useless woman! Thou woman belonging to worthlessness. Thou root of lying and lack of thought, who carest neither for thy husband's tabus nor for his child." Rising, he poured out the stream of expletive upon her. Still she lingered over her supper, tearful, sullen, convinced that the child wasn't hungry, until the enraged husband seized his lime gourd and flung a pint of powdered lime into her eyes. The scalding tears slaked the lime and burned her eyes horribly as she stumbled blindly from the house, wailing. One of the women who gathered at the sound of trouble took her home with her, and the little baby with her. Ndrosal went to his sister's house to sleep, and when the younger boy sleepily cuddled his father and asked why his adopted mother was crying, he was told gruffly that his mother was a bad woman who refused to feed his little sister.

Or let us go into the house of Ngamel. Ngamel and his wife Ngatchumu got on quite well together. Once Ngamel brought a second wife home but Ngatchumu was so cross that he sent her away to keep peace. Years ago Ngamel used to keep a piece of cordlike vine specially for beating his wife. Those were the days when their first five children all died as babies, owing to some evil magic which clung to a borrowed food bowl, lying forgotten among the rafters. But now Ngatchumu had borne him four beautiful children; one he gave away to his brother, three were at home. Ngamel was ageing, a quiet man who loved to sit on his verandah at twilight and play with the children. But one afternoon Ngatchumu took Ponkob, aged three, with her to a house of death, where her sister lay struck down by the ancestral spirits of Ngamel's clan for aiding remarriage of a widow of a dead brother of Ngamel. The house was close, filled with the odour of death, and the maddening wail of many voices. Little Ponkob pressed close between his mother and another woman, wilted, and finally fainted quite away. The frightened mother carried the sick child home in desperate fear over her husband's anger. His ancestral spirit's vengeance had been flouted by a member of his family attending the dead woman. For two days neither he nor their eight-year-old boy spoke to her who had loved her dead sister so much that she had not thought of the possible wrath of her husband's avenging spirit.

Or take the feast for ear piercing held in Pwisio's house. The house is full of visitors, all the relatives of Pwisio's wife are there, with laden canoes to celebrate the ear piercing of Pwisio's sixteen-year-old son, Manuwai. In the front of the house all is formal. Manuwai, in a choker of dogs' teeth, painted and greased, sits up very straight. His father's two sisters are waiting to lead him down the ladder. But his mother is not there. From the curtained back of the house come sounds of weeping and the low-voiced expostulation of many women. In the front sits Pwisio, facing his guests but pausing to hurl insult after insult to his wife whom he had caught sleeping naked.

(There were strangers in the house and during the night an unwedded youth, a friend of her son's, had stirred the house fire into a blaze.) So Pwisio overwhelms his wife with obloquy, fearful to beat her while so many of her kin are in the house, and she packs her belongings, tearfully protesting her innocence and angrily enumerating the valuables she's taking with her. "This is mine. I made it and my sister gave me these shell beads. These are mine. I traded the materials myself. This belt is mine; I got it in return for sago at the birth feast last week." Her little adopted daughter Ngalowen, aged four, stands aside in shame, from her mother whom father brands thus publicly as a criminal. When her mother gathers up her boxes and marches out the back door, Ngalowen makes no move to follow. Instead, she slips into the front room and cuddles down beside her self-righteous and muttering father. After the long confusion, the ceremony is resumed, the absence of the mother who would have had no official part in it receives no further comment.

In order to understand such dissensions it is necessary to go back of the marriage to the engagement period and follow a Manus girl from her betrothal to motherhood.

Ngalen is eighteen; for seven years she has been engaged to Manoi, whose very name is forbidden to her. She had seen him once as a very small child when her mother had taken her children to her own village of Peri. She remembers that he had a funny nose and a squint in one eye and had worn a bedraggled old *lap*

lap. But she has tried not to think of these things, for her mother had taught her that it was shameful to think of her husband personally. She might dive for *lailai* shells of which winglike ornaments would be made for her small back. She might bend all day over the bead frame, straining her eyes to make beadwork for her sister-in-law. She might think of the thousand of dogs' teeth, of the yards of shell money which had been paid for her betrothal feast, or feed the pigs with which those payments were being met. But of her husband himself she might not think. She was forbidden to go to Peri, her mother's home village, except on very important occasions, like the death of a near relative. Then she must go about very circumspectly, wrapped in her mantle of cloth lest she encounter her betrothed's father or brother. If a Peri canoe passed her father's canoe at sea, she must hide within the penthouse or double up in the hull. When she was very tiny, she had sometimes forgotten to avoid some words which contained syllables like the names of her husband's relatives and had cowered in shame before her elders' sense of outrage. Once the spirits had mentioned in a séance how careless she was in not hiding properly from a distant cousin of her betrothed, a boy who had been her playmate since childhood. But that was several years ago. Now for two or three years she had been very careful. Her village was full of boys returned from working for the white man with who knew what evil magic in their possession. One had a curious bottle which he carried in his betel bag. He said it was only ringworm medicine but every one knew it was love magic. Her own people did not make these evil charms which led a girl to forget her betrothal and wander into sin. But the inland people of the great island had charms which could be slipped into tobacco leaves, or whispered over betel nut, or secretly muttered into a purloined pipe. These they sold to the young men of her people, the young men who sat up all night in their club house, laughing and beating drums and plotting evil. Long ago these young men would have gone to war and captured a foreign girl to minister to their pleasure. But there had been no such prostitute in the village since Ngalen was a little girl, and the youths were very dangerous.

When she went abroad she took care never to let the wind blow from these young men to her. For there were charms which could be sent upon the wind.

There were a few boys in the village with whom she was friendly, her brothers, her cross cousins, the younger cousins of her betrothed. To these last she was "mother," and must only be careful not to eat in their presence.

All day she made beadwork for her sisters-in-law and mother-in-law. After she was married they would give her beadwork to give to her brothers. In her husband's house she would work hard and feel secure. She would learn to understand the intricate financial exchanges. She would learn to make the great square pancakes used in ceremonies, and how to cut cocoanut meat into lilies to decorate the ceremonial food dishes.

She would bear children to her husband. Once a mother she would be no longer a fair and desirable woman, for the Manus consider childbearing, not virginity, the dividing line between youth and experience. Ten times the Pleiades would pass over the sky and she would be old.

Already she knew what the marriage costume was like, for twice she had been decked out in heavy aprons of shell money, her arms and legs laden down with dogs' teeth. But to-morrow she is to be married indeed to the man whose name she mustn't pronounce, of whose squint eyes it is wrong to think. She is going to a village of strangers. True, it is the village of her mother's people, but some of these, because they are closer kin to her husband, are tabu to her. In all her life she may not say their names. And they are to live in the house of her future husband's paternal uncle; he will be her father-in-law. She must always refer to him as "they," never as "he." When he comes into the house she must hide behind the mat curtains and never raise her voice lest he should hear her speak. All her days she will not look upon his face unless as an old man, bald and with shaking hands, he decides to lay aside the tabu by making a large feast for her.

All the men in the village will comment on her, she knows. Uneasily she plucks at her long pendulous breasts, the breasts of an old woman. Fortunately the heavy bindings of dogs' teeth will hold them up into the semblance of a young girl's breasts. Will her husband hate her for her breasts? She has heard the men of her own village talk and she knows how women are valued for their youthful looks. Will she be quick enough to suit her sisters-in-law, make thatch with a steady hand, design pleasing beadwork, and cook efficiently? Her sisters-in-law will hate her, as she and her sisters hate her brother's wife. She can never expect them to love her, only to tolerate her, only to forbear to provoke her too far.

All this she thinks as she sits huddled in her tabu blanket under the pent-house of the canoe. Her relatives are taking her to Peri; all about her is a lively chatter of dogs' teeth and shell money, pigs and oil, unpaid debts, possible contributors, trade opportunities. Her father is well pleased with the match. Ten thousand dogs' teeth will be paid, ten thousand dogs' teeth which he can very well use to pay for a wife for his brother's son who is turned fifteen and unbetrothed. Talk shifts to the financial status of his nephew's bride-to-be.

She looks at her mother, sitting with her sister's baby on her lap, at her older sister, who frowns sullenly into the sea. It is a month since her older sister left her husband, and he has sent no messenger to ask her to come back. Her sister has not told them what happened, only that her husband beat her. A sharp word of command arouses her to the approach of a canoe and she crawls quickly inside her robe.

At last they are in the village itself. Muffled from hand to foot, she climbs hastily into her grandmother's house. Her grandmother is very old, the muscles in her neck are stringy like uncooked pork. She has seen three husbands into the grave. Her voice is cracked and weary as she bids them hurry to dress her granddaughter, for the party will be here soon to fetch her for "the journey of the breast." The cedar boxes are brought in from the canoe and the heavy ornaments spread on the floor. Her father and brothers go away and she is left alone with the women, who dye her hair red, paint her face and arms and back orange, wrap the long strands of shell about her limbs. Two heavy shell aprons are fastened under a belt of dogs' teeth; crescents of shell are stuck in the breast bands. In her arm bands are hidden porcelain pipes, knives and forks and spoons, combs and small mirrors, the foreign property which is never used except to deck out a bride. A bristling coronet of dogs' teeth is fastened about her forehead. Inside it are ranged a dozen tiny feather combs. Yards of trade cloth and bird of paradise feathers are stuck in her arm bands. Her distended ear lobes are weighted down with extra clusters of dogs' teeth. Finally, a slender bit of bone is thrust through the hole in her septum and from her nose hangs an eighteen-inch pendant of shell and bone and dogs' teeth.

Like a rag doll she submits to the dressing process, or obediently turns and twists at command. Meanwhile there is a sound of many voices outside. The women of her future husband's house have come to fetch her. She bends her laden head still lower. But they do not come in. Instead a violent quarrel ensues as to whether the canoe is big enough or not. More women keep arriving in little skiffs, but all must return in the bride's canoe. After a violent altercation two women set out to get another canoe. The others wait on the verandah. Ngalen can distinguish among their voices that of her husband's aunt who is a noted medium and has a spirit dog to do her bidding; all the other voices are strange to her. There are no young girls, only married women, she knows. She has seen canoes set out for "the journey of the breast" before.

At last the larger canoe is at the door. Her mother and aunt pull her to her feet. She stoops a little under the weight of wealth which covers her. With bowed head she is hustled down the ladder onto the canoe platform. She looks at no one and is greeted by no one. A storm is coming up and the overcrowded canoe rides precariously, low, shipping water. She sees the punts flash quickly in muscular hands and notes a new bead design on one wrist, but she does not look above the wrists to their faces.

It is a short journey through the lagoon to the home of her betrothed, a home from which he is banished for the night. At a word from the mother-in-law she climbs up the ladder and sits down, miserable, abashed, in a corner. Immediately all of her betrothed's paternal aunts and female cousins fall upon her; they pull the feather comb from her hair, they tug and tear at her armlets to find combs, mirrors, pipes. One pipe is broken in their haste. The ragged porcelain edge cuts the girl's arm. No one notices, but bitter comment is made on the useless broken pipe, the stinginess of the bride's relatives in giving broken pipes. One old crone remarks that they probably needn't expect a very fine display with the bride to-morrow, a lot of the pots looked pretty small and cracked, and she's heard that there are only ten pieces of cloth. Another old woman mutters unamiably that the men of the bride's family aren't good for much: the bride's older brother hasn't begun to pay for his wife yet, and her younger brother isn't even betrothed. Shamed, furious, the girl sits in a corner, her bristling coronet of dogs' teeth sagging over one eye. Meanwhile, the women leave her, as birds of prey leave picked bones, and turn to the next business of the day, the distribution of the big green bundles of sago which the bride's kin loaded into the canoe. There is a furious argument as to who will preside, for the woman who presides must see that every one has a good share, even if she suffers herself. All of the women gather around the pile of sago. The bride sits forgotten in a corner, stripped of her finery, alone among hostile, grasping strangers. Later, some of the women will go home; most of them will stay to sleep with her. They will offer her food which she will refuse to eat; the fires will die low and they will sleep. No one will have spoken to her; she will have spoken to no one. If one wakes in the night and stirs up the fire for a moment, she will see that the bride is not sleeping, naturally "because she is ashamed."

Early in the morning her own kin fetch her home, surreptitiously. Again she is dressed and anointed.

An incantation is pronounced over her to make her a strong rich woman, active in the accumulation and exchange of property. This time, on the canoe which receives her stands a high carved bed, one leg of which is cracked and sagging. Her husband's kin will mention that defect later. The canoe proceeds slowly through the village, past crowded verandahs, to her betrothed's house. His aunt comes down on the verandah to receive her, and half drags her up the steps. She huddles at the top, with her back to the inmates of the house. She has just caught a glimpse of a bedizened youth sitting behind her, with feet stretched out stiffly in front of him. For a moment there is silence, then a hurried sound of footsteps. The bridegroom has left the house, to be seen no more until after nightfall. Every one breathes freely, the children are allowed to run about again. Her parents' canoe returns to the landing. She is hustled out upon her platform, and the party proceeds to the little islet where the day will be spent in speech-making, in the distribution of property. The drums will boom, the men will dance. But the bride will sit veiled in her canoe.

Late at night the bridegroom will return to the village and take his bride. He has no attitude of tenderness or affection for this girl whom he has never seen. She fears her first sex experience as all the women of her people have feared and hated it. No foundation is laid for happiness that night, only one for shame and hostility. The next day the bride goes about the village with her mother-in-law to fetch wood and water. She has not yet said one word to her husband. All eyes turn towards her, and everywhere she hears the words "breasts," "breasts of an old woman." "The breast bands held them up yesterday." Late in the afternoon she breaks her silence to scream angrily at a child who has followed her into the back of the house. This too is reported throughout the village, the village where she must now live but to which she in no sense belongs.

And this sense that husband and wife belong to different groups persists throughout the marriage, weakening after the marriage has endured for many years, never vanishing entirely. The father, mother and children do not form a warm intimate unit, facing the world. In most cases the man lives in his own village, in his own part of the village, near his brothers and uncles. Near by will live some of his sisters and aunts. These are the people with whom all his ties are closest, from whom he has learned to expect all his rewards since childhood. These are the people who fed him when he was hungry, nursed him when he was sick, paid his fines when he was sinful, and bore his debts for him. Their spirits are his spirits, their tabus his tabus. To them he has a strong sense of belonging.

But his wife is a stranger. He did not choose her; he never thought of her before marriage without a sense of shame. Because of her he has many times lain flattened out under a mat while his canoe passed through her village or by the house of one of her relatives. Hot with embarrassment, he has lain sometimes for half an hour prostrate on his stomach, afraid to speak above a whisper. Before he married her he was free in his own village at least. He could spend hours in the men's house, strumming and singing. Now that he is married, he cannot call his soul his own. All day long he must work for those who paid for his wedding. He must walk shamefacedly in their presence, for he has discovered how little he knows of the obligations into which he is plunged. He has every reason to hate his shy, embarrassed wife, who shrinks with loathing from his rough, unschooled embrace and has never a good word to say to him. They are ashamed to eat in each other's presence. Officially they sleep on opposite sides of the house. For the first couple of years of marriage, they never go about together.

The girl's resentment of her position does not lessen with the weeks. These people are strangers to her. To them her husband is bound by the closest ties their society recognises. If she is away from her people, in another village, she tries harder than does her husband to make something of her marriage. When he leaves her to go to his sister's house, she frets and scolds, and sometimes even commits the unforgivable sin of accusing him of making a second wife of his sister. Then the spirits send swift punishment upon the house, and the breach between husband and wife widens. If the bride has married in her own village, she goes home frequently to her relatives and makes even less effort at the hopeless task of getting along well with her husband. For her marriage her face was tattooed, her short curly hair was dyed red. But now her head is clean shaven and she is forbidden to ornament herself. If she does, the spirits of her husband will suspect her of wishing to be attractive to men and will send sickness upon the house. She may not even gossip, softly, to a female relative about her husband's relatives. The spirits who live in the skull bowls will hear her and punish. She is a stranger among strange spirits, spirits who nevertheless exercise a rigid espionage over her behaviour.

All this is galling enough to the young girl and she grows more and more sulky day by day as she sits among her relatives-in-law, cooking for feasts, or goes with them to the bush to work sago. If she does not conceive promptly, she is very likely to run away. Sometimes her relatives persuade her to return and she vacillates back and forth for several years before a child is born. When she does conceive, she is drawn closer, not to the father of her child, but to her own kin. She may not tell her husband that she is pregnant. Such intimacy would shame them both. Instead, she tells her mother and her father, her sisters and her brothers, her aunts and her cross cousins. Her relatives set to work to prepare the necessary food for the pregnancy feasts. Still nothing is said to the husband. His wife repulses his advances more coldly than ever and his dislike and resentment of her increases. Then some chance word reaches his ears, some rumour of the economic preparations his brothers-in-law are making. A child is to be born to him, so the neighbours say. Still he cannot mention the point to his wife, but he waits for the first feast when canoes laden with sago come to his door. The months wear on, marked by periodic feasts for which he must make repayment. His relatives help him but he is expected to do most of it himself. He must go to his sisters' houses and beg them for bead work. His aunts and mother must be importuned. Here where he has always commanded, he must plead. He is constantly worried for fear his repayments will not be enough, will not be correctly arranged. Meanwhile his pregnant wife sits at home making yards of beadwork for her brothers, working for her brothers while he must beg and cajole his sisters. The rift between the two widens.

A few days before the birth of the child the brother or cousin or uncle of the expectant mother divines for the place of birth. If he does not have the power to handle the divining bones himself, a relative will do it for him. The divination declares whether the child shall be born in the house of its father or of its maternal uncle. If the former is the verdict, the husband must leave his house and go to his sister's. This is usually only done when the couple have a house of their own, a very rare occurrence in the case of a man's first child. His brother-in-law and his wife and children move into his house. Or else his wife is taken away, sometimes to another village. From the moment her labour begins he may not see her. The nearest approach he can make to the house is to bring fish to the landing platform. For a whole month he wanders aimlessly about, sleeping now at one sister's, now at another's. Only after his brother-in-law has worked or collected enough sago, one or two tons at least, to make the return feast, can his wife return to him, can he see his child.

Meanwhile the mother is very much occupied with her new baby. For a month she must stay inside the house, hidden by a mat curtain, her food must be cooked on a special fire in special dishes. Only after dark may she slip out and bathe hastily in the sea. Life is more pleasant for her than it has been since before her marriage. All of her female relatives stop in to chat with her, those with milk suckle her child for her during their call. Her brothers' wives cook for her, bring her betel nut and pepper leaf, humour her as an invalid. Her husband, whom she has not learned to love, is not missed. She hugs her baby to her breast, runs her pursed lips along its little arms, and is happy.

The day before the big feast of sago and pots, a small feast is made within the household. Her brothers and their wives and sisters all prepare special foods, all kinds of shell fish, taro, sago, a white fruit called *ung*, and two kinds of leaf puddings. One of these called *tchutchu* is nine or ten inches square and an inch thick. After the food is cooked it is dished up in carved wooden bowls, and set away on the shelves until after the mother is dressed. Her hair, which has been allowed to grow during pregnancy, is painted red. She puts on beaded anklets and strings of dogs' teeth; all this is finery, not heavy money for her husband's relatives. The food is arranged on the platform of a canoe and the whole party of women and the small girls of the family proceed to one of the small islands in the village, an island belonging to one of her ancestral lines. Here her father's sister or her father's mother solemnly slaps her on the back with one of the *tchutchu* cakes, invoking the family spirits to make her strong and well and keep her from having another child until this one can walk about and swim. Then all the party partakes of the feast; the mother returns to her baby; the others go about the village leaving bowls of food at the homes of relatives. For the last time the mother sleeps alone with her child.

The next day is one long tiring round of ceremonies. The morning is spent in cooking for the feast. Here and there in the village sago is being loaded onto canoes, pigs are being caught ready for transfer. The mother is again dressed, this time in the heavy kind of money costume she wore as a bride. Her hair is painted for the last time. To-morrow it will be shaved off as is befitting a virtuous wife.

The long procession of canoes, sometimes fifteen or twenty strong, forms outside the house. On the most heavily laden canoes are slit gongs upon which the owners beat vigorously. The heavily clad young mother steps into the last canoe and as the flotilla moves slowly, pompously about the village, she steps from one canoe to another. She is expected to walk from end to end of the sago which has been collected in her honour. The heavy money skirts drag at her body, wearying her. This festival of return to her husband gives her no pleasure. Very often on the plea that she is ill or that her child is crying for her she leaves the procession and goes home. The feast goes on merrily. Her absence is not missed. She is only a pawn, an occasion for financial transactions.

Finally, after dark, the time has come to make "the journey of the breasts": to return her to her husband. This is a profitable business for the women who accompany her so there is much wrangling among the women of the house as to which kindred shall punt the canoe. The quarrelling may go on for an hour while the young mother sits sullen and bored. The house of feasting is dark now, except for flickering fires. Food bowls and children crowd the floor. The voices of the greedy women crack in the stifling smoke-charged air. At last a compromise is reached and a group of women lead the young mother down the ladder and bundle her into a canoe. A storm has come up; the canoes rock and bump one another by the landing. Not a house can be seen. The practised women punt the laden canoe to the house of her husband's sister, where her husband has lived since their separation. The wife climbs upon the platform and sits there quietly. Her husband may be within the house but it is not necessary that he be there. He gives no sign. After a little she climbs back into the canoe and returns to her baby, to the crowded house and the new wrangling over the sago payments involved in the journey. Only after the last reckoning is settled will the guests disperse. Her brother's wife is the last to go, gathering up her belongings and muttering because her own children have fallen ill among the spirits of strangers. The young wife goes to sleep, wearily, and late that night the husband returns.

Now begins a new life. The father takes a violent proprietary interest in the new baby. It is his child, belongs to his kin, is under the protection of his spirits. He watches his wife with jealous attention, scolds her if she stirs from the house, berates her if the baby cries. He can be rougher with her now. The chances are that she will not run away, but will stay where her child will be well cared for. For a year mother and baby are shut up together in the house. For that year the child still belongs to its mother. The father only holds it occasionally, is afraid to take it from the house. But as soon as the child's legs are strong enough to stand upon and its small arms adept at clutching, the father begins to take the child from the mother. Now that the child is in no need of such frequent suckling, he expects his wife to get to work, to go to the mangrove swamp to work sago, to make long trips to the reef for shell fish. She has been idle long enough for, say the men, "a woman with a new baby is no use to her husband, she cannot work." The plea that her child needs her would not avail. The father is delighted to play with the child, to toss it in the air, tickle it beneath its armpits, softly blow on its bare, smooth skin. He has risen at three in the morning to fish, he has fished all through the cold dawn, punted the weary way to the market, sold some of his fish for good bargains in taro, in betel nut, in taro leaves. Now he is free for the better part of the day, drowsy, just in the mood to play with the baby.

From her brother too come demands upon the woman. He worked well for her during her pregnancy. Now he must meet his obligations to his wife's people. His sister must help him. From every side she is bidden to leave the baby to its doting father and go about her affairs. Children learn very young to take advantage of this situation. Father is obviously the most important person in the home; he orders mother about, and hits her if she doesn't "hear his talk." Father is even more indulgent than mother. It is a frequent picture to see a little minx of three leave her father's arms, quench her thirst at her mother's breast, and then swagger back to her father's arms, grinning overbearingly at her mother. The mother sees the child drawn further and further away from her. At night the child sleeps with the father, by day she rides on his back. He takes her to the shady island which serves as a sort of men's club house where all the canoes are built and large fish traps made. Her mother can't come on this island except to feed the pigs when no men are there. Her mother is ashamed to come there but she can rollick gaily among the half-completed canoes. When there is a big feast, her mother must hide in the back of the house behind a hanging mat. But she can run away to father in the front of the house when the soup and betel nut are being given out. Father is always at the centre of interest, he is never too busy to play. Mother is often busy. She must stay in the smoky interior of the house. She is forbidden the canoe islands. It is small wonder that the father always wins the competition: the dice are loaded from the start.

And then the mother becomes pregnant again, another baby which will be her own for a year is on its way. She withdraws more from the struggle and begins to wean the present baby. The weaning is slow. The child is spoiled, long accustomed to eating other foods, it is used to being given its mother's breast whenever it cries for it. The women tie bundles of hair to their nipples to repel the children. The weaning is said to last well into pregnancy. The child is offended by its mother's withdrawal and clings still closer to its father. So on the eve of the birth of a new baby, the child's transfer of dependence to its father is almost complete. The social patterning of childbirth reaffirms that dependence. While the mother is occupied with her new baby, the older child stays with its father. He feeds it, bathes it, plays with it all day. He has little work or responsibility during this period and so more time to strengthen his position. This repeats itself for the birth of each new child. The mother welcomes birth; again she will have a baby which is her own, if only for a few months. And at the end of the early months the father again takes over the younger child. Occasionally he may keep a predominant interest in the older child, especially if the older is a boy, the younger a girl, but usually there is room in his canoe for two or three little ones. And the elder ones of five and six are not pushed out of the canoe, they leave it in the tiny canoes which father has hewn for them. At the first upset, the first rebuff, they can come swimming back into the sympathetic circle of the father's indulgent love for his children.

As the father's relation to his child is continually emphasised, so the mother is always being reminded of her slighter claims. If her father is ill in another village, and she wishes to go, her husband cannot keep her, but he keeps her two-year-old son. Some woman of his kin will suckle the child if he cries and the father will care for him tenderly. The woman goes off for her uncertain voyage, torn between her blood kin and her child. This is in cases of perfectly ordinary relations between husband and wife. In case of a quarrel she will take her young children with her if she runs away from her husband. But even here five- and six-year-olds make their own choices and often elect to stay with their father.

Or a woman will come with her husband and children to visit in her own village during a feast. The husband will put up a ban against her father's house. One of the children got sick there before; the spirits are inimical, none of his children shall enter that house again. Instead, the whole family must stay with his relatives in the other end of the village. The grandparents must come there to see their grandchild. The mother may go if she wishes but, says the husband, *his* child shall not.

A man's attitude is the same whether a child be adopted or his own child. One fourth of the children in Peri were adopted, in about half of the cases the parents were dead. In any event, the real parents relinquished all hold on the child if the adoption had taken place in infancy. An elder brother's child adopted by a younger brother called the younger brother "father" and his real father "grandfather." A little girl adopted by her older sister called her sister "mother," her mother "grandmother." In one striking instance the foster father had died and the real parents took back their son whom they always addressed formerly as "child whose father is dead," a special mourning term. Children adopted by elder members of the family called their true parents by their given names. An adopted child belonged to the clan of his foster father; the spirits and tabus of that house were his. But to his foster mother he had no bond except that she it was who gave him food. And with this denial to the woman of her share in the rewards of providing a home for the foster child goes a curious change of emphasis.

Much has been written to prove that mother-right is natural because maternity is unmistakable. Paternity being always questionable, is a less firm basis for descent. Native statements are quoted in support of this view.

Manus presents a vivid contrast to this attitude which seems so credible to many modern authors. Physical paternity is understood; the natives believe that the child is a product of semen and clotted menstrual blood. But physical paternity does not interest them in the least. The adopted child is considered to be far more his foster father's than his true father's. Does he not belong to his foster father's spirits? Men marry pregnant women who are widowed or separated from their husbands and when the children are born welcome them as their own. The real father makes no claim upon his child born to a runaway wife. Although the whole village may know the true father of a child, they will never mention it unless pressed, and never to the child unless the child remembers its adoption.

But maternity is a very different matter. Blood or adopted, the father's claims, the father's rewards are the same. But to her child the mother has very little claim except the claim of blood. So we find not disputes about paternity but disputes about maternity. A woman will declare, holding a child fiercely to her bosom, "This is my child. I bore him. He grew in my body. I suckled him at these breasts. He is mine, mine, mine!" And yet every one in the village will tell you she is lying and point to the real mother of the child adopted in early infancy. An aspersion on a woman's maternity rouses all the shamed defensive rage usually associated among us with throwing doubt upon paternity.

This passionate attitude may also be due to the relation between mediumship and maternity. Only women who have dead male children can act as mediums and acting as a medium is the only way in which women can exercise any real power in their husband's households. Where upon her rests the ultimate determination of the will of the spirits, a woman can, innocently enough, read into the odd whistling sounds which the spirit makes through her lips, motives and counsels congenial to her. And a child spirit will not act as a control for a foster mother. It is of course equally possible that the insistence upon real maternity of mediums may have flowed from the attitude towards blood motherhood.

Even the blood tie between mother and children is likely to be disrupted. Salikon and Ngasu were two of the brightest, best dressed little girls in the village. Salikon was about fourteen, so near to puberty that her foster father had already stored the coconuts away for the puberty feast. Ngasu was eleven, curly-haired, bright-eyed, quick-limbed. She could swim as well as the boys and she fought almost as many battles. Their mother was a widow, a plump, buxom woman, still comely, and highly skilled in every native industry. Her husband, Panau, had been a man of wealth and importance in the community. He had just been on the verge of making the important silver wedding payment for his wife when he died suddenly. One so cut off in his prime was bound to feel angry, and fear of Panau's spirit was strong in the village. His younger brother Paleao inherited his house, the care of his widow, whom he called mother, and the guardianship of his daughters. Salikon was betrothed and it was Paleao who collected the pigs and oil to meet her betrothal payments. The widow was much respected in the village and very much attached to her daughters. She disciplined them more carefully than any other mother in the village, and dressed them better. Their grass skirts were always nicely crimped; they always wore beaded bracelets and armlets which "mother made." The widow was such an expert worker that she was in great demand everywhere and she moved about the village, sometimes living in the house of Paleao, sometimes in the house of one brother, sometimes of another. Wherever she went the two little girls went with her instead of settling in the house of their foster father and mother. It was a pretty picture of mother and daughter devotion.

But the day came when the charming picture was shattered. The widow of Panau was still young. Many men sought her hand, all clandestinely, for her kin did not dare to connive at her remarriage for fear of her dead husband's ghostly wrath, nor did they wish to lose such a good worker. Finally the widow found a suitor of her own choice and in great secrecy she eloped with him to another village. All the amiability of her relatives and relatives-in-law vanished. Furious at her desertion, desperately afraid of Panau, they all vied with each other in loud-mouthed condemnation of her flight. And loudest of all were the two little daughters, who refused to see their mother and spoke of her with the greatest bitterness. Now their dead father would be angry. Once before their mother had planned to elope and Ngasu had nearly died of fever.

This time one of them would surely die. Oh, their wicked, wicked mother, to think of her own happiness instead of theirs! They lived on in the house of their father's brother and thrust their mother's image from their hearts.

THE CHILD AND THE ADULT SOCIAL LIFE

MANUS children live in a world of their own, a world from which adults are wilfully excluded, a world based upon different premises from those of adult life.

To the Manus adult, trade is the most important thing in life; trade with far-away islands, trade with the land people, trade with the next village, trade with his relatives-in-law, trade with his relatives. His house roof is stacked with pots, his shelves piled with grass skirts, his boxes filled with dogs' teeth. The spirit of his ancestor presides over his wealth and chastises him if he fails to use it wisely and well. When he speaks of his wife he mentions the size of the betrothal payment which was made for her, when he quarrels with his neighbours he boasts of the number of large exchanges he has made for her. When he speaks of his sister he says, "I give her sago and she gives me beadwork"; when he speaks of his dead father he mentions the huge burial payment he made for him. When he angers the spirit of a neighbour's house he atones in pigs and oil, or boxes and axes. The whole of life, his most intimate relation to people, his conception of places, his evaluation for his guarding spirits, all fall under the head of *kawas*, "exchange." He has no other word for friend, naturally friendship too falls under the spell—friends are people with whom one trades, or who help one in trade. A specially beautiful food bowl or well woven grass skirt is praised as "belonging to *kawas.*" Pregnancy, birth, puberty, betrothal, marriage, death, are thought of in terms of dogs' teeth and shell money, pigs and oil. The chief events in the village life are these exchanges and the accompanying pomp and ceremony, oratory and ceremonial jesting. Trade widens and narrows through the generations, so a man and his sister help each other for a *quid pro quo*, but are not conceived as actually exchanging wealth. But the sons of the brother and sister become formal traders as the financial backers of the arranged marriage between their sons and daughters. These businesslike cousins are permitted to jest with one another, to refer lewdly to each other's private life, to break every convention of sobriety of speech, to shatter every reticence. Thus the strain of economic antagonism is ceremonially broken. A man who is receiving advance payments from his cousin of ten thousand dogs' teeth, payments which it will take him years to meet, is permitted to dance an obscene defiance to his creditor. When the children of these two men marry, the gap made by property is complete, the wife is on one side of the exchange, the husband on the other. Business rivals, they are careful to betray no secrets, one to the other.

The attention of adults is fixed upon trade: when the canoe will be in from Mok with coconuts; when that landsman will bring the promised and paid-for-in-advance sago; if all the preparations have been adequately made for next week's post-birth ceremony. All day they bustle to and fro in the village, consulting relatives, dunning creditors for small repayments, giving orders, making requisitions on property. In every exchange fifteen or twenty people take part, relatives of each of the principals exchanging with a partner on the opposite side. The exchange may be a mere three hundred pounds of sago, but it is an individual stake, not a contribution to the good of the whole, and so of vast importance to the person making it.*

During the days before a big exchange, the village is in a fever of expectancy. For instance, Pomasa is to make a *metcha,* the silver wedding payment which a rich and successful man makes for a wife to whom he has been married fifteen or twenty years. For three years Pomasa has been preparing for this great event. He is an expert turtle fisher, and turtle after turtle he

* As we invest in factories or stores or export companies, so Manus financiers invest in marriages, or more accurately the economic exchanges which centre about marriage. In the initial betrothal payment for a male child, a large number of relatives invest dogs' teeth and shell money and the recipients on the bride's side pay these amounts back later in pigs and oil. At each new economic exchange resulting from a betrothal or marriage new investors may come in provided they can find partners on the opposite side. Sometimes would-be investors of little economic importance are seen cruising about the edges of a ceremony looking for partners. And just as our financiers hesitate to back a man who has gone bankrupt or a store which is forever being shifted from one location to another, so the Manus are canny about backing a man who has been often divorced. They centre their investments about tried and enduring marriages and the marriages so substantially endorsed by society assume greater prestige; their stock goes up, so to speak.

has sold to the land people for dogs' teeth and shell money. He has trade friends on the north coast, and he has made long expeditions there to fish for dugong. All his sisters, his aunts, his brothers, have helped him collect the necessary property. To do this they have had to call in all their debts, dun and dun their creditors for repayment. Now it is only a month until the great day. Pomasa kills a turtle and punts it through the village, drumming triumphantly, boastfully, upon his slit drum. He cooks the turtle and sends it to all his relatives who are helping him in the exchange. That night, in their presence, he counts his dogs' teeth and measures his fathoms of shell money.

For the rest of the month he does no work, neither he nor the members of his household. Instead, resplendent in dogs' teeth and ornament, they voyage here and there in search of more contributions of wealth. A great wooden bowl is placed on the canoe; the canoe stops at the landing platform and the woman relative in the house brings out her contribution and drops it into the bowl. Each contributor will receive an exact return in pigs, oil and sago, when the return payments are made. Another day, Pomasa will hang the jaw bone of his father down his back, fasten a specially large and ornamental bag over his shoulder, and set out overland to call on some distant relatives among the land people. Or the whole household will sail off to another village, coming back this time with a couple of new canoes, collected from some cousins.

Meanwhile the relatives of his wife to whom he

will make the spectacular payment are busy cooking. Day after day they send bowls of food to the house of Pomasa, that he and his wife may be free of any need to think about their daily bread. Pomasa is always dressed up, always portentous in manner, the centre of public interest. As the time for the *metcha* approaches, all the members of his wife's family are invited to an inspection of the payments they are later to receive. In the crowded house, lit by blazing torches, kindled in the low fireplaces, men and women crowd eagerly about the display of wealth. "Oh, Nali, Panau's sister-in-law, is to have this string of dogs' teeth!" Carefully, avariciously, she notes its special characteristics, five teeth and then a broken one, blue beads between the teeth except in the middle, where there are five red ones, blue and red tags on the ends. If two weeks later there is a mistake and Nali does not receive this very string, she will clamour loudly for her rights. After this exhibition the in-laws go home to cook bigger and better meals for the household of Pomasa.

When the great day comes Pomasa is arrayed in yards of ornament. His sad-eyed wife is dressed in bridal finery. Her tenth child is within a month of being born. Five of her children are dead. Popitch, the last to die, died only six weeks ago. Her long, worn breasts sag in spite of the supporting ornaments. Her face is lined and haggard and she stoops awkwardly beneath the weight of the bridal aprons. This is a great day for Pomasa, her husband, and a great day for Bosai her brother who will receive Pomasa's spectacular payments. It is her silver wedding.

The village is crowded, strangers come from all parts, every house is filled with guests. Canoes are clustered about the little islets, the thousands of dogs' teeth are hung on lines, and both sides dance and make long speeches. An event of major significance and interest has taken place. For years this *metcha* will be mentioned: who did or did not make a good showing; how Pomasa smugly refused to make the secret extra payments usually made at dead of night. When Pomasa quarrels with his neighbors who have not made a *metcha*, he will boast of his great achievement. And with the pigs and oil in which his creditors gradually repay him, he and his family will feast and pay their debts.

In this complex pattern of dog tooth finance, every person who owns property is involved, weekly, almost daily. Where a pig changes hands half a dozen times in a morning, the participation of many individuals is inevitable. Every *metcha*, every betrothal, every marriage, has reverberations through many villages, affects the plans of scores of households.

From this world the children are divided completely by a very simple fact: they own no property. They have neither debtors nor creditors, dogs' teeth nor pigs. They haven't a stick of tobacco staked in the transaction. True, the exchange may be made in the name of one of them. Kilipak's father may be paying twelve thousand dogs' teeth to his cousin, the father of Kilipak's future wife. This brings the question of Kilipak's one-day marriage before the minds of the other children. They chaff him a little, suddenly stop using his personal name and call him instead "grandson of Nate," the name of his bride's grandfather. Kilipak turns hot and sullen under their teasing but he takes no extra interest in the ceremony, although in the name of it his elders will some day bring him to account. To-day he simply goes off fishing with the other boys.

Afterwards Kilipak will feel this payment in which he takes no interest: henceforth he must avoid his bride's name and the names of all her relatives, and he must lie hidden if his canoe goes through her village. So to the child's eyes, the elders have a great economic show which takes up all their time and attention, makes mother cross and father absent-minded, makes the food supply in the house less subject to the child's insistent demands, takes the whole family away from home, or separates him from the large pig which he used to enjoy riding in the water. Then there is a great deal of beating of drums, speech making, and dancing. Every ceremony is just like every other. It may be of huge interest to his elders that for a *kinekin* feast for a pregnant woman the packs of sago are stacked in threes, while for a *pinpuaro* feast after birth the sago packs are stood upright. To the elder such important bits of ceremonial procedure are sign and symbol of intimate knowledge, like the inside knowledge on the stock market which the new speculator displays so proudly.

But to the child as to the non-investor, this is all so much unintelligible rigmarole.

His version of the whole spectacle is brief and concise. There are two kinds of payments—the payments made on a grand scale and the small gradual repayments made individually. The big ones may be canoes of sago and pigs and oil, or they may be hundreds of dogs' teeth hung up on the islet, in which case there may be dancing. Sometimes, for wholly inexplicable reasons, there is no dancing. At other times a pig changes hands and a drum is beaten about that, most annoyingly. The drum beat may turn one from one's play in anticipation of some interesting event. And it turns out to be nothing but the payment of a debt. Afterwards there are always quarrels, insults, and recriminations. If mother is very much involved in the transaction, so involved that it would be inconvenient to go home—in the children's words, if mother "has work"— father will be especially nasty to her, knowing she won't dare leave him. But if it's "father's work," mother is likely to be extra disagreeable, to weary of it in the middle, and go off to her own kin. The fact that a lot of this "work" is ostensibly in his name only serves to set the child more firmly against it, as a most incomprehensible nuisance. To all questions about commerce, the children answer furiously: "How should we know —who's grown up here anyway, we or you? What do you think you are to bother us about such things! It's your business, not ours."

The parents permit their children to remain in this

happy state of irresponsible inattention. No attempt is made to give the children property and enlist their interest in the financial game. They are simply expected to respect the tabus and avoidances which flow from the economic arrangements, because failure to do so will anger the spirits and produce undesirable results.

In the child's world property, far from being garnered and stored, is practically communal in use if not in ownership. Property consists of small canoes, paddles, punts, bows and arrows, spears, spider-web nets, strings of beads, occasional bits of tobacco or betel nuts. These last are always shared freely among the children. One poor little cigarette of newspaper and Louisiana twist trade tobacco will pass through fifteen hands before it is returned to its owner for a final farewell puff. If among a group of children one name is heard shouted very frequently above the rest, the listener can be sure that that child has a cigarette which the others are begging. Similarly a string of beads will pass from child to child as a free gift for which no return is expected. Quarrels over property are the rule in the adult world, but they are not frequent among children. The older children imitate their parents' severity and chastise younger children for even touching adults' property, but this is more for a chance to start a fight and from force of habit than from any keen interest in protecting the property.

Quarrels which spring up from other causes will be justified in terms of property, if an adult inquires into them. The children know that to say "He took my canoe" will elicit more sympathy than "I wanted to make cat's cradles and he didn't"; and the child is an adept at translating his world into terms which are acceptable to the adult.

The constant buying and selling, advance and repayment in the adult world is a serious obstacle to any cooperative effort. Individually owned wealth is a continual spur to self-centred individualistic activity. But among the children, where there are no such individual stakes, much more co-operation is seen. The boys of fourteen and fifteen who stand at the head of the group organise the younger children, plan races, on foot or in canoe, organise football teams, the football being a lemon; or institute journeys to the river for a swim. Surface quarrelling and cuffing is fairly frequent, but there is little permanent ill humour. The leadership is too spontaneous, too informal, and has developed no strong devices for coercing the unwilling. The recalcitrant goes home unchastised, the trouble-maker remains. The older boys scold and indulge in vivid vituperation but they dare not use any appreciable force. A real fight between children, even very tiny ones, means a quarrel between their parents, and in any case the child always finds a sympathiser in his parents. Irritation over missped plans or a spoiled game takes itself out, very much as dominoes fall down one upon another. Yesa tells Bopau to get his canoe. Bopau refuses. Yesa slaps him, Tchokal slaps Yesa for slapping Bopau and Kilipak slaps Tchokal for slapping Yesa. Kilipak being the largest in that group, the scuffle degenerates into a few wailing or sulking individuals. In five minutes all is fair weather again unless some child feels so affronted that he goes home to find sympathy. These teapot tempests are frequent and unimportant, the consequence of a large number of aggressive children playing together without devices for control. At that, they are far sunnier and less quarrelsome than their elders, more amenable to leadership, friendlier, less suspicious and more generous. Deep-rooted feuds and antagonisms are absent. Among the elders almost every person has definite antagonisms, always smouldering, always likely to break out into open quarrels. But the size and the varying ages of the children make a fluid unpatterned grouping in which close personal attachments and special antagonisms do not flourish.

Although the parents take violent part for their children, their children do not reciprocate. Children whose parents are making the village ring with abuse, will placidly continue their games in the moonlight. If the quarrels between the parents grow so serious that the spirits may be expected to take a hand, the children are warned against going to the house of the enemy, a prohibition which they may or may not obey.

The whole convention of the child's world is thus a play convention. All participation is volitional and without an *arrière pensée*. But among the adults casual friendliness, neighbourly visiting is regarded as almost reprehensible. Young men without position or standing go to the houses of older relatives to ask for assistance or to render services. Men may haunt their sisters' homes. But visiting between men of the same status, or between married women who are neither sisters nor sisters-in-law, is regarded as trifling, undignified behaviour. A man who goes about the village from house to house must have considerable prestige to stand the raillery which such behaviour calls for. The only man in Peri who habitually visited about had been given the nickname of "Pwisio," Manus for the white man's cat, whose wandering ways are known to the natives. Social gatherings are for purposes of exchange, either to plan the exchange or to execute it, or about the sick, the shipwrecked, the dying, or the dead. To leave one's own home and go to sleep in the house of trouble is regarded as the highest expression of sympathy. Men, women, and children crowd the floor of the house of mourning, men sleeping in the front of the house, women in the rear, husbands and wives separated, sometimes for a month at a time. To sleep in the house of another is a solemn matter, not to be undertaken lightly.

Manus men, uninterested in friendship themselves, are intolerant of friendship on the part of their wives. As one woman phrased it: "If a man sees his wife talking for a long time with another woman or going into another woman's house, he will look at her. If she is her sister or her sister-in-law, it is well. If she is an unrelated woman, he will scold his wife. He may even beat her." But with her own feminine relatives a woman must always speak circumspectly. Her husband is tabu to them; their husbands are tabu to her.

She cannot mention any intimate matter about any one who is tabu. A daughter cannot comment upon her married life to her mother who has never even been allowed to look her daughter's husband in the face. The tabus between relatives-in-law act most efficiently in keeping such relatives not only out of the social scene but also out of the conversation.

With her sister-in-law she is on even more formal terms. The sister-in-law is devoted to her brother, resents the wife, will not hear the most casual complaints against him. Sisters-in-law may not use each other's names; a certain reserve in conduct is always enjoined upon them, and remarks from one to the other are prefaced by the vocative: *"Pinkaiyo"* (sister-in-law)! As a man's relations to his sisters, a woman's to her brothers, are one of the strongest threats against the stability of marriage, cultural insistence upon the appearance of friendship between sisters-in-law and between brothers-in-law has important results.

All through adult life in Manus there is a struggle between a man's wife and a man's sister for his allegiance and his gifts. This struggle is far keener than between brothers-in-law. The obscenity in which a jealous and outraged wife accuses her husband of making his sister into her co-wife has no parallel in the relationship of brothers-in-law. It is the wife who is the stranger, who is at a continual disadvantage in fighting the vested interests of the sister. So the community votes it good for these two traditional enemies to sign a continuous public truce. And it is true that in lasting marriages brothers-in-law learn to be good partners if not good friends and sisters-in-law become adjusted to working together with some show of co-operation. But the societies' insistence upon those friendships which are most difficult as the friendships which are most admirable hampers free choice and regiments human relations.

A man's formal relationships with his brothers and brothers-in-law is in strong contrast to his joking relationship to his cross cousins.* Wherever he goes he is almost sure to find a man who can address him as "Cross cousin," and straightway make mock of whatever solemnity he is engaged in. Although often embarrassing and often provoking, this ceremonial intimacy gives a sort of outlet which is not permitted in other relationships. And to his female cross cousin a man who is a widower may even talk about his matrimonial plans in fairly personal terms.

But between female cross cousins this jesting does not obtain. It is permitted but never used. And the woman, although she receives the confidences of her male cousin, does not reciprocate; better drilled in prudery than he, she is silent.

The children, especially the boys, act as cavalierly towards all these ceremonial prescriptions of the adult world as they do towards the economic exchanges. Small children class older relatives indiscriminately as fathers, mothers, and grandparents. The special terms

* The children of a mother's brother, or a father's sister, i.e., first cousins whose sibling-parents are of opposite sex.

[94]

for mother's brother and father's sister are treated with complete neglect, and a boy of fourteen or fifteen cannot even give the proper term for father's paternal aunt, although she and her female descendants will be the principal mourners when he dies. The adult world is divided for the children into father's clan, mother's clan, people who are related to father and mother in some way which brings them within the circle of attention, people whom mother avoids, people whom father avoids, people whom one must avoid oneself. The most conspicuous fact about a grandmother may be the way she runs when father approaches, and father's blushing fury if her name is mentioned in his presence. There is no word for relatives in general use; instead one says, "I belong to Kalat.* He belongs to Kalat," or, "We two belong to Kalat." Children under seven or eight will simply know the houses of their mother's clan as friendly places, but older children can usually give the fact of their mother's clan membership as an explanation of this fact. Sharply singled out from the host of relatives are father and mother and semi-foster fathers who have adopted one in name or are in process of adopting one. These elders are the ones most compliant to one's whims. So Langison, who had been informally adopted as an older child by his father's mother's sister's husband and by his father's younger brother was said to have "three fathers," or, as the other boys put it, "three places where he can cry out

* Kalat is a localised paternal clan group, the houses of whose members stand near each other in one part of the village.

[95]

for food." The houses of grandparents are also places where one can "cry out for food" without bringing shame and opprobium upon oneself and one's parents, for the rule against asking for food is part of the training in respect for property.

The adult's general tolerance of negligence on the part of children permits the child to reap all the advantages of his kinship arrangements but requires him to pay very slight attention. If a household of the clan of Motchapal is giving a ceremony, all the children belonging to it may ride in the canoes, dress up in dogs' teeth, nibble greedily at the feast, if they wish to. But their presence is never required. Even in mourning ceremonies no demands are made upon children under fifteen; only slight demands are made on the unmarried. The whole adult scheme is phrased in terms of children's claims upon it. The strongest claims it makes on the child are the demands for avoidance.

Nor are the strictly delimited friendships of the adult demanded or even expected from the children. The play groups include the village. If one clan is a little isolated from the others, as is the case with Kalat, the younger children of Kalat will play together more than they will play with the children at the other end of the village. Children use no kinship terms among themselves and are not conscious of exact relationships. Adults will laughingly point out the infant uncle of a lusty ten-year-old or comment on the way in which the adoption of a little girl makes her her own sister's titular cross cousin. But the children themselves pay no attention. The first consciousness of relationships outside the household group comes with the recognition of some common avoidance. I saw this happen in the case of four boys, Pomat, Kilipak, Kutan and Yesa, boys who had played together constantly from childhood. Pomat knew that his mother called Kilipak's mother "sister," but he never addressed Kilipak as "cross cousin." He knew that Kutan's father, Pomasa, called his own father, Kemai, "grandfather," but he had never been accustomed to calling Kutan "son" on that account. He knew that Yesa had been adopted by his mother's clan brother and still he never addressed Yesa as "cross cousin," either. All four boys thought first of each other as individuals. They had not learned the adult habit of thinking first of relationships. Then the husband of Pomat's sister, Pwondret, came to live in the village. This youth, named Sisi, was a tabu relative of all four boys because he had married Pwondret, the sister of Pomat, cross cousin of Kilipak and Yesa and "mother" of Kutan. Sisi's marriage with Pwondret had been sudden and without a long betrothal so for years all four boys had known him as an occasional visitor whom they called by his name. Now all four had to give up using his name and call him "husband of Pwondret." This annoyance brought to their attention that they were all related one to another and laboriously they traced out this relationship and the kinship terms which they should use to one another.

So the simplified canons of the child's world may become complicated by contact with the adult world, but the gulf between the two worlds is not thereby narrowed. Rather age-class consciousness is increased; all four boys realised their common inconvenience under this adult convention. There is no real attempt to induct the child into this alien adult world. He is given no place in it and no responsibilities. He is permitted to use it for his own egocentric purposes and only made to feel its pressure when the observance of tabus is felt to be absolutely necessary for the safety of the community.

VI

MANUS religion is a special combination of spiritualism and ancestor worship. The spirits of the dead males of the family become its guardians, protectors, censors, dictators after death. The skull and finger bones are suspended from the roof in a carved bowl, and the desires and preferences of the spirit of the house consulted upon all important occasions. Severe disaster falling upon the household discredits the principal spirit, who is then either demoted to the rank of spirit guard of some young man or small boy or else expelled altogether from the house. Without a house, a spirit is as much a social nonentity as a man would be. He roams, impotent and vaguely malicious, in the open spaces between the houses, finally degenerating into some low form of sea life. Meanwhile a new spirit is set up in the house. This regnant house spirit is the special guardian of the male head of the family. Unless requested to remain at home, he accompanies the house father on his overseas expedition or on his trips to the mainland. His spirit wife or wives, who are of little importance, and are not represented by skulls, remain at home. Women and girls have no personal guardians and are therefore spiritually unequipped for venturing into dangerous places. But little boys, from the time they are four or five, are usually given guardian spirits who are supposed to attend them everywhere. These guardians may be the spirits of dead boys, or children born to spirits on the spirit plane, or occasionally the slightly discredited or outmoded adult spirits of their fathers.

In Manus there is neither heaven nor hell; there are simply two levels of existence. On one level live the mortals all of whose acts, each of whose words, are known to the spirits, provided the spirit is present and paying attention. The spirit is not conceived as omniscient. He, like a living man, can only see and hear within the range of his senses. A spirit will disclaim knowledge of what went on in a house during his absence. Spirits are invisible, only rarely are they seen by mortals, but they occasionally make their presence manifest by whistling in the night. They are more powerful than mortals, being less dependent upon time and space and having the power to translate material objects into their own sphere of invisibility. They act upon mortals by extracting bits of the soul stuff. If all of a mortal's soul stuff is taken by a spirit or spirits the mortal will die. Spirits can also hide things, steal things, throw stones, and otherwise manipulate the material world in a capricious, unaccountable fashion. This, however, they very seldom do. In spite of their greater powers they are conceived very humanly. So a man will beseech his spirit to drive an expected school of fish into a particular lagoon. He will not ask his spirit to multiply the fish, only to herd them. The chief duties of a spirit are to prosper the fishing of his wards and to preserve their lives and limbs against the machinations of hostile spirits. It is the spirits' privilege to demand in return the exercise of certain restraints and virtues. In the first place, the living must commit no sex offences which interfere with the Manus social order (i.e.: a spirit will not object to an intrigue with a woman of another tribe). This is a rigorous prohibition; light words, chance physical contacts, evil plans, careless jests, non-observance of the proper avoidance reactions towards relatives-in-law, all these may bring down the spirits' righteous wrath, either upon the sinner or upon some one of his relatives—perhaps pushing a decrepit old man from his lingering death bed into death, perhaps afflicting a new born baby with the colic. Additionally, the spirits abhor economic laxity of any sort: failure to pay debts, careless manipulation of family properties, economic procrastination, and unfair allotment of funds among the needs of several relatives, as when a man uses all the wealth which comes into the family to make spectacular payments for his wife and fails to make betrothal payments for his younger brothers. Insubordination within a family, quarrels between in-laws also stir their wrath. And bad housing annoys the critical spirits, who object to presiding over unsafe floors, sagging piles, and leaky thatch.

In addition to their obligations to their dutiful wards and their stern rôle as upholders of a moral order, the spirits engage in various activities which may be said to be the results of their mortal natures carried over into the spirit level: they marry or strive to marry, they beget children, they quarrel among themselves, they shirk their obligations, they maliciously vent old grudges upon the living, or transfer enmities arising on the spirit plane to the mortals connected with the hated spirits. So a spirit will punish his mortal wards who fail to treat as in-laws the mortal relatives of his spirit wife, or he will strike ill the living younger brother of a spirit who has seduced his spirit wife. Also, while yet newly translated to the spirit plane he will work havoc among the living in revenge for his own death. If he is a youth, he will try to kill other youths who are living while he is dead; if he died for adultery he will constitute himself official executioner of all adulterers. If he died before making a large feast, he will afflict others who give promise of successfully making the same kind of feast. Or he will exercise special malice towards any who arrange or assist in the remarriage of his widow.

The will of the spirits is conveyed to mortals through séances, women with dead male children acting as mediums. The spirit child acts as a messenger boy upon the spirit plane. He speaks through his mother's mouth, in a whistling sound which she translates to the assembled questioners. At her bidding he goes about interrogating the various spirits who may be responsible for the illness, misfortune, or death, or he collects the bits of purloined soul stuff and returns them to the sick person.

Men are able to hold less satisfactory converse with their own guardians by a kind of divination—a question is propounded and a bone hung over the shoulder. If the back itches on one side the answer is "yes," on the other, "no." Thus the man often determines the direction which the medium's responses in the séance will take.

So a Manus village is seen as the abode of mortals and spirits. There in the house of Paleao is the newly translated spirit of his dead adopted brother, Panau, still smarting from his sudden demise in the midst of preparations for a feast. He has a bad habit of striking people with a hatchet. The afflicted person spits up blood and is likely not to recover. In the little house next door lives Paleao's mother-in-law presided over by the guardian spirit of Paleao's small son, Popoli, his namesake. The spirit Popoli, restive after he had been displaced by the newly dead Panau, systematically afflicted the household, making ill Paleao's pig, Paleao's wife, Paleao himself, until Paleao built a separate house for his mother-in-law, where his son's spirit could reign supreme. Just down the way is the house of a man whose guardian spirit has two spirit wives who get on very badly together and who vent their continual quarrels upon the child of the house.

So it goes; the personalities, prejudices, marital arrangements, of the spirits are known as well as are those of their living wards. Most of them are the recently dead; their very faces are still fresh in the memory of the living. But this spirit world is a world in which adult values and adult values alone are current, where the chief preoccupations are work, wealth and sex—ideas with which the children are essentially uncon-cerned. Furthermore, the children do not recognise that the spirits are still exercising the tenderness and humanity which they were accustomed to receive from fathers and uncles while they were still on earth. The children are little in need of protection—they are not permitted to wander abroad, they do no fishing which needs spirit supervision, they have no economic affairs to prosper. So the spirits of the dead appear to them in a stern, inimical light. Panau was a beloved father, but since he died he made his daughter Ngasu sick be-cause her mother wanted to marry again. Popitch was a jolly little comrade, a romping, scatter-brained boy of eleven, up to any prank, undeterred by authority. Dead, he is suddenly elevated to be the chief spirit of his father's house, and makes his fourteen-year-old brother Kutan sick, in a spirit quarrel as to who shall be Kutan's spirit. The children forget their grief for Popitch the comrade, in dread and resentment towards Popitch the hostile spirit. Father or comrade, the spirit is usually no longer felt to be the children's friend.

Furthermore, although the adults are accustomed to bear almost any exaction or take any trouble to meet their children's whims, they dare not anger the spirits, nor expose their beloved children to the hostile spirits' malice. A father will usually take a child along fish-ing, although it means extra trouble and delay, pos-sibly a smaller catch. But he will not take a child out ot the shelter of the village if illness or recent death has tainted the very air with fear. Then the child's pleadings and rages are equally powerless to move the usually compliant father. In the name of fear of the spirits, obedience is forced upon the child. Usually this is quite sincere. The adult really delights in gratifying the child where he can, but occasionally it is an alibi behind which the father, unwilling to take the child and afraid to say so outright, hides. In the hands of the impious young people of the village, it becomes much more alibi than truth. The small fry are bidden to stay at home because "the place is full of spirits." The ten-year-olds proceed to try the same game upon the five-year-olds, and complete lack of faith and conscious mendacity usurps the place of the adults' genuine anxiety and solicitude. The spirits seem to the younger children a factor in the adult world which is especially troublesome and unkind.

Of the existence of the spirits the children have as little doubt as have the adults. They do not know them as well, many of the names which recall personalities to their elders are only empty names to them. Those spirits whom they do remember seem to have changed their very natures. The account of a spirit adultery as revealed in the night séances is a long, tedious business; the children go to sleep and do not listen. Affairs on the spirit level generally lack vividness and do not command their attention. Furthermore, séances usually turn upon the economic arrangements of adult life, which they do not understand and in which they take no interest. The occasional séance with a straight plot of adultery or an alleged spirit attack on a mortal with a hatchet, the children discuss casually among themselves. They know that Kutan is sick because Popitch fought with another spirit brother and that Pikawas no longer wears a betrothal cloak because her spirit aunt objected to the proposed marriage. Kisapwi of fourteen knows that her dead father made her uncle sick because he wanted Kisapwi to go and live with her uncle instead of remaining with her mother. She knows too that her mother refused to let her go, professing to fear harm for the child herself. But more often the children do not know the substance of a séance which explains their own illnesses.

The boys of five to fourteen, who have special guardian spirits of their own, might be expected to find in them imaginary companions of power and compensation. But they make singularly little use of them. They neither see them nor talk with them, although they have heard their fathers utter long chatty monologues to their spirits. They don't ask them to do things for them, as one boy explained, "The spirit only hears if he's right beside you, and he probably is not, so it's no use bothering to talk to him." Sometimes they do not even know their names. They never quote the fact that they have spirits and the girls none as evidence of masculine superiority, although the men do that very thing. Instead they tend to push away from them, to neglect, ignore, depreciate, the importance of the most powerful factor in the adult world.

Besides the formal religious system there are bits of magic, legends of the land devils, stories of water devils. The magic the children know little about; it again is concerned primarily with the accumulation of property, success in love, the demolition of an economic rival, or the prosecution of a fight between cross cousins. The blessing and cursing powers of fathers' sisters and their descendants in the female line are not even known to children under fifteen. Children are never taught charms of any sort, and if an incantation is being recited over the sick, a new baby, or a bride, they are either chased away or constrained to perfect quiet. The children view these occasional magical scenes with annoyance.

The legends of land devils and water serpents played a slightly different part. Manus legends are dull, truncated, unelaborate accounts of encounters between human beings and "*tchinals*"—the supernaturals of the land people, whom the Manus regard as mischievous inimical devils. There are also some myths of the origin of natural phenomena. But the tales are not knit up in any way with the life of the people, they neither explain religious ceremonies nor validate social position. They are not even a device for filling unused time. The elders count them dull and unimportant. It never occurs to any one to tell them to children. However, the adults do describe the devils occasionally to intimidate the children and keep them from going to the mainland. These devils are said to have fingernails as long as their fingers and matted hair falling thickly over their eyes. They will kidnap children or tear out their eyes. Here again, the children give only half credence. The grown ups so obviously pay no attention to the devils but go freely about their business; they so transparently use them as nurses among ourselves use the bogie-man to persuade reluctant children to go to bed, that the children hold them in amused contempt. They occasionally embody them in their games, calling any one who is dressed strangely or gesticulating queerly a "devil," and usually naming a poor attempt to draw a man a "devil." In their drawings they did not elaborate the "devils," invent special characteristics for them, or give them names. They have developed no legends or haunted spots or dangerous water holes. The imaginative faculty which our children spend upon such ideas is not called into play by a society which provides them with a ready-made set of spirits, ghosts, devils, dragons, and then uses these same dreadful and marvellous creatures as instruments of oppression, as alibis for seemingly irrational behaviour. Where our children react to a militantly matter-of-fact world with compensatory interest in fairies and ogres, derived from fairy tales, Manus children, also acting contra-suggestibly, reject the supernatural in favour of the natural.

These long-nailed devils are not especially congenial to the child mind. They are an adult device, and the child is traditionally uninterested in the adult world. So legends play no part at all in the child life, and the people of legend are given contemptuous tolerance.

THE CHILD AND THE SUPERNATURAL

It is also interesting to note the relationship between early childhood conditioning, the family situation, and the religious system. The Manus attitude towards the spirits is composite of the attitudes of the child towards the father and of a man towards his children. To the very small child the father is the indulgent protecting parent who exists primarily to gratify the child's desires. This intensity is modified somewhat as the child grows older and turns to other children for some of his social satisfactions. But behind the knocks and blows of contact with his fellows stands his father, always willing to take his part, make him toys, take him as a companion and friend, quarrel with his mother over him. It is his father who makes the first payments for his wife, who is taking anxious thought for his little son's future, at the time when this financial solicitude has not yet become a burden to the son. But the father seldom lives to carry through his obligations, to complete the payments for his son's wife, to see his daughter-in-law safely installed in the rear of the house. The father-in-law tabu which forbids a man's seeing his daughter-in-law is felt as a poignant deprivation where the own father is concerned.

This is one of the few situations which the Manus feel as romantic, the adventure of looking upon the face of a loved son's wife. "Should I die," says an old man, "and never see the wife whom I have purchased for my son?" So the old father, tottering towards death, beyond the age when disrespect could lurk in his glance, is allowed to make a feast for his daughter-in-law. After thus publicly showing his respect for her, the tabu is removed forever and father, son and daughter-in-law live as one household.

But this is a situation which very seldom occurs: there were only two men in Peri who had lived long enough to see the wives of their own sons. Both had removed the tabu. Usually the father dies while his son is in the late teens or early twenties, often while the son is away at work. The Manus way of life is hard and exacting and Manus men die very young.

The duty of paying for the son's wife passes to a younger brother, or cousin, a man for whose wife the father has paid. Thus the taskmaster who can capitalise the newly married man's ignorance and poverty is a man sometimes ten or fifteen years his senior, a man who is just emerging from servitude himself. For years he has worked for the boy's father, who financed his marriage. Now he will finance the son in return and the son must work hard for him. The complication of this system can be seen in the family of Potik.

Potik adopted Panau, who was to him as a son. Later Potik married Komatal, who had adopted her cousin's baby boy, Paleao. Paleao grew up to call Potik father. Later Komatal bore him two sons, Tunu and Luwil. Potik lived to see Panau married, and died. Panau paid for Paleao's wife and began payments for Tunu and Luwil. He adopted a young son, Kutan. As long as Panau lived, Paleao worked for him and owed him allegiance, as did the young Tunu and Luwil. Panau died just after Kutan went away to work. Paleao continued to finance Tunu and Luwil and took over the financing of Kutan's marriage. Paleao was now paying for his own marriage entirely; he had no financial backers and was therefore an independent citizen. He now made the first payments for his young son, Popoli, which he may not live to complete. In that case Tunu, or more probably Luwil, who is the more intelligent, will continue helping Kutan and finance Popoli's marriage. Throughout this whole chain only one son, Panau, and he an adopted son of a man's old age, was married before his father died. In every other case the kind indulgent father was replaced by an older brother or uncle, to whom the young man owed no affection and from whom he could expect no paternal solicitude.

But in the whole organisation of the family in its relation to little children, the brother relationship is never stressed. Older children do not take care of younger ones. Younger ones are not allowed to accompany the older ones because, say the mothers, "If the babies cried to be brought home it would interrupt the older children's play." This terrible intrusion upon the children's leisure must be avoided at any cost. The household constellation is therefore not a series of children each dependent upon the next older, each cherishing the next younger, as in Samoa, but a group each of whom centres his or her interest in the father, and, secondarily, in the mother. The first seven or eight years of delightful dependence upon the devoted father determine the child's pattern response. This is over-

laid by his interest in his companions but it is not fun-
damentally changed. His father's death leaves him
bereaved, perhaps permanently. Children under four
or five are adopted and made to feel that the foster
father is their own. Girls of any age are adopted more
easily because their participation in the household life
is more continuous. The loneliest children in the village were the boys whose fathers were dead.

Banyalo was one of these. His father had died
when he was seven. He had passed into the care of
his father's sister, an old widow living alone. No new
man took his father's place. His mother went to live
with her brother and later married again. When the
recruiting officer came through looking for school children, Banyalo was given to him. Fatherless, there was
no one to object to his going. When he returned to
the village after six years in Rabaul, he came home as
a stranger. His mother he hardly knew. His mother's
brother extended a formal welcome to him. He might
of course sleep in his house, but he did not feel himself
as having real part in his household. After wandering
about from place to place he finally settled down in
the home of his mother's younger sister's husband,
Paleao, who took upon himself the duty of paying for
Banyalo's wife. To the constraint and embarrassments
which belonged to the brother-in-law relationship was
added the invidious dependence of the wifeless upon
him who bought his wife. Banyalo turned finally to
a warm friendship with a younger boy and so staved
off his loneliness for a little.

[112]

Even lonelier was little Bopau, the son of the dead Sori. Sori had been a gentle, firm man, respected by every one, peaceful, unaggressive. It was said that only after much urging would he ever state a request and that he had been silent and abashed among men younger and poorer than he. Bopau's mother had died when Bopau was born and Sori had devoted long and tireless care to him. The child took on his father's personality like a perfectly fitting glove, grew up quiet, soft spoken, unaggressive. Sori married again, but the child did not form any attachment for his new mother, who brought with her an uncouth deaf child whom Bopau disliked. And then Sori died while still a youngish man of thirty-five or so. His second wife had quarrelled with him before his death. She lived with her people without any interest in her unmourned husband's seven-year-old son. It fell to the lot of Pokenau, Sori's younger brother, to care for the little orphan. Pokenau took Sori to be his own guardian spirit and grew very proud of his exploits. To Sori's credit he laid the success of the month's fishing for the entire village. But he did not love Sori's son. His own little boy Matawei, Bopau's junior by three years, was very near Pokenau's heart. Pokenau's wife was occupied with two young children and had no time for Bopau. He lived in the house, a patient, undemanding lonely child. His foster father was of so vociferous, aggressive a nature that the government officials had christened him "Big-mouth." Matawei imitated his father's every gesture. But Bopau remained faithful to Sori's personality. On the playground he never fought. If difficulties arose he simply retired from the field and sat quietly by himself. When nightfall came, he often curled up to sleep on our floor. There was no one to worry about him, to seek for him.

For one brief month, in his ninth year, Bopau tasted again the importance, the enveloping affection which he had known as a younger child. He was adopted by Pataliyan, himself a lonely stranger, a native of another place who had been captured in war as a child by Sori's father. Pataliyan was a widower, without any true relatives, lonely in this place, and yet not wishing to return to his own people of the island of Nauna, whose language he had forgotten. A great friendship sprang up between him and the fatherless little boy, and finally he took Bopau to live with him in his bachelor quarters. Bopau grew prouder, more self-confident, held his head higher. But his happiness was short-lived. Pataliyan eloped with a widow, an elopement which shook the village. The widow had been the wife of Sori's cousin. In the séances and dreams which followed, Sori violently took his dead cousin's part. Pataliyan had fled to another village with his bride. He had not trusted Bopau with his secret. Pokenau and all his relatives pointed out to Bopau how angered his father was by Pataliyan's conduct, how all of them were in danger of death if they spoke to Pataliyan. Bopau, hurt by Pataliyan's desertion, held by long habit to his father's will, repudiated Pataliyan as firmly as the rest. When

Pataliyan's canoe passed through the village, Bopau turned his head away.

Kapeli was the third boy whose father was dead and who had no new father to take his place. He was fifteen, a stocky, loyal little youngster, always ready for a fight or an adventure. He lived with his mother Ndrantche, an old virago, in her widow's hut. The head of his clan, his half-brother Tuain, had quarrelled with his mother and his other brothers over a projected marriage. A man with whom old Ndrantche had had an affair fifteen years before and who had fled from the village to avoid marrying her, now wished to marry her daughter. Furiously the old woman fought the idea; the younger members of the family sided with her. Kapeli, ever loyal, took her side. He had nothing in common with either the eldest male of the family, Tuain, or the weak, shifty-eyed Ngamasue, his other brother. In his fiery-tongued mother he recognised something of his father's indomitable spirit. His father had kept two wives in order within one house.

Kapeli was too old to shift his affection to one of his brothers and these older brothers repaid his lack of allegiance with an equal lack of responsibility. Kapeli had no wife paid for. Tuain and Ngamasue paid their own debts and took no thought for him. And he, alone of all the adolescent boys who worked for us, never ran away. Each of the others, when he became bored or annoyed with our establishment, followed the usual pattern and ran away for a few days. But as

Kapeli explained, he "had no father to receive him and so he might as well stay."

These were the loneliest boys, the most unplaced. Their fathers died too late for their reabsorption into some other household. This in itself is good indication of the degree to which a child's personality is fixed by the age of five or six. None of these three had yet learned to depend upon the spirits, though little Bopau stoutly maintained, in the face of Pokenau's contempt, that Sori was to be his special guardian. The spirits do not begin to play a rôle in the lives of young men until after marriage, when they have economic obligations to fulfil, and fishing is of great importance to them. It is after marriage also that the average youth feels most keenly his father's death, a death which usually takes place while he is a young man absorbed in young men's pursuits or else while he is away at work. The harshest reality he has ever faced comes to him with marriage, and his father's care is no longer there. Here it is that he turns to the spirits, sometimes his father's, sometimes others of the family dead who take on the same supervisory tenderness which the father displayed towards him in childhood. He lives in the care of these omnipresent, paternalistic spirits, who care for him as well as they are able and who frown upon him if he fails in his moral obligation and forgive him if he makes amends for his faults. Towards the spirits he continues to play the capricious, unfilial part which he played with his father, now threatening to withhold or transfer his allegiance. taunting them with the loneliness which will be theirs should he reject them.

As in childhood the child clung to his father, dependent upon his father's affection and care in a one-sided relationship which always emphasised the child's right to receive love, never the father's right to filial devotion, so it is with the spirits. The Manus do not love their spirit guardians who after all are only doing their proper spirit duty in looking after them. The more alert natives who consider quite calmly the future entrance of Christianity know that this means that all the ancestral skulls will be thrown into the sea, the spirits ejected forever. But they look upon this with the naughty glee of bad children contemplating the overthrow of their parents, with only a passing regret, and a great feeling of relief. Spoiled children in early life, they are spoiled children to their spirits, accepting every service as their due, resenting discipline, quick to desert a spirit which has not been powerful to protect them.

VII

THE major issues of the adult world are thus ignored by Manus children. They are given no property and they acquire none. There are none of those collections of shells, odd shaped stones, fish spines, seeds, etc., which clutter the secret caches of American children and have led to the construction of theories of a "collecting stage" in childhood. No child under thirteen or fourteen had any possessions except his canoe or bow and arrow, furnished him by adults. Spinning tops of seeds are made with some labour, only to be discarded after an hour's play. The short sticks used as punts, the mock spears, the dart, serve a few hours' use and are thrown away. The beaded anklets and armbands are made by the parents, placed on the children and taken off again at the parents' whim. The child does not complain. Even the new and strange objects which we brought to the village were not hoarded. The children scrambled eagerly for bits of coloured ribbon or tinsel, the tin wrappings of films or rolls of exposed and used film, but they never kept them. After I threw away about one hundred wooden film spools, an accidental discard left one camera without a spare spool. I asked the children to bring back one of the dozens they had picked up in the preceding weeks.

After an hour, a fourteen-year-old boy finally found one which had been put away in his mother's work box; all the others had disappeared.

But this dissipation of property, so eagerly clutched and so swiftly relinquished, was not due to destructiveness. Objects were lost far oftener than broken. Indeed, the children showed a touching care of a toy while they were still interested in it; a respect for property far exceeding our children's. I shall never forget the picture of eight-year-old Nauna mending a broken penny balloon which I had given him. He would gather the edges of the hole into a little bunch and painstakingly, laboriously, wind it about with raffia-like grass. The hole made temporarily fast, he would inflate the balloon, which a moment later would collapse and have to be mended again. He spent three hours at this labour of love, never losing his temper, soberly tying up the rotten flimsy material with his sturdy grass string. This was typical of their care of material things, an attitude instilled into them as children. But their elders had been at no pains to give them any pattern of collecting things for themselves or hoarding their small possessions.

Similarly in social organisation, the children found no interesting adult pattern upon which they could draw. The kinship system with its complex functions and obligations of relatives was not taught them, it was too complicated for them to grasp readily themselves. Their habitual contempt for grown-up life kept them from drawing on it for play purposes. Occasionally, about once a month, a group would make slight mimetic play with it—stage a payment for a marriage, or pretend that one of their number was dead and that tobacco must be given away for his death feast. Just once I saw the small girls pretending to keep house. Twice the fourteen-year-old boys dressed up as girls, donned grass skirts and calico cloaks and dashed about in gay imitation of betrothed maidens avoiding tabu relatives. Four times the six-year-olds built imitation houses of tiny sticks. When one stops to compare this lack of imaginative play with a large, free play group among our own children—with its young pirates, Indians, smugglers, "sides," its clubs, secret societies, pass words, codes, insignia, initiations, the difference is striking.

Here in Manus are a group of children, some forty in all, with nothing to do but have a good time all day long. The physical surroundings are ideal, a safe shallow lagoon, its monotony broken by the change of tide, by driving rains and occasional frightening whirlwinds. They are free to play in every house in the village, indeed the reception section of the house is often hung with children's swings. They have plenty of materials ready to hand, palm leaves, raffia, rattan, bark, seeds (which the adults make into tiny charm cases), red hibiscus flowers, coconut shells, pandanus leaves, aromatic herbs, pliant reeds and rushes. They have materials in plenty with which they could imitate any province of adult life—playing at trade or exchange, or the white man's trade store which a few of them have seen, of which all of them have heard. They have canoes of their own, small ones, entirely their own, the larger ones of their parents in which they are always free to play. But do they ever organise a boat's crew, choose captain and pilot, engineer and helmsman, reproduce the crew of the white man's schooner of which they have heard so many tales from returned work boys? Never once in the six months I spent in close contact with them did I see this happen. Or did they pluck large shrubs, fashion spears, whiten their bodies with lime, advance in a war fleet formation upon the village as their elders did at great ceremonies? Did they build themselves small dancing pole platforms in imitation of their elders? Did they catch small turtles and beat miniature drums in triumph over their catch? They never did any of these things. They put on seeds instead of shells and practised with the little blunt spears their elders had taught them to make. They beat toy drums when the young men drummed for a dance, but they held no dances of their own.

They had no sort of formal organisation, no clubs, no parties, no codes, no secret societies. If races were held, the older boys simply divided the children up into fairly equal teams, or selected pairs who were matched physically. But there was nothing permanent about these teams, no continuous rivalry between the children. Leadership there was, but only the spontaneous, free sort due to intelligence and initiative. Very loose age groups, never exclusive, never permanent, tended to form about special activities, as a fishing trip a little afield of the village for part of an afternoon; stepping-stone groups also formed for a few minutes' play—of one adolescent, a twelve-year-old, a seven-year-old, and possibly a baby brother. These serial groupings were partly dependent upon neighbourhood or relationship, but even these were fluid—the smaller children retained no permanent allegiances to older ones.

Their play was the most matter of fact, rough and tumble, non-imaginative activity imaginable; football, wrestlings of war, a few round games, races, boat races, making figures in the water, distorting their shadows in the moonlight while the person who was "it" had to guess their identity. When they were tired they gathered in groups and sang long monotonous songs over and over:

> I am a man.
> I have no wife.
> I am a man. I have no wife
> I will get a wife in Bunei.
> From my father's cross cousins,
> From my father's cross cousins.
> I am a man,
> I am a man,
> I have no wife—

Or they made string figures, or burnt decorative scars on each other's arms with red hot twigs.

Conversation turned on who was oldest, who tallest, who had the most burned beauty spots, whether Nane caught a turtle yesterday or to-day, when the canoe would be back from Mok, what a big fight Sanau and

Kemai had over that pig, how frightening a time Pomasa had on the shipwrecked canoe. When they do discuss events of adult life it is in very practical terms. So Kawa, aged four, remarked, "Kilipak, give me some paper." "What do you want it for?" "To make cigarettes." "But where's the tobacco coming from?" "Oh, the death feast." "Whose?" "Alupu's." "But she's not dead yet." "No, but she soon will be."

Argumentative conversations sometimes ending in fisticuffs were very common. They had an enormous passion for accuracy, a passion in which they imitated their elders, who would keep the village awake all night over an argument as to whether a child, dead ten years, had been younger or older than some person still living. In arguments over size or number attempts at verification were made, and I saw one case of attempted experiment. In the midst of several exciting days, during a death in the village, I had less time than usual for meals, and a can of fruit, of a size usually consumed at one meal, did for two. Pomat, the little table boy, commented on it, but Kilipak, the fourteen-year-old cook, contradicted him. I had never divided a can of peaches between two meals. All the other boys, the children who haunted the house, the married couple who were temporarily resident, my two adolescent girls, were drawn into the argument, which lasted for forty-five minutes. Finally Kilipak declared in triumph, "Well, we'll try it out; we'll give her another can of the same kind to-morrow. If she eats them all, I'm right; if she doesn't, you are."

This interest in the truth is shown in adult life in various ways. Pokenau once dropped a fish's jawbone out of his betel bag. Upon being questioned, he said he was keeping it to show to a man in Bunei who had declared that this particular fish had no teeth. Another man returned from working for a scientific-minded German master to announce to his astonished companions that his master said New Guinea was once joined to Australia. The village took sides on the question and two young men fought each other over the truth of the statement. This restless interest in the truth takes its most extreme form when men try out the supernatural world; disbelieving the results of a séance, they will do something which, if the séance were true, would endanger their lives.

So the form of children's conversation is very like their elders'—from them they take the delight in teaching and repetitious games, the tendency to boasting and recrimination, and the violent argument over facts. But whereas the adults' conversation turns about feasts and finances, spirits, magic, sin, and confession, the children's, ignoring these subjects, is bare and dull, preserving the form only, without any interesting content.

The Manus have also a pattern of desultory, formal conversation, comparable to our talk about the weather. They have no careful etiquette, no series of formal pleasantries with which to bridge over awkward situations; instead meaningless, effortful chatter, is used. I participated in such a conversation in the house of Tchanan, where the runaway wife of Mutchin had taken refuge. Mutchin had broken his wife's arm, and she had left him and fled to her aunts. Twice he had sent women of his household to fetch her and twice she had refused to return to him. On this occasion I accompanied her sister-in-law. The members of her aunt's family received us; the runaway remained in the back of the house, cooking over a fire. For an hour they sat and talked, about conditions at the land market, fishing, when certain feasts were to be held, when some relatives were coming from Mok. Not once was the purpose of the visit mentioned. Finally a young man adroitly introduced the question of physical strength. Some one added how much stronger men were than women; from this the conversation shifted to men's bones and women's bones, how easily broken the latter were, how an unintentional blow from a well-meaning man might shatter a woman's frail bone. Then the sister-in-law rose. The wife spoke no word, but after we had climbed down into the canoe, she came slowly down the ladder and sat in the stern. This oblique conversational style is followed by some children when talking with adults. They make prim little statements which apply to any topic under discussion. So Masa, when her mother mentions a pregnant woman in Patusi remarks, "The pregnant woman who was at our house has gone home." She is then silent again until some other topic gives her a chance to make a brisk comment.

The adults give the children no story-telling pattern, no guessing games, riddles, puzzles. The idea that children would like to hear legends seems quite fantastic to a Manus adult. "Oh, no—legends are for old people. Children don't know legends. Children don't listen to legends. Children dislike legends!" And the plastic children accept this theory which contradicts one of our firmest convictions, the appeal of stories to children.

The simple narration of something seen or experienced does occur, but flights of fancy are strictly discouraged by children themselves. "And then there was a big wind came up and the canoe almost upset." "Did it upset?" "Well, it was a big wind." "But you didn't go into the water, did you?" "No-oo." The insistence on fact, on circumstantial accounts, on accuracy in small points, all serve as checks upon the imagination.

So the story-telling habit, the delight in story, is entirely absent. Imaginative speculation about what is happening on the other side of the hill, or what the fish are saying, is all completely lacking. And the "why?" element in children's conversation with adults is superseded by the "what?" and "where?" questions.

Yet this does not mean a lack of intelligence on the children's part. Pictures, advertisements in magazines, illustrations of stories, they greeted with interest and delight. They pored for hours over an old copy of *Natural History*, explaining, wondering, admiring. Every explanatory comment of mine was eagerly remembered and woven into new interpretations. Their alert minds had been neither dulled nor inhibited. They took to any new game, new pictures, new occupations, with far greater eagerness than did the little Samoans, smothered and absorbed in their own culture. Drawing became an absorbing passion with them. Tirelessly they covered sheet after sheet of paper with men and women, crocodiles and canoes. But unused to stories, unpractised in rearing imaginary edifices, the content of the realistic drawings was very simple: two boys fighting, two boys kicking a ball, a man and his wife, a crew spearing a turtle, a schooner with a pilot. They drew nothing with plot. Similarly, when I showed them ink blots and asked for interpretations, I got only straight statement, "It's a cloud," "It's a bird." Only from one or two of the adolescent boys whose thinking was being stimulated by the thought of the other lands they would see as work boys, gave such interpretations as "a cassowary" (which he had never seen), a motor car, or a telephone. But the ability of children in this society of developing whole plots from the stimulus of an ambiguous ink blot was lacking.

Their memories were excellent. Trained to small points and fine discriminations they learned to distinguish between beer bottles of medicines in terms of slight differences in size of label or number of words on the label. They could recognize each other's drawings of four months before.

In other words they were in no sense stupid children. They were alert, intelligent, inquisitive, with excellent memories and receptive minds. Their dull unimaginative play life is no comment upon their minds, but rather a comment upon the way in which they were brought up. Cut off from the stimulation of adult life, they were never asked to participate in it. They took no part at feasts or ceremonies. The grown ups did not give them patterns of clan loyalty or chieftainship which they could use in their organisation of their children's group. The intricate interrelations of the grown-up world, the relationships between cross cousins with its jesting, cursing, blessing; the ceremonial of war, the mechanics of séances, any one of these would have given the children amusing material for imitation if only the adults had given them a few hints, had aroused their interest or enlisted their enthusiasms.

The Plains Indian life with its buffalo hunt, its pitching and breaking up of camp, its war conventions, does not provide any more vivid material for its children than does the Manus life. But the Cheyenne mother makes her child a little tipi in which to play house. The Cheyenne household greets the diminutive hunter's slain bird as a great addition to the family cook pot. In consequence the children's camp of the Plains, which reproduces in mimetic play the whole cycle of adult activities, forms the centre of Cheyenne children's play interest.

If on the other hand, the Manus had wilfully, aggressively excluded the children, shut doors against them, consistently shooed them off the ceremonial scene, the children might have rallied to positive defensive measures. This has happened with Kaffir children in South Africa where the world of grown ups treat children as little nuisances, lie to them, pack them off to watch the grain fields, forbid them even to eat the small birds of their own catch. This play group of children, put on its mettle by adult measures, organises into a children's republic with spies and guards, a secret language, outlaw conventions of its own, which reminds one of city boys' gangs to-day. Either active enlistment of the children as on the Plains, or active suppression, as among the Kaffirs, seems to produce a more varied, richer child life. Even in Samoa, which does neither but gives every child tasks graded to its skill, the children's life is given content and importance because of the responsibilities placed upon them, because they are part of a whole dignified plan of life.

But the Manus do none of these things. The children are perfectly trained to take care of themselves; any sense of physical insufficiency is guarded against. They are given their own canoes, paddles, swings, bows and arrows. They are regimented into no age groups, made to submit to no categories of appropriate age or sex behaviour. No house is denied to them. They frolic about under foot, in the midst of the most important ceremonies. And they are treated as lords of the universe; their parents appear to them as willing, patient slaves. And no lord has ever taken a great interest in the tiresome occupations of slaves.

As in the social organisation, so with the religious life. There is a ready-made adult content in which the children are given no part. Their invisible playmates are given them, pedigree complete, making no appeal to the imagination and no plea for its exercise.

GROWING UP IN NEW GUINEA

In the less formal thought and play of children, which seems more spontaneous than their attitudes towards the finished system of religion which they have to learn by rote, a contrast with our own children is also seen. The habits of personalising inanimate things, of kicking the door, blaming the knife, apostrophising the chair, accusing the moon of eavesdropping, etc., are lacking in Manus. Where we fill our children's minds with a rich folklore, songs which personalise the sun, the moon, and the stars, riddles and fairy tales and myths, the Manus do nothing of the sort. The Manus child never hears of "the man in the moon," or a rhyme like Jean Ingelow's:

"Oh, moon, have you done something wrong in Heaven,
  That God has hidden your face?
  I hope if you have, you will soon be forgiven,
  And shine again in your place."

nor hears his older sister dance to:

"Turn off your light, Mr. Moon Man,
  Go and hide your face behind the clouds.
  Can't you see the couples all spooning?
  Two's a company and three's a crowd.
  When a little lad and lady
  Find a spot all nice and shady,
  It's time to say good-night.
  When you want to spoon,
  Say, 'Please, Mr. Moon,
  Be a good sport and turn off your light.' "

His parents and grandparents have given him no rich background upon which to embroider ideas about the moon, and he thinks of the moon as a light in the sky which is there and not there, periodically. He does not think the moon is a person. He believes it cannot see because "it has no eyes." His view of the moon is a matter-of-fact, naturalistic view, uncorrected by science, of course, for, like his untutored father, he believes that sun and moon alike proceed across the sky. His folklore gives him no help and the Manus language is cool and bare, without figures of speech or rich allusiveness. It is a language which neither stimulates the imagination of children nor provides material for adult poetry. It is a rigorously matter-of-fact language where ours is filled with imagery and metaphor.

So where we give the moon sex and speak of her as "she," the Manus language, which makes no distinction between he, she, and it, all of which are "third person singular," gives no personalising suggestion. Nor are verbs which apply to persons applied to the moon. The moon "shines," but it never smiles, hides, marches, flirts, peeps, approves; it never "looks down sadly," or "turns away its face." All the impetus to personalisation which our rich allusive language suggests to a child are absent.

I couldn't even persuade children to cast the blame upon inanimate objects. To my remarks, "It's a bad canoe to float away," the other children would reply, "—but Popoli forgot to tie it up" or "Bopau didn't tie it fast enough." This suggests that this "natural" tendency in our children is really taught them by their parents.

Their attitude towards any sort of pretense or make believe is symbolised by the reply of a small girl when I questioned the only group of children which I ever saw playing house. They were pretending to grate coconuts and the little girl said *"grease e joja,"* "this is our lie." The word *grease* is pidgin English for flattery or deceit. It has found its way into the native tongue as a deceit or lie. The little girl's answer contained a condemnation of their make believe play.

From this material it is possible to conclude that personalising the universe is not inherent in child thought, but is a tendency bequeathed to him by his society. The young baby's inability to differentiate or at least to respond differentially to persons and things, is not in itself a creative tendency which makes an older child think of the moon, the sun, boats, etc., as possessed of will and emotion. These more elaborate tendencies are not spontaneous but are assisted by the language, the folk lore, the songs, the adult attitude towards children. And these were the work of poetic adult minds, not the faulty thinking of young children.

Whether or not an adult philosophical system of religion or science will appeal to the child is not a function of the child mind but of the way the child is brought up. If the parents use matter of fact methods of suppression and invoke the child's size, age, physical incapacity, the child may respond with seven league boots and attendant genii, ideas drawn not out of its head, but from the folk lore which it has been taught. But if an unscientific point of view is used as a disciplinary method, as when the child tears a book and the adult says, "Don't pull the cover off that book. Poor book! How would you like to have your skin pulled off like that?" the same aged child can reply in the most superior tone, "Pooh, don't you know that books can't feel? Why, you could tear and tear and tear and it would never feel it. It's like my back when it's numb." The naturalistic approach is no less congenial to the child than the supernatural; his acceptance of one rather than of the other will depend on the way they are presented to him and the opportunities which arise for their use.

Children are not naturally religious, given over to charms, fetishes, spells, and ritual. They are not natural story tellers, nor do they naturally build up imaginative edifices. They do not naturally consider the sun as a person nor draw him with a face.* Their mental development in these respects is determined not by some internal necessity, but by the form of the culture in which they are brought up.

The Manus play life gives children freedom, wonderful exercise for their bodies, teaches them alertness, physical resourcefulness, physical initiative. But it gives them no material for thought, no admired adult pattern to imitate, no hated adult pattern to aggressively scorn, no language rich in figures of speech, no

* In thirty thousand drawings, not one case of personalising natural phenomena or inanimate objects occurred.

wealth of legend and folk tale, no poetry. And the children, left to themselves, wrestle and roll—and even these games are stimulated by passing adult interest— tumble and tussle, evolving nothing of interest except general good spirits and quick wits. Without food for thought, or isolation, or physical inferiority to compensate for, they simply expend their boundless physical energy, and make string figures in the shade in complete boredom when they are weary.

VIII

WHILE Manus permits its children to spend their formative years in such a good-natured vacuum, its treatment of very young children does make for the development of marked personalities.

So differences in personality are seen very early. This is true not only of the idiosyncrasies of manners, speech and gesture which play so pronounced a rôle in giving individuality, but in the more fundamental aspects of personality,—aggressiveness, dominance, recessiveness, etc. Although the play group is an important factor in their lives from four to fourteen for girls, from five to twenty or so for boys, it does not have the levelling effect upon personality which was so conspicuous in Samoa. There children were more like their playmates than they were like the members of the family—in Manus it is just the opposite. There is the most vivid correspondence between the personality of children and their real or foster fathers. If it were a matter of father and own children only, the likenesses could be put down to heredity but the number of similar resemblances between fathers and foster children rules heredity at least partly out of the question.

The children, real or adopted, of older men with strong wills and dominant natures are aggressive, vociferous, sure of themselves, insatiable in their demands upon their environment. They are noisy, unabashed. As babies they stamp their feet, shout their every intention, slap any one who refuses to pay attention to them. As children of six or seven they bully and scrap with their companions, rage up and down the lagoon in exact imitation of their fathers. As boys of fourteen or fifteen they are the leaders of the group. Children of timid young men who are still economically unimportant, unskilled in finance and abashed in the presence of their elders, and children of older men who are failures, are recessive, timid, untalkative. Between these two extremes are the children of men who though young and temporarily under a social eclipse, were aggressive children and will become aggressive again as soon as they gain financial independence.

These differences are so conspicuous that it is possible to watch a group of children for half an hour and then guess at the age or status and general demeanour of their parents, particularly of their fathers. In the cases, of which there were several, where the mother was the more dominant personality, the mother's behaviour was reflected in that of the child.

Pwakaton was a mild, good-humoured, stupid man. He was one of the best drummers in the village and a passable fisherman, but he had no head for planning and he muffed his financial obligations so badly that he was a nonentity in the village. He had one little girl, a mild child who aped his unsure manner and his timid ways. But his younger child had been adopted by the leading older man in the village, Talikai, a man much given to stamping, and to making loud statements of his intentions. This child at almost two years of age was a small counterpart of his foster father. Talikai had another adopted son, a boy whose real father had been of no note in the community, and he, Kilipak, was the leader of the fourteen-year-old group.

Among the eight- to eleven-year-olds, there were a group of small boys whose parents were of small importance. Tchokal was a clever little gamin, lacking neither in wit nor resource, but his father was a despised waster and defaulter without prestige or self-respect. Polum was the son of a man who had failed to make any financial mark. Kapamalae's father was a mild good-natured bear, whose younger brother dominated and managed him. Bopau's father, recently dead, had been a mild, soft-spoken man, who died in debt. This group was dominated by Nauna, the son of Ngamel, one of the most respected elders of the village. Ngamel was neither as aggressive nor as voluble as Talikai, but he was firm, self-assured, rich, powerful, and reliable. Nauna imitated his father's virtues and his father's manners and led a group of boys older than himself.

In some cases it was possible to see a child's personality change under adoption. Yesa, Kapamalae's older brother, was a quiet, abashed child of twelve when I came to the village. Like his younger brother he took his colour from his mild, unremarkable father. Shortly afterwards he was adopted by his father's younger brother, Paleao, one of the most enterprising men in the village. Paleao had a small foster son, Popoli, whom he had adopted as a baby from another tribe, and who showed a great resemblance to him now in every gesture. Yesa, the quiet, immediately took colour from the decisiveness of his new father: his real father became "grandfather," relegated to unimportance, and his shoulders squared beneath his new prestige. But the correspondence was less marked and would probably be less marked always than if he had been adopted in babyhood.

Kemai was the most substantial man in the village, sound, reliable, slow of speech, routine in his thinking. His wife's sister's son, Pomat, whom he had adopted as a baby, reproduced not only his mannerisms, but his character traits.

There were two brothers, Ngandiliu and Selan. Ngandiliu was the elder, but he lacked the definiteness, the assurance, which makes for success. Having no children of his own, he adopted Selan's child Topal, on the death of Selan's wife. Topal grew up, like Ngandiliu, quiet, persevering, never taking the initiative, never making his own points.

Selan was still a young man, too young to be permitted much importance in the social scheme. Ngandiliu had paid for his wife and Selan had not yet assumed full economic status. But he was restlessly ambitious. He became a medium, an unusual thing for a man; he even engaged in furious altercations with the old men of the village. Although usually preserving a subdued mien, suitable to his years, beneath it he was quietly aggressive, persistent, self-assured. And so was Kawa, his five-year-old daughter, who broke her silences only to make carefully calculated demands. Three years younger than Topal, she was already a more poised and vigorous person.

But the sum total of the cases is more impressive than is any individual case. Differences between one set of brothers, brought up in different circumstances, can be explained away on other counts, hereditary differences, accident, and so on. But when the children of young or unsuccessful people as a group exhibit one type of personality, and the children of older, successful people exhibit another, the matter assumes significance.

There is a great deal of inbreeding in Manus, both the inbreeding which results from the prescribed marriage between second cousins and the inbreeding inevitable in small communities, where there is much common ancestry. It may therefore be argued that all the children have similar potentialities upon which environment has only to play in order to develop striking differences. Nevertheless, it is important to note that the leading lines in the community represent the inheritance, not of blood, nor of property, which is largely dissipated at death, but of habits of dominance acquired in early childhood. Let us follow, for a moment, the family tree of one group of leading men in the village history.

Malegan, a man of importance, adopted Potik, a

nephew. When he died Potik became a leading citizen in the village. Potik adopted Panau, and later Paleao, dying while Paleao was very young and leaving two blood sons, Tunu and Luwil. Panau and Paleao had been the adopted children of Potik's years of power; they grew up under his influence. Luwil was reared by a maternal uncle of no consequence, Tunu by Panau while Panau was still a young and unimportant man. Panau attained prestige and importance and died at its height. His position in the economic scheme was taken over by Paleao, his adopted father's second wife's adopted sister's son. Paleao's own blood brother was adopted not by the powerful Potik, but by a mild maternal uncle, and remained a mild, though not at all unintelligent, nonentity.

This discussion might seem to depreciate the rôle of intelligence. It is not meant to do so. But personality is a more powerful force in Manus than is intelligence. The man of force with average intelligence gets on better than the less-assured man of higher intellect. And it is this very matter of force, of assurance, which seems so heavily determined by the adult who fosters the child during its first seven or eight years.

This means that the scales are most unevenly weighted against the children of a man's youth and the children, real or adopted, of unsuccessful older men. It also means that a dominant man can be far surer of a satisfactory successor than he could be if he had to depend upon an accident of native endowment which would persist through the levelling process of a different kind of education.

This latter is the case in Samoa. The care of young children by slightly older children, themselves without defined personalities, perpetuates a far lower level of development of social individuality. The gifted man in Samoa does rise to the top, but he never comes in contact with his young children. He is given no opportunity to pass on the assurance which he has gained after years of apprenticeship.

The same result would be likely to obtain where children were left to the care of nursemaids, or slaves, or of old or infirm dependent female relatives of a household. Such a fostering group, whether of children, servants, or old women, may present an effective barrier through which the influence of father or mother does not penetrate. This may be as powerful a factor in producing the startling discrepancies between fathers and sons in our own society as the more popular explanation of inferiority complexes.

The successful identification of the child with his father's personality in Manus, is also made possible by the father's tender regard for the child and lack of domineering in the parent-child relationship. Talikai, haughty and uncompromising in his attitude towards adults, left an important ceremony in the middle to come and beg a balloon from me for his two-year-old child. The child's cry turned the most dominant person in a roomful of people into an anxious servitor. It is no wonder that that child did not develop an inferiority complex. But constant association with Talikai led him to imitate his manner, to take over and make his own Talikai's assurance. Nor are the children of shy, quiet, abashed fathers given an inferiority complex, it is rather a question of acquiring a habit of inconspicuous, socially unimpressive behaviour.

In the case of girls the effects are less impressive. In girls under eight or nine the father's personality is reflected almost as completely as it is in the personality of little boys. But the break of identification with the father tends to confuse the girl's later development. The girl's spirit is broken at an earlier age by the tabus. She never makes as strong an identification with any woman as she made with her father. Her individuality is allowed full play only up to thirteen or fourteen, instead of up to twenty to twenty-four, as in the case of boys. So, although early association with an important father turns a small girl into an assured little tyrant, there are more social forces at work to blur her aggressiveness, to tone down her individuality. The most aggressive girls in the village were the daughters of prominent widows, the first identification with the father had carried over peacefully to an identification with strong self-sufficient personalities of their own sex.

The children's play groups are sharply influenced by this early development of individuality. Any group of children of the same age tends to break in two, the passive, quiet children of the young and unsuccessful falling on one side, the noisy, aggressive children on the other—with the children of young men of dominant character in the middle.

The earliest play groups are of pairs or trios of children of two or three. As soon as a child can wade with safety, the attraction of the water life brings it into the company of other children. Three-year-olds may still hesitate or have difficulty in climbing up the slippery piles to seek out companions in strange houses, but it is easy for two or three children to gravitate together beneath the houses—in the low tide shallows. Play pairs are found often where one child is aggressive and one passive. The differences in social personality are much more pronounced than other differences —of skill or intelligence, and it is possible for the aggressive children to gratify their urge to leadership most simply if they select another child of a different temperament. Alliances between two aggressive children are much less frequent. The children are too spoiled to enjoy having any point contested by another will of equal strength. Sometimes two meek, passive children will drift into an association—for there seems to be no similar will to be commanded. But these associations are less firm, fall apart quickly at the word of one of the more aggressive children.

Ponkob and Songau were a typical play pair. Ponkob, Nauna's younger brother, was a strong, lusty child, imperative in gesture, wearisomely expansive in conversation and manner. He was lord of the world and particularly lord of Songau, the son of an anxious unreliable failure, Pomat. Pomat came of a line which had once played an important part in village life—his shiftless ways called forth much comment from his fellows. He himself was a furtive and occasionally honey-tongued man; when delirious with fever, he spoke incessantly of fulfilled obligations. His wife had been married before, and lost her first baby because she had tattooed her face, arousing the virtuous anger of her husband's spirits. Her marriage with Pomat was a step down. She was abashed by life and wholly inefficient in dealing with it. Little Songau was a bright child, he often showed more knowledge of his surroundings than Ponkob, who was too busy exclaiming over them, fighting them, manipulating them, to observe them properly. Songau's whole trend was towards silence, quiet little activities of his own, slow wondering at the things he found in the water or saw in the sky. But Ponkob wanted an audience. The pair would pass a whole hour together in a companionship which could hardly be called co-operative play. Ponkob would decide to push his canoe into the water, and call Songau. Songau would go, help him for a minute, wander away, find a stick, throw it into the water, swim after it, apparently oblivious to Ponkob's continuous: "Come and help me. Help me put the boat, put the boat in the water. Songau, Songau, come here. What's that? I'll fix it, this boat. Just me. Just me. It's my boat. Oh, it's stuck. Songau!" At the tenth "Songau!" Songau would wander back, help him for a minute, then lose interest and go off about his own affairs. This would go on for an hour, Ponkob shout-

ing, commanding, doing purposeful things, Songau saying little and most of that to himself, only half co-
operating with Ponkob, losing interest half way through.
Ilan was a small girl who sometimes was present at
their play, sitting on the side lines, with her finger in
her mouth, hardly moving, rising only at an insistent
command and never remaining engaged in activity long.
If Ponkob were not there and Ilan and Songau played
together, Ilan emerged a little more from her shell,
and the two of them would meander about the shallows,
picking up his seaweeds, Songau occasionally comment-
ing on it to himself, "Mine—seaweed. It's mine";
Ilan saying nothing and doing little.

Another type of association—a less common one—
was like that of Ponkob and Ngalowen. Ngalowen
was his sister, a year older than he, who had been
adopted in babyhood by their uncle, whom she called
father. But Ngamel, her true father, she addressed by
his first name and she called her true mother by the
mourning term, "One whose baby died while newborn."
Her adopted father was an older man, self-assured,
devoted to Ngalowen. His only son was nearly grown
and all the affection of his old age he expended on this
winning, adopted child, who at four was an accomplished coquette, the darling of all the men in the village. Pwisio, her adopted father, was vain but not
talkative. He demanded a hearing when he spoke.
Ngalowen's picture of the world was of one which responded to her, made way for her, by virtue of her
mere presence. Any person who was not responding

to her, every smile not directed at her, was anathema.
She was too vain to like the company of strong willed,
aggressive children, too accustomed to adulation to be
willing to lead a group of unaggressive ones. So she
played very little with other children, but spent most
of her time with her father or paddling or swimming
about the village by herself, looking for adults who
would pay attention to her. But when she wearied of
these precocious activities and wanted a good play in
the water, she turned for a playmate to Ponkob—he
was younger and less adept than she, and his running
line of chatter, his constant appeal to her, gave her the
needed sense of calling forth a response. Ponkob
meanwhile was perfectly contented with a companion
who let him talk and boss, and gave far more efficient
co-operation than did his crony, Songau. Ngalowen
carried her mania for personal recognition further than
any other child—she was the only child who usually
refused to draw. When she did draw, for each stroke
on paper, she made half a dozen self-conscious moves,
wasted the paper, ran about, climbed on adults' laps,
pouting, flirting, drawing attention to herself. Her
one foster brother had been away all her life so that
she had no competition from brothers and sisters.

Masa belonged to the silent, unaggressive type. She
had lost one eye in an attack of conjunctivitis and her
father had never cared as much for her as for her half-
brother, three years her senior. She had stayed with
her mother, a quiet, efficient woman without self-im-
portance or pretentiousness. Masa hardly ever spoke.

She played about with the other children, in a small canoe, waded contentedly about the edges of the little islet, a round-faced homely child with a bad eye. Very infrequently she would ask a question of an adult, never of a child. She seemed to have no desire to make an impression on other children, or to draw their attention to herself. Her favorite companion was Posendruan, a little boy with a club foot. His infirmity, which he handled amazingly well, and his attachment to his mild-faced young father made him unusually quiet and un-aggressive. Older than Masa, he followed where she aimlessly, unimpressively led. Yet Masa in a group of grown people would participate in the conversation in a completely adult manner. If a strange woman, talking to her mother, would ask, "Has that woman going by in the canoe ever been pregnant?"—after her mother's negative answer, Masa would add, "The pregnant woman who was at our house has had her child; father took sago to her husband," in a cool, clear little voice. She never monopolised the conversation, only contributed to it brief, apposite remarks when they seemed called for. Her behaviour was in striking contrast to that of Ponkob, Songau, Pokus, Bopau, Piwen, Ngalowen, Salaiyao and Kawa, all of whom regarded a group of adults as an audience. If one or several grown people entered their group, the children gave up contending with one another and all concentrated on gaining the adults' attention, using varied techniques: Ponkob, Pokus and Manoi by rapid fire conversation; Piwen by stubbornness and active intractability, Salai-

yao by fits of temper; Ngalowen and Songau by flirta-
tiousness, and Kawa by persistent teasing for some particular object. Each of these techniques for gaining
attention was firmly fixed in the particular child; every
child of three had developed a definite line for dealing
with the adult world. And so fixed is the Manus tradition that the child should be the centre of the group,
that the children found their methods almost invariably
successful, even when directed towards the busier and
less docile women instead of the indulgent men.

This constant orientation towards an adult prevents
the development of co-operativeness among the small
children, but also makes them particularly amenable
to the leadership of older children. When a group
of five-year-olds are loitering, splashing, scuffling aimlessly about on the edges of an islet, it is easy for an
older child of nine or ten to come along and organise
a race or a game of ball. The organisation does not
last long among children less than six or seven, but
the ten-year-olds are indefatigable in attempting to
put over in the younger group the play methods of
their seniors. This again is a pattern taken from the
older men, who are always ready to act as referees,
cheer leaders, beasts of burden, in a children's game.
The more usual play group, in which there are round
games, races, tugs of war, etc., consists of one or two
older children and a mass of younger ones. The older
ones, lacking the docile adult psychology, act as tyrants,
choose sides, assign partners, decide who shall play and
who not, and the others agree good-naturedly. The

habit of being taught and ordered about in play by older children is fixed quite young.

But it is not until the growing children begin to feel the adult world as slightly inimical, until there comes over them a faint premonition of the subservience which must supersede their present gay insouciance, that group consciousness forms. A boy of ten drifts—now teaching a baby to count, now organising a game of "kick ball" among the eight-year-olds, turning from that to a canoe race with a number of age mates, joining two older boys to chase a group of small girls; home, to stamp his foot and scream until food is cooked specially for him, back in the lagoon, to wade placidly about all alone with a toy pinnace.

This easy give and take, group play, partnership, individuality activity, now as teacher, now as leader, now as slavey, gives the child a maximum opportunity to develop those personality traits set in babyhood. A greater preference for following than for leading, for playing with the baby, or tagging after an older boy, docs not set him off from his fellows, because of the lack of age norms and fixed age groups. Each child's active potentialities are stimulated to the full.

The result of this form of social life is seen in the fourteen-year-old boys, not yet sullen and shamed, harried by financial obligations, nor struggling for freedom. They are attractive, self-sufficient children, without feelings of inferiority, afraid of nothing, abashed by nothing.

The capacities of this group were shown when our

household was turned over to five boys, Kilipak, Pomat, Taumapwe, Kapeli, and Yesa. Kilipak was cook and head boy, Pomat, butler, Taumapwe, bedroom boy, Kapeli, cleaner of fish, hewer of wood, and drawer of water, Yesa, dish washer and kitchen knave. With hardly any directions or advice—for I wished to see what they made of the strange situation—they ran the house, divided up the work, scrupulously parcelled out tasks and rewards, with a minimum of quarrelling. Primitive children, unused to any type of apparatus, unused to punctuality, unused to regular work, they came regularly day after day, learned to handle lamps, take temperatures, handle a stop watch, wash negatives, expose the printing frame for sun prints, fill and light a tilly lamp. In a few years their culture will have claimed them, turned their minds to commerce, tangled up their emotions in a web of shame and hostility. The roots of their future are already laid in their lack of affection for any one, their prudery, their awed respect for property, their few enjoined avoidances. Emotionally they were warped in early childhood to a form of egocentricity, against which the fluid child world is helpless; but in active intelligent adjustment to the material world, they have had years of excellent training.

IX

THE father treats his young children with very slight regard for differences in sex. Girls or boys, they sleep in their father's arms, ride on his back, beg for his pipe, and purloin betel from his shoulder bag. When they are three or four he makes them small canoes, again regardless of sex. Neither boys nor girls wear any clothing except tiny bracelets, anklets, necklaces of dog's teeth, and beaded belts. These are usually only worn on state occasions, as continued wear chafes the skin and produces an ugly eruption. The adults emphasise sex differences from birth in their speech—a boy is a *nat*, a girl is a *ndrakein*, at an hour of age. Before birth only is the term *nat* used to denote child. These terms are used so frequently by women—who are likely to wax voluble about "boy of mine," or "girl of mine"—that a child of three will gravely correct the misapplication of a term to the baby of the house.

But before three, no other distinctions are made between the sexes. At about three maternal pride makes a new bid for the small girl. A tiny curly grass skirt is fashioned with eager hands and much comment, and the solemn-eyed baby arrayed in it for a feast day. The assumption of this costume unites the daughter with the mother in a way that has never happened be-

[151]

fore. Her mother is addressed as *pen*, woman, but she is a *ndrakein*, similarly her father is called a *kamal*, and her brother is a *nat*. The differences between her body and her brother's is obvious, as both sexes go naked. But as adults are clothed and most prudish about uncovering, and her undeveloped breasts are more like her father's than her mother's, mere anatomy does not give her nearly as good a clue to sex as does clothing.

The children were asked to draw pictures of men and women, or of girls and boys; where differences were shown—far more often they were ignored—the male anatomy was drawn correctly and the female was indicated by drawing a grass skirt.

From the moment when the baby girl and her slightly older sisters are dressed identically with their mother, although it is only for an hour, the girls begin to turn to their mothers more, to cling to their older sisters.

Little girls are not forced to wear grass skirts until they are seven or eight; they put them on, go swimming, get them wet, put on green leaves instead, lose the leaves, run about naked for a while, go home and put on dry skirts. Or they will take their grass skirts off and wade through the water at low tide, grass skirts high and dry on top of their curly heads. Not until twelve or thirteen is the sense of shame at being uncovered properly developed.

At about the age of three little boys begin to punt their fathers to the lee of the island which all the men of the village use as a latrine. Girls and women never go there, and the boy child learns thus early to slip apart from the women to micturate.

But little boys' great realisation of maleness comes when they learn the phallic athleticism practised by their elders in the dance. A child grown suddenly proficient wriggles and prances for days and the adults applaud him salaciously. This is learned at about the age of three or four. Soon after this age, the boys are given bows and arrows and small fish spears; very tiny girls and boys wander about the lagoon at low tide playing with sticks and stones, imitating the more purposeful play of the older children without regard to sex. But little girls are never given real fishing toys. They are given small canoes and are as proficient in paddling and punting as the boys, but they never sail toy canoes of their own. From the time of this differentiation in play and dress the sex groups draw apart a little. There is no parental ban upon playing together nor is there any very deep antagonism between the groups. The line is drawn more in terms of activities. Round games and water games are played by both groups; fist fights as frequently cross sex lines as not; on moonlight nights boys and girls race shrieking over the mud flat of the lagoon laid bare by tide.

But as the adolescent girls are drawn more and more into the feminine activities of their households, the twelve-year-olds, eight-year-olds, five-year-olds, tend to follow in a long straggling line. When a girl reaches puberty all the younger girls down to the age of eight or nine go to sleep in her house for a month. This draws the girls closer together. There was one little island in the village reserved for the women. Here they went occasionally to perform various industrial tasks, and here on a grass plot at the peaked summit of the small steep cone, the little girls used to dance at sunset, taking off their grass skirts and waving them like plumes over their heads, shouting and circling, in a noisy revelry, high above the village.

The boys would be off stalking fish in the reedy shallows and sternly schooling the crowd of small boys who followed in their wake. Between the boys' group and the girls' there would be occasional flare ups, battles with sea animal squirt guns or swift flight and pursuit. Very occasionally, as we have seen, they united in a semi-amorous play, choosing mates, building houses, making mock payments for their brides, even lying down cheek to cheek, in imitation of their parents. I believe that fear of the spirit wrath over sex prevented this play from ever developing into real sex play. Each group of children believe that the young people who are now grown engaged in much more intriguing play when they were young. But as this golden age theme is investigated, each group pushes it back a generation further to the days just before their time when the spirits were not so easily angered. This play is always in groups. There is no opportunity for two children to slip away together; the group is too clamorous of all its members.

With the child's increased consciousness of belong-

[154]

ing to a sex group and greater identification with adults of the same sex comes a rearrangement of the family picture. Up to the time a little girl is five or six, she accompanies her father as freely as would her brother. She sleeps with her father, sometimes until she is seven or eight. By this time she is entering the region of tabu. If she is not engaged herself, younger sisters and cousins may be engaged, and she will be on terms of avoidance with the boys to whom they are betrothed. If she is engaged herself, there will likely be several men in the village from whom she must hide her face. She is no longer the careless child who rode upon her father's back into the very sanctuary of male life, the ship island. More and more her father tends to leave her at home for her younger brothers and sisters, or to go more staidly, babyless, about his business. But she is used to adult attention, dependent upon the sense of pleasant power which it gives her. Gradually deserted by her father, she comes to identify herself either with her mother or with some older woman of her kindred. It is curious how much more frequent this latter adjustment is, except where the mother is a widow. It is as if the girl had so thoroughly passed over her mother in preference to her father that she could not go back and pick up the dropped thread. These attachments to older women have nothing of the nature of a "crush" in them; they are very definitely in terms of the family picture. Often a grandmother is chosen. The older women are freer to teach the girls beadwork, to start them at work for their trousseaux.

The younger women are more preoccupied with baby tending, which does not interest the little girls and in which their help is not enlisted. Little girls have no dolls and no pattern of playing with babies. We bought some little wooden statues from a neighbouring tribe and it was the boys who treated them as dolls and crooned lullabies to them.

This shift is not made without some unhappiness and rebellion. The little girls kick off their grass skirts and rebel against the domestic tasks in which their more frequent presence at home involves them. Gathering firewood, fetching water, stringing beads,—these are dull activities compared with following their father about and playing noisy games in the lagoon. At play with the other children they are still gay, but those who are engaged are ridden with anxiety. A calico veil or a pandanus rain mat is a clumsy thing to carry about, but the fourteen-year-old who leaves hers behind her may find herself crouching for fifteen minutes in the wet hull of a canoe, head bowed between her knees, while her betrothed's father stands near by, chatting unconcernedly. For it is the women and the very young boys who must make the positive moves of avoidance; a grown man will always stand his ground unconcernedly while a group of women flutter away like frightened birds. If the young girl goes to the house of a friend she has no guarantee that at any moment the cry of "Here comes a tabu relative of yours," will not send her scurrying from the house, conversation interrupted and beadwork forgotten. Only in her own house will she receive adequate warning. If she goes on a fishing expedition, the same thing may happen. So the happy friendships formed among the ten- and twelve-year-olds tend to break up. Association between older girls is too troublesome. Also, any absence from home and the company of reliable relatives, is looked upon with suspicion.

All this is reflected even in the play group. Solemn-eyed children of eight will comment upon the free and easy ways of their comrades, and add, "But we married women must sit at home and do beadwork to give to our husbands' sisters." More with their mothers now, they become increasingly conscious of the speech tabus, and learn to avoid all the words tabu to the elder women of the group, remarking proudly, when questioned, "No; that is not my tabu, it is my grandmother's. But I help my grandmother with her tabu." It is the small girls who become conscious earliest of the social organisation, and who know all the engagements in the group. "Kutan is going to marry a boy in Patusi. Pikewas was engaged but there was a séance, and they took away the engagement." This type of running social comment is never volunteered by boys, and usually they do not have the necessary information to make the simplest comments on the social organisation.

At menstruation the girl's pact with her sex is sealed forever. She learns that not only must she endure first menstruation, but the strange fact, the fact that no man in all Manus knows, that she will menstruate every moon and must hide all trace or knowledge of her condition from every one. Here is a new handicap to a free untrammelled life. The girl is not told that the menstruation of unmarried girls is a secret which no man knows. Indeed, few Manus women realise clearly that this is a complete secret. The sense of shame is so deep that the subject is hidden away without the mental process being rationalised. The mother has only to communicate this shame to her daughter and the secret is safe for another generation. If the children were told it as a secret, some one might have betrayed it long ago. But secrecy enjoined as a shamed precaution works infallibly. Manus men, told that among other peoples girls not only menstruate initially, at puberty, but every moon, wed or unwed, until the menopause, simply shrug and reply, "Manus women are different."

But this close identification of the girls with the women is neither voluntary nor enthusiastic. For the women of her group she has no such enthusiasm as she had for her father, her father who still is fond of her but is separated from her by so many necessary reticences. If the women huddle closely together, it is as prisoners, under a common yoke of precaution and tabu. But the early conditioning to receive rewards from men, to look for affectionate care and response from men, still lingers in the girls' minds. How much they confuse this partially lost picture with the husbands they are to marry, it is hard to say. Marriage is of course identified with tabus and avoidances, with the life they are leading now, not with the happier life of childhood. But a girl's comments upon marriage are placidly expectant, as if a little of the peace of childhood coloured them. The disappointment is all the ruder when marriage comes. In the home of her husband, her fellow females are enemies and her husband regards her as fit for forced intercourse, child-bearing, and housework. Nor can she reproduce her relationship to her father in her relationship to her children, for they belong to a different clan, are more her husband's than hers. And never in her life has she learned to know shared emotion, from the days when her father and mother fought over her cradle.

When the small boy wearies of riding on his father's back, he wanders away to play with his companions, but he is never thrust away by his father, nor forced away by convention. The relationship between fathers and sons of six and seven is particularly satisfactory. The child has learned motor control and respect for property—there are no more unpleasant lessons to learn. Indeed, these lessons are principally taught by the mother, in the child's first eighteen months. To the father fall all the pleasanter tasks. He treats his six-year-old son like a tyrannous and favourite boon companion, indulges his every whim, gaily, as if it were his greatest delight.

Pokenau and Matawei presented a most attractive picture. The mother was occupied with a new baby, and Matawei was his father's constant companion. Pokenau had given him, as guardian spirit, the spirit of his grandfather Gizikau. Matawei knew that the skull of his grandfather hung in the wooden bowl near the door, while the skull of Sori, his father's guardian ghostly elder brother, was kept in the other bowl. Father and son used to laugh about their spirits, threaten each other with the spirits' wrath. Pokenau would tease Matawei, saying Gizikau's skull was so old it would fall to pieces, and Matawei would make gay rebuttal. If Matawei awoke to find his father gone fishing without him, his wail sounded through the village. For his mother he had not even tolerance, but his father he followed everywhere.

If his father went out in the evening, Matawei accompanied him and fell asleep at his feet. When the conversation was finished, his father lifted him on his shoulder and bore him home, still sleeping, to rest by his side until dawn. Matawei had mastered whole passages of pidgin, and went about reciting them in imitation of his father's truculent manner. One day Pokenau struck his wife and she fled from the house with the two young children. All day he was in a flutter of anxiety for fear Matawei would follow his mother. There would be food with his mother. Pokenau had no sisters, and his uncle's aged widow had gone with his wife, for it would have been improper for her to remain alone with him. There was no one to cook. Perhaps Matawei would be hungry in the fireless, cheerless house. But the next morning Pokenau appeared beaming. Matawei had elected to stay with him. He reported his happiness as proudly as a lover relates his triumph over his mistress's heart.

But the slightly older boys spend less time with their fathers, more time with other boys. They grow tired of the rôle of demanding spectator and plunge into activity. Any difficulty sends them back again, crying for sympathy. So the boys have no sense of being pushed out of their father's affections. Their fathers are there, glorious but humble before their sons, waiting to give all that is asked. And the fathers demand nothing in return; no item of work, no little chore is asked of them. Only at sea are they ever made to perform tasks and this is marine discipline, not parental exaction. The boys, spending less time with adults than do the girls, know far less of the social organisation.

The relationship between the sexes becomes more complicated as the young people grow older. The engaged girls avoid some youths as in-laws, some as possible seducers. With the others, their relatives, they are free to go about the village, joke, exchange presents, and non-embarrassing confidences. Here is laid the foundation of the strong brother-and-sister tie which lasts through life. The only feminine society permitted young men is that of "sisters" for whom they must show tenderness and respect, and "cross cousins," with whom they are allowed to engage in rough, semi-sexual play. During this period the threefold division of attitudes towards women which is to govern a man's thinking all his life is developed. For sisters tenderness, solicitude, a sense of mutual obligation, the duty of helping each other economically are emphasised. "We are brother and sister. He gives me food, and

[161]

I give him beadwork. We work for one another. When he dies I will lament for him a beautiful lament." So a woman will describe her relation to her brother. "It is well to have sisters who will make beadwork for you and wail you well at your death," say the men. "Unfortunate is the man who has no sisters." When the son of Talikatin seduced an engaged girl in Taui, it was the girl's brother who attacked her furiously with a wooden pillow, declaring he would kill first her and then himself. This is the only emotional tie which is truly reciprocal, for the equally strong tie between father and child is very one-sided in its emphasis.

Furthermore, this brother and sister relationship provides a pleasant outlet for puritanical feelings; sex forbidden, the community approving, a slight sentimentality is permitted. If the relation between brother and sister seems to us a little commercial, with a strong flavour of beadwork and sago about it, it should be remembered that where wealth is the dominant interest, loyal assistance in matters of wealth is the strongest of bonds. It is comparable to the feeling of an American whom I once heard define "a friend" as "a man who will lend you any amount of money without security." To his sister's verandah goes the man who needs financial aid and he does not go in vain.

From this brother-and-sister relationship specific mention of sex is sternly excluded. As the Manus phrase it, "A father may tell his daughter that her grass skirt is awry, but her brother may not. However, if her grass skirt is often awry, he may upbraid her formally for her carelessness." Similarly, a brother may discuss with his sister the financial details of her marriage, but when she flees to his protection after a marital quarrel, he asks no questions. The relationship upon which adult men and women rely for comfort, support, understanding, is a relationship from which sex is specifically debarred. One possible component of the rounded attitude which we expect between husband and wife has been extracted and labelled "non-sexual" and "belonging to the sister."

The feminine cross cousin receives yet another attitude which a man might entertain towards his wife. This is the element of play, of light laughter, of familiarity. Her he can accuse of marriage with impossible mates, to her he can attribute conception and childbirth —points which he can never mention to his own wife. He can seize her by her short curls, or grasping her under the armpits swing her roughly back and forth. He can hold her pointed breasts in his hands. All this is play, which must not be carried too far, or the spirits will be angry. But it is nevertheless permitted. Habits of rough and tumble sex play, established in youth, persist into the maturer years, and it is a curious sight to see a stout burgher of forty playfully mauling a worn widow, or making sprightly accusations against her character. Among the few and scattered sex offences which outrage the spirits and terrify the living, occasional liaisons between cross cousins are recorded, but they seem few enough to be non-significant. I found nothing to suggest that this sex play sets up patterns which have a tendency to work themselves out in more complete sex relations. Rather another split is accomplished: playfulness and easy casual familiarity are marked as inappropriate to the sex relation by their permissible presence in this cross cousin relationship, where sex is tabued.

The effect of this distribution of possible sex attitudes upon the marriage relation itself is hard to overestimate.* A man gives the allegiance of dependence to his father, occasionally to his mother, mutual affection and feeling of reciprocity and co-operativeness to his sister, playfulness and easy give and take to his female cross cousin, anxious, solicitous, sedulous care to his children. For his wife he reserves—what? Unrelieved by romantic fictions or conventions of wooing, untouched by tenderness, unbulwarked by co-operativeness and good feeling as between partners, unhelped by playfulness, preliminary play or intimacy, sex is conceived as something bad, inherently shameful, something to be relegated to the darkness of night. Great care is taken that the children should never be witnesses. In the one-room houses it is impossible to accomplish this, but the children soon learn the desirability of dissembling their knowledge. Their clandestine

* It is interesting to compare these disassociated sex attitudes in this primitive setting where arranged marriage is the backbone of the social order, with the conditions in Europe, where prostitution, homosexuality and adultery all drain off emotional attitudes incompatible with arranged marriages. For a vivid analysis of European conditions, see Floyd Dell's "Love in the Machine Age."

knowledge is as shamed, as marred by a sense of sin, as is their parents' indulgence. Children sleeping in another house will say formally to their host or hostess upon leaving a house, "We slept last night. We saw and heard nothing." But children of six are sufficiently sophisticated so that one small boy remarked about a marital quarrel, "Why doesn't he copulate with his wife instead of beating her all the time?"

Married women are said to derive only pain from intercourse until after they have borne a child. The implications of this statement are obvious. They confide little in each other. Each conceals her own humiliating miserable experience as did the Puritan women of the Victorian era. Every woman, however, successfully conveys to her growing daughters her own affective reaction to the wearisome abomination which is sex. And most women welcome children because it gives their husbands a new interest and diverts their unwelcome attentions from themselves. The husband's growing interest in the child which often means that he will sleep all night with the child clasped in his arms, is welcomed as a diversion. As one woman phrased the common attitude, "That house is good in which there are two children, one to sleep with the husband on one side of the house, one to sleep with the wife on the other. Then husband and wife do not sleep together."

Variations of the sexual picture are slight. The spirits are not concerned at all with any aspect of sex which does not involve heterosexual activity on the part of Manus women. All other types of sex behaviour are enveloped in the prevailing atmosphere of shame, but escape the stigma of sin. Masturbation is practised by the children but always in solitude, and solitude is hard to find. It seems to have no important psychological concomitants; engendering as it does no very special shame in a society where every act of excretion is lamentable and to be most carefully hidden. The girls' superficial masturbation does not seem to diminish their frigidity at marriage. Homosexuality occurs in both sexes, but rarely. The natives recognise it, and take only a laughing count of it, if it occurs between unmarried boys, in which cases it is sometimes exploited publicly in the boys' houses. Sodomy is the only form of which I received any account. Homosexual relations between women are rare and frowned on as inappropriate. I neither saw nor heard of any definite inverts, but mental instability in several cases frequently took a sexual form, with manifestations of exhibitionism and gross obscenity.

The utilisation of other erogenous zones, and variations of the sex act in heterosexual relations do not seem to occur. (All my comments on sex must be so qualified because in such a puritanical society it is difficult to rely upon any kind of information about sex.) Sex play is barred out, because of the specialisation of the cross cousin picture. A woman asked if her husband is permitted to touch her breast indignantly replies, "Of course not; that (privilege) belongs to my cross cousin only." The unwillingness of the women and the untutored brutality of the men give little encouragement to experimentation.

Unmarried men of over twenty are a definite menace to the inflexible sex code of the village. Affairs with young girls or with married women are almost the inevitable result of an unattached young man in the village. In Peri there were two such youths, one a boy of low mentality, brutal, unreliable, dishonest, the son of a shiftless father, descendant of a shiftless line. His short-lived affair with his cross cousin Lauwiyan had caused the illness of little Popitch, brought the stately Lauwiyan to shame and disgrace. He also prated of affairs with two visiting girls. Unbetrothed because his father was so poor and improvident, he was a real problem in the village. The other youth was Tchokal, lately fled from the village which accused him of adultery with the head man's wife, which had caused her death. He likewise was unbetrothed: no one was willing to give his daughter or even to enter into negotiations with him because he refused to confess his sin.

For the Manus carry the doctrine of confession to its logical conclusion. A sin confessed, is a sin wiped out. There is no word for virgin, and disgrace following confession is temporary. An arranged marriage is not broken off because of the lapse from virtue of the bride; instead the marriage date is hastened. It is the concealed sin only which angers the spirits; a sin confessed and paid for in a fine to the mortal wards of the avenging spirits is no more cause for illness and death. A man will describe an affair with a woman in the quietest, most impersonal terms, giving name, date, and place, if he can add something like, "Later on my brother was ill. I confessed my sin and paid for it and my brother got all right again."

To the sinner who steadfastly refuses confession the community turns a cold, distrustful face. To make an alliance with such a one is courting death. So Tchokal goes unwed, but for the time being too hurt to be dangerous. Some day the people say he will marry a widow. He can never hope to get a young wife now.

The obligation to confess sins committed is accompanied by an obligation to confess sins accidentally discovered. Thus when Paleao was a small boy he climbed up unannounced into his cousin's house, only to find his cousin, a man of thirty-five, copulating with his uncle's wife, a woman of fifty. Paleao climbed hastily down and slipped away, trembling with shame and fear. Where would the wrath of the spirits fall? He had not long to wait. In a week his cousin fell ill of cerebral malaria. He lay at the point of death, too ill to confess his own sin, and his uncle's wife had gone on a visit to another village. The ten-year-old boy proudly rose to the occasion and "saved his cousin's life." "Had I not done so," says he, "he would surely have died and as a spirit, angry over his death, he would have killed me, who had known the truth and concealed it."

Sometimes the consequences of sin become so complex that the ordinary marriage arrangements are upset. So it was with Luwil and Molung. These two lived in the same house, the house of Luwil's mother's brother and Molung's father's sister. Both were betrothed. Mutchin, the head of the house, went off on a long expedition to Mok, in a canoe heavily laden with sago. While he was away and the house in charge of a deaf old woman, Luwil and Molung slept together. This went on for three nights undiscovered and then the sounds of mourning broke out in the village. A canoe had come in from Mok and reported that Mutchin had never arrived. Drums were beaten as for the dead, a dreadful wailing sounded through the village, three search parties set out at once. For two days doubt and misery lay over the village. Then news was brought that after being overturned in a gale, losing all their food, and floating helplessly under water for two days, the canoe had arrived safely. Neither Molung nor Luwil doubted that their sin was responsible; afraid to face the angry Mutchin, they did a most unusual thing, they eloped to the shelter of an inland village where Luwil had a friend.

Angry and disgruntled as their elders were, they ratified the marriage with an exchange of property. To leave the young couple living in sin for another day would invite further disaster. By a quick rearrangement of debts, a marriage was planned between the fiancée of Luwil and the fiancé of Molung, so that some of the cherished financial arrangements were saved from the wreckage. But such rewarding recklessness is rare: it is seldom that one has good friends among another tribe, and no Manus home would dare to give the eloping pair shelter. The offended spirit of that house would immediately punish the inmates. Luwil and Molung were one of the rare cases where husband and wife get on fairly happily together, perhaps because the affair began by their own choice.

The observance of the sex mores of the community is based upon no respect for personal relations, no standard of love or of loyalty, but simply upon property rights and fear of the spirits. The ideal of every man in the community is the golden age, which each believes to be just a generation behind him, when the spirits took no interest in mortal amours and whenever one met a woman alone, one could take her by the hair. Rape, the swift and sudden capture of an unwilling victim, is still the men's ideal.

They tell with gusto the story of how Pomalat got his large, dour wife. She had had a mixed career: seduced by her cousin, carried off by a man from Rambutchon, then returned to her village, she knew far more of sex than did the average woman. Her uncle wanted her to marry Pomalat, a slender, under-sized, indeterminate youth. This she refused to do. Now an unwilling widow, and as such Ngalowen ranked, commands a higher price than a willing one, possibly to compensate her relatives for their troubles. Ngalowen refused to marry Pomalat. Pomalat did not wish to make a higher payment for her. Finally he and three other youths captured her and carried her off for three days with them on the mainland. After the third day, the men say sagely, "She was no longer unwilling." This only happened once within memory but it appealed to all the men as an excellent way to make the women see reason.

In the village there were only two women of bad character—one was Ngapan, one of Poiyo's two wives, the other was the widow Main. Ngapan had had a secret intrigue with Selan and become pregnant. The women accused her of pregnancy but she flouted their questions, affirming that a magical charm had made her body swell. Then Selan's small sister fell ill and in desperation he confessed to his cousin, only insisting that his sin be not proclaimed abroad until after he had left the village. When Ngapan's pregnancy became unmistakable, her family dressed her as a bride and took her to the house of Selan's older brother. But the older brother, advised of their purpose, barred the door, and fled to the bush. The rejected bride had to be taken home again. A little girl was born and died soon after. The spirits could not be expected to protect such a brazen child. For two years Ngapan lived sullenly at home and then became involved in an illicit affair with Poiyo, who already had one wife, a dull, industrious woman. Again she became pregnant. Her family threatened to take the matter to the white man's court and Poiyo married her as his second wife, legitimising his son, and saddling a licensed quarrel upon the village. The little boy was regarded as legitimate, so there was not a single illegitimate child in the village.

The other woman, Main, had been five times widowed. Her only child had died at birth. Her first husband had died, her second she had left, her third had taken her by force. From him she had returned to the second, who died soon after. A fourth and fifth, first as intrigues, later solemnised, had followed. Her path was strewn with infidelities. Of the Pontchal clan only two men still lived, all the rest had died in the influenza epidemic. In native belief the two who lived, lived only because they had confessed to what the others no doubt had concealed, intrigues with Main. She was a jolly, impudent woman, self-sufficient, sensuous, sure of herself, devoted to various nieces and nephews— those who remained after their brothers and sisters had died for her sins. She was a little stupid and went about at night in fear of the spirits of her five dead husbands.

She would have been a woman of easy virtue, quick compliance, in any society. Given her reputation, acquired early in youth, the young men gravitated towards her, the older men boasted that they had resisted her evil attempts, for had she not killed off all Pontchal and would she not like to finish off their clans also? Her veniality was regarded not a sin of the flesh but as a definite malicious attempt directed against mankind. She was the incarnate wicked feminine principle of the early Christian fathers. Where frigidity up to first childbirth and distaste and weariness with sex were the rule, and illness and death followed sex indulgence, men could only conceive her as a sort of pursuing fury, and hope for strength to avoid her. But a Manus community is too democratic, too unorganised to make any concerted move against such a social evil as Main.

The whole picture is one of a puritan society, rigidly subduing its sex life to meet supernaturally enforced demands, demands which are closely tied up with its property standards. To interfere with marriage arrangements for which thousands of dogs' teeth have been paid, is blasphemy. Accompanying this banishment of the sex motive in life are various other social traits. Casual profanity takes the form of references to the private parts or sex adventures of the dead. The commonest of these expressions which fall from every lip are, "Inside my mother's vagina," and "Copulate with my father who is dead." And this is a society where the sex activity of the living is only referred to between jesting relatives or by outraged elders dispensing punishment.

Dress and ornamentation, removed from any possibility of pleasing the opposite sex, become a matter of economic display and people only dress up at economic feasts. Sweet-smelling herbs are seldom used. Faces are painted in mourning and as a defence against inimical spirits. The elaborate forms of ornamentation are interpreted either as money or as mourning. Although the people are moderately cleanly because of their water lives, they are seldom spick-and-span. The young men, in the boys' house, occasionally dress up, piling their compliant hair into great structures on top of their heads, winding necks and arms with leaves. So dressed, they parade through the village, beating their drums the louder, as if to drown the aimlessness of their proceedings. There is no word for *love* in the language. There are no love songs, no romantic myths, no merely social dances. Characteristically, the Manus dance only when a great deal of property is given away, and after a period of mourning, "to shake the dust from the house floor." An hibiscus in the hair is a sign of magic making, not of love making. The village lies fair in the moonlight, the still lagoon holds the shadow of houses and trees, but there is no sound of songs or dancing. The young people are within doors. Their parents are quarrelling on the verandas or holding séances within doors to search out sin.

X

PUBERTY for girls means the beginning of adult life and responsibility, the end of play, careless companionship, happy hours of desultory ranging through the village. The tabus begun some years earlier if a girl has been betrothed as a child, now settle upon almost every girl, for there are seldom any girls past puberty unbetrothed. But puberty does not mean the beginning of a new life, only the final elimination of play elements from the old life. The girl performs no new tasks, she simply does more beadwork, works more sago, does more fishing. She makes no new friends, but she sees less and less of her old friends.

The hour of puberty itself is marked by ceremony and public observance. When the girl has her first menses, her father or guardian (that is, the elder male relative who is bearing the onus of her marriage exchanges) throws great numbers of coconuts into the sea. All the neighbours' children leap in after them shouting, struggling with one another for the nuts. So word circulated quickly through the village that Kiteni had attained puberty. The event is regarded without embarrassment as important to the adults because a whole round of ceremonial is set up, important to the children because a sort of house party will be instituted in the house of the pubescent girl.

Kiteni herself was placed in a little cubby hole made of mats near the centre of the house. About her neck were dogs' teeth, her hair was combed to a glossy perfection. For five days she had to sit in this little room without stirring thence.

She might not eat puddings of taro leaves or the pudding known as *tchutchu,* taro, the fruit called *ung,* or shell fish. All that she ate had to be prepared for her on a separate fire, in separate cooking vessels, by her mother. She might not talk aloud, nor might any one address her in a loud voice, or pronounce her name audibly. Every night most of the girls of the village, especially the younger ones, came to sleep with her. They came after sunset and lay down to sleep on the floor slats, one recumbent little figure curled close to another. At dawn they slipped away before breakfast, for a family has no obligation to feed this horde of visitors. If young married women come to sleep, they are fed before leaving. During the day some of the girls returned to play cat's cradle with Kiteni, or simply to lie contentedly upon the floor murmuring scraps of song.

Meanwhile all the elders of Kiteni's household were very busy. Each day tall black pots of *bulukol,* a coconut soup, had to be taken to the family of her betrothed. Extra hot stones were dropped in just as the canoe reaches the house, so that the gift arrived in a flare of steam. (Throughout the observances for puberty runs the pattern of heat and fire.) The family of her betrothed had to bring fish each day, her future mother-in-law bringing it to the house platform at dawn, but not entering the house. Kiteni's own brothers and paternal uncles had to fish for her; the heads of these fish were eaten by her father's mother and her father's sisters. After she has eaten the bodies of the fish, the skeletons were hung up above her head, as a boast to visitors of the family's success in fishing. These men had to set to work to make sago, to trade for sago, to travel overseas to collect debts of sago due to them. All of those who were parties to Kiteni's projected marriage were involved. Kiteni had a brother in the island of Mok; he had to be warned to prepare his quota of sago. This could be no mean offering. For Kiteni was to marry Kaloi, the younger brother of the dead Panau. Paleao, a man of great economic consequence, was financing the marriage. Every inland trade partner of the family was importuned for sago; the men worked sago by day and fished by night to obtain fish to pay for more sago.

At the end of five days the first feast for relieving the girl of her tabus was held. This was a feast looked forward to by all the girls and regarded by the men as particularly daring and spectacular behaviour on the part of womankind. It was held after nightfall. A great quantity of bamboo torches and large lumps of raw sago were prepared. The house was crowded with women and girls and brightly lit by torches piled in each of the four fireplaces. On this particular occasion last to arrive was Kiteni's paternal grandmother. Kiteni, who giggled and held back, was bidden to stand up and run the length of the house pursued by her grandmother, waving a burning torch over her. But Kiteni ran without conviction and the whole party laughed as the grandmother perfunctorily pursued the girl. The torch was held overhead as the grandmother pronounced an incantation over her.

Meanwhile the girls seized the bowls of raw sago and the bundles of burning torches, loaded them upon a large canoe, and set off through the village. As they went they waved the torches and showered sparks into the sea. Three small girls encountered on the way were bidden to splash vigorously as the canoe passed. At the houses of brothers, grandparents, uncles, a cake of sago and a torch were left on the platform. The village streets were empty of canoes. Attracted by the shouting or by the gleam of the torches reflected through the floor slats, people came to the doors and peered out, shouting hilarious greeting. The last sago distributed, the last glowing torch laid quickly on a doorstep, the party returned, only slightly sobered, to the house of Kiteni where a feast was spread.

Kiteni was now free to walk about the house and to go out on the platform or into the sea near by, in the dark or in the rain. She still was not allowed to go about the village or leave the house when the sun was shining.

Seven days later a second feast was held, "The Feast for the Ending of Coconut Soup." Three kinds of food, a taro and coconut oil pudding, cakes of sago and coconut, and puddings of taro and grated coconut, were prepared. The women of Kiteni's family took these, carefully laid out in carved bowls on canoe platforms, to the house of Kiteni's future mother-in-law, who received them formally and distributed them to all her sisters-in-law who were to help with the return payment of beadwork. For each bowl of food a bead belt was expected in return. This ended the exchange of soup and fish.

Five days later a third feast was held. This is the most thoroughly feminine and most amiable feast held in Peri. No debts are contracted, no old debts paid off. It is a feminine feast for all the women of the clan and all the women who have married into it. At the centre of the house with a mat spread before her sat Kiteni, the *piramatan*, literally, "female owner," of the feast. Over the distribution presided the wife of her uncle, who was paying for her marriage. About the fireplaces sat the women of the clan. At one end of the house sat her mother's sisters-in-law, at the other, her young sisters-in-law who had married her "brothers." Bowls of food were set aside for the girls betrothed to sons of the house. Every guest brought a bowl of food. These were spread out on the mat in front of Kiteni, and her aunt garnished each with shiny betel nuts and pepper leaves, pronouncing as she did so, "This is for the wife of Malean"—"This for the wife of Pokus." Then the bowls of each group were formally passed over to the other group. Followed a friendly argument between Kiteni's paternal aunt and grandmother as to which one should perform the taro feeding ceremony. The aunt prevailed and the grandmother washed her hands carefully, and taking up a large handful of taro, she worked it into a ball, saying:

"Pomai!
Tchelantune!
I take the taro of Paleiu—he is strong!
I take the taro of Sanan—he is strong!
The two grandfathers are strong!
For the descendant of Pomai,
For the descendant of Tchelantune.
She eats our taro.
May fire be in her hand.
May she kindle forehandedly the fire of her mother-in-law
In the house of the noble one who receives this exchange.
May she blow the housefire,
Providing well for the funeral feast,
    the marriage feast,
    the birth feast.
She shall make the fire swiftly,
Her eyes shall see clearly by its light."

(Here the grandmother thrusts a handful of taro into the girl's mouth.) Taking up another handful she continues:

"I give this to her mouth in order to brighten
    the funeral fires with it,
    the fire of gift exchange with it,
    all that belongs to it."

(Again she feeds her taro.)

"I give taro to the daughter of Paleiu,
To the grandchild of Sanan,
To the grandchild of Posanau."

(She eats our taro.)

"When she keens she must not merely cry,
'My mother, my mother,'
She must first cry on the names of people,
Then all will understand."

(She feeds her taro. Then the widow Polyon, sister
of Kiteni's dead father, takes up the chant:)

"I give her this food,
I give her this taro.
She will eat our taro,
She will recite our mourning songs.
By eating it her mouth will become flexible.
She will keen because of it.
As for us of (the clan of) Kamatachau,
We are all dead,
Only I remain.
We give taro to the mouth of this one.
I give my fire,
She will take my fire in her hand.
It will be the fire of the gift exchanges.
All that belongs to the gift exchange
She will give to her mother and her fathers, her sisters, her
    brothers."

Now it was the turn of Ngatchumu, another aunt.
Ngatchumu was unaccustomed to the ceremony. She
stumbled and halted, and was prompted by Kiteni's
grandmother. Halfway through, she paused and said
hopefully, "Is that all?"

Her chant:

> "Ponkiao,
> Poaseu,
> Ngakeu,
> Ngatchela,
> This is your grandchild.

(She feeds her taro.)

> "Let her take my fire to kindle her fire with it.
> All the women of her father's side,
> All the women of her mother's side,
> Let them all give her shell money quickly.
> In her own hands there are no possessions."

The hilarity occasioned by Ngatchumu's ignorance continued. Women began to feed each other taro and utter mock incantations; a most unusual good humour prevailed. Once a woman raised her voice to hush a group of small children who were playing under the house. When the feast was ended the women left the house to find a flotilla of canoes waiting to take them home, a flotilla of canoes punted by husbands who had the sheepish air worn by men waiting outside a woman's club house.

The kin of the betrothed later makes a feast in which the food is specially decorated. Coconut meat is cut into star-shaped flowers and fastened on the ends of sticks giving the effect of tall stiff lilies. Among them single betel nuts are placed, also on little standards. These flower and bud decorations are arranged in bowls of taro.

This ended the small ceremonies. There only remained the great exchange with the betrothed husband's
family. Kiteni had to stay about the house until that
was completed. The days dragged on. The little
girls wearied of sleeping in Kalat. She had fewer companions and she had to get about her business, making
beadwork for her trousseau. Finally, after nearly two
months the sago, the pigs, and the oil were ready. The
day before the big exchange Kiteni was finally released
from her tabus. The women of her household had prepared scores of sago balls, about the size of grapefruit.
These were placed in large carved bowls on the canoes.
Kiteni was dressed in a few simple bits of finery—dogs'
teeth, beaded leglets—and carried down the ladder
on her grandmother's back. The canoe was punted out
into a weedy shallow far from any houses. Here all
the women of the village had gathered. The flotilla
of canoes stretched for five hundred feet—mothers and
children, old crones and little girls. Kiteni stood in
the shallow lagoon while her grandmother poured oil
over her head, chanting.

Then she broke a young coconut, spilling the juice
over the girl, repeating another incantation.

This concluded, all the girls leaped into the water
and splashed Kiteni laughing, shouting, making as
much of a foaming confusion as possible. Afterwards
they swam about, damp blinking little servers passing
the refreshments, balls of sago, among the different
canoes. Now the whole convoy returned to the house.
Kiteni was dressed in the heavy finery of a bride, and

[183]

all the boxes of the village were ransacked to dress up the other girls in shell money or bead aprons. Finally, in a long slender canoe, Kiteni's slender charm completely obscured by her heavy trappings, they paraded the village in solemn procession. The next day all the accumulated sago was also paraded through the village, piled upon the little islet and presented to the opposite side with impressive orations.

Older girls when they speak of their own adolescence ceremony, always emphasise the same points, the number of girls who came to sleep with them, the splashing in the sea, and the size of the display of property which was made in their name. Poor Ngaleap alone in the village was betrothed after her first menstruation, so she had had a very poor ceremony indeed. It stands out in the girls' minds as a rather gay social event, an occasion for pride and display without the unpleasant connotations of the similar great display at marriage. The association with menstruation does not seem very fundamental. Menstruation is a point which is never discussed, about which young boys know nothing beyond this first event. The fact of its recurrence is locked away in the girl's mind as a guilty and shameful secret and is automatically separated from the public ceremonial of which she is so proud. A similar ceremonial, including the torchlight distribution of fire and raw sago and the water party, marks the *memandra*, a feast held just before marriage.

There is a period of tabu and a gift exchange between her father's relatives and her mother's relatives when a girl's ears are pierced, but this ceremony which will be described in detail for the boys, is entirely overshadowed in the case of girls by the longer, more impressive puberty ceremonial.

Past puberty, betrothed, tabu, and respectable, the girl is expected to settle down peacefully to her labours, to submit silently to eternal supervision. The slightest breath of scandal means a public scene and exaggerated ignominy. The majority of girls prefer to submit like Ngalen, to go soberly about their tasks and look forward to becoming resigned and virtuous wives. No girl can manage a long career of rebellion. While she sins, all of her kin, her betrothed's kin, her betrothed, her partner-in-sin, she herself, are in danger of death from the ever observant spirits. But occasionally tempted, a girl will become involved in a swift, surreptitious sex affair. Ngaleap was a buxom, laughing girl, stout, good-natured, quick-tongued, at eighteen quite unable to take life seriously. She was engaged to marry a boy who had been adopted into the next village, a boy whom she had never seen and whom she cared nothing about. She was sick to death of snatching up her cloak and hiding her head at the approach of someone from Patusi. Patusi was only half a mile away: Patusi men were continually coming and going, interrupting her at her fishing, making the houses of other girls intolerable to her. These were men she had known all her life; why should she not joke with them? And the village shook its head and said Ngaleap kept her tabus in a most slovenly fashion. Two years before Kondai had come to visit in Peri. Kondai was tall and arrogant, twenty-three and unwed, used to loose living from many moons spent upon a small trading schooner. More than once his master had had to weigh anchor quickly to escape the rage of the local natives because Kondai had been allowed ashore. Ngaleap slept in the house of her uncle, and in the early morning Kondai was seen slipping from the house. No one could prove that anything had happened, but Ngaleap was soundly whipped. Two illnesses were attributed to her sin; Kondai was bidden to go home to his own village. Two years later the little schooner anchored within the reef, and Ngaleap, Ngaoli, and a grass widow who had been away among white men, surreptitiously went out to the schooner and spent an hour aboard, while Kondai borrowed their canoe and went fishing. His boys told the white trader, who told Ngaleap's uncle. It was also said that Kondai was boasting that he was going to marry Ngaleap. The uncle shouted the girls' names through the village. They came to the little islet, abashed, sullen, wrapped in their tabu cloaks. They admitted nothing, except the visit to the steamer, out of the corners of their mouths sullenly denying all else. The uncle stormed, "This Kondai—he possessed thee before. Now I know he possessed thee before. And thou still dost think of him. Did I not warn thee that his magic was strong, that thou shouldst beware when he came into the village? Thou girl belonging to worthlessness, I have paid five pigs and one thousand sago for thy marriage.

Who dost thou think paid these? I, even I, thy uncle. Where is thy father? He is dead. Where is thy mother? She is dead. Who will finance thy marriage if I desert thee? Wilt thou bring disgrace upon my house?"

The foster father of Ngaoli took a different vein. He was little and insignificant and unstable. His four successive wives had borne him no children. His brothers were dead. In uncontrollable hysteria he danced about on the islet, shouting to Ngaoli that he had fed her, he had cared for her, he had cherished her, and now her sin would kill him, the spirits would kill him, he would die, he, the last of his line, slain by her fault.

After these two had finished, other male relatives joined in the abuse. The crowd grew thicker. Finally almost the whole village was assembled, the women huddled in their cloaks. After the men, the women joined the girls, adding their upbraiding, lower keyed only because of the presence of so many men; the girls were sullen, defenceless, miserable. For weeks they went about with eyes cast down, especially avoiding each other's company. The village waited—no illness followed, and gradually the furore died down. The girls must have told the truth after all or the spirits would have expressed their anger. But this pragmatic test is no salve to injured feelings. A girl who has not sinned is helpless in the face of the damning evidence contained in the illness or death of a relative. Whether she confesses to an uncommitted sin or stubbornly refuses to confess is a measure of the depth of her shame.

From puberty until marriage a girl is given no greater participation in village life: she is less free but no more important. She never cooks for feasts, she makes no exchanges. In the big gift exchanges she is simply dressed up and pushed about like a dummy. Unless some overbold youth catches her alone, sneaks into the house unobserved or intercepts her between sago patch and river, the years between puberty and marriage are uneventful. She learns a little more about sago working, she learns to sew thatch, she finishes a few lots of beadwork, she does more reef fishing, she fetches wood and water.

Around her, across her beading frame, over her head, behind her bent shoulders, goes the gossip of gift exchange, of shrewd planning, anxious devices, chatter of the market place. She does not participate, she is given no formal instruction, but day by day she absorbs more of the minutiæ of adult life, learns the relationship, the past economic history, the obligations of each member of the community. When a ceremony takes place she attends it perforce because she is working in the house. She sees the magicians brew their leaves and spit their henna-coloured betel juice over the sick, she sees the red paint of the property-eliciting magic poured over the head of the bride or bridegroom; she helps dress her married sisters and sisters-in-law for the birth ceremonials. Less sleepy than in her childhood, forbidden to go abroad in the dark night, she lies awake and listens to the hour-long colloquies between mortals and spirits. She can no more learn the medium's art than she can engage in gift exchange. Marriage is required for both occupations. But perforce she listens.

Thus three or four years are spent as a rather bored, very much inhibited spectator to life, years during which she gets the culture by heart. When she marries she will know far more than her husband, especially as the woman's rôle in economics is a private one. The woman is expected to plan, to carry debts in her head, to do the quiet person-to-person canvassing for property. Upon the shrewdness, social knowledge, and good planning of his wife a young or stupid man is very dependent, for in all his dealings she is his adviser. So the young married woman who has never cooked for a feast takes her place unerringly among her sisters-in-law. She has seen each dish made a hundred times. She plans and selects the beads or the food for exchange with equal sureness. She has had four or five years of education by contemplation.

Except for the unusual intrusion of a brief, penalty-ridden sex affair, these years are not years of storm and stress, nor are they years of placid unfolding of the personality. They are years of waiting, years which are an uninteresting and not too exacting bridge between the free play of childhood and the obligations of marriage. In so many societies the late teens are a time of some sort of active sex adjustment. Whether it be the many love affairs of the Samoan, the studied social life of the débutante, or the audacious technique of the flapper, ways of attracting the opposite sex form an absorbing occupation. In Manus, a girl has no need to seek a husband; he has been found. She may not seek a lover; she is denied the outlet of close friendship with other girls. She simply waits, growing taller and more womanly in figure, and in spite of herself, wiser in the ways of her world.

XI

THE ADOLESCENT BOY

FOR the Manus boy there is no one puberty ceremony. At some time between twelve and sixteen, when
his family finances suggest the advisability, his ears are
pierced. The feasts of ear piercing pay back the great
display which his father made at his silver wedding.
Much property must be collected, many plans laid.
The boy's size or age are relatively unimportant. But
some day a boy comes home from playing with his
companions, to be told that his ears will be pierced in
a month. If he is the first among his age mates to
undergo the tiresome ceremony, he rebels. Occasionally
a father will follow his pattern of indulgence, more
often he insists. The wives of the boy's mother's
brothers come in a body to stay in the house with
him. His father's family prepares a feast of cooked
food. He himself is dressed in his very best—his
small neck bristles with dogs' teeth, a gorgeous new
laplap proclaims his special state. He sits beside his
father, very stiff and straight, divided between embarrassment and pride. None of his friends come to
the ceremony, only grown people and little children.
His father's sisters take him by the hands and lead him
down the ladder to the platform. Here his mother's
brother pierces his ears with a sharpened bit of hard

wood. Bits of soft wood are inserted in the newly made hole, and small protectors of sago bark are placed over each ear. Now the boy is under strict tabu. He cannot cut with a knife; he cannot kindle a fire; he cannot bathe for five days. He must eat only of the food which his mother's brothers' wives cook for him. When he leaves the house, he sits very erect and gaudy upon the canoe platform while the other boys punt him. His companions are very impressed with his strange state. They gladly act as oarsmen. They take him all the tobacco they can beg. At the end of the five days, he may wash, and he is free to move quietly about the village. The other prohibitions hold until his mother's relatives make a big feast for his father's relatives. Until then his ears are in danger should he be unobservant of the tabus.

The adolescent girl observes her tabus out of a general vague fear that something will happen to her if she does not. But of the boy (or girl) at ear piercing no such vague precautions are required. If he fails in the tabus, his ears will break, his beauty will be forever marred. He can never have the long ear lobes, heavy with ornament. So he is docile, walks carefully like some one trying a broken foot after a month on crutches. During this period he is given no instruction, he is not made to feel more adult. He is simply being quiescent for beauty's sake.

If his relatives are very slow in making the feast, he becomes restive. When the feast is made, he is taken in a canoeful of women—his paternal grandmother and paternal aunts and cousins—to the family island, and his grandmother calls on the family spirits to bless him, make him strong in war, clever in exchange, active in finance. Then he is released to go back to his companions. No new duties are required of him, no new knowledge has been given him. He returns to play leapfrog on the islet, to run races by moonlight, to catch minnows in spider web scoops. When his ears heal he sticks rolls of leaves in them as a bit of swank and the next boy for whom an ear piercing is planned will be less unwilling.

In the life of the fifteen-year-old boy only one change is shown. His play group—over which he and three or four of his age mates are petty lords—is deprived of the girls of his own age. Instead, he must lord it over twelve-year-olds, chase and pretend to capture giddy ten-year-olds. It is much easier to manage the play group than of old.

Girls of his own age who were well-developed physically, strong of arm and swift of tongue, formed a real obstacle to supremacy. These are all gone. The small boys are independent but devoted slaves. There is no work to be done, only the same old games. The boys form closer friendships, go about more in pairs, make more of the casual homosexuality current in childhood. There is much roughhouse, arm linking, whispered conferences, sharing of secret caches of tobacco.

These close friendships are broken into by the chance absence of one of the boys, who is permitted to go on an overseas voyage with his father, or on a turtle hunt with the young men. The boys grow taller, heavier. They are skilled in navigation; racing their canoes about the lagoons, they have learned the details of sailing. They are ready for adult life, but under no constraint to enter it.

And here at sixteen or seventeen there must come a sharp break in the description of the old way of life and the new. Twenty years ago, before government was established in the Admiralties, this group of youths was proficient in the arts of war. They had learned to throw an obsidian-pointed spear with deadly aim and dodge spears directed at themselves. They were lusty, full of life, anxious for adventure. And the motive for war was present. They cared nothing for the economic quarrels of the elders nor for the compulsion under which various adults lived to kill a man or at least take a prisoner for ransom. But they followed gladly where the older men led for the fun of it and to capture women. Their spirits forbade love-making directed towards Manus girls, but like most gods, they were not interested in the women of the enemy. Usiai girls, Balowan girls, Rambutchon girls, were fair game. Even the girls of other Manus villages with whom an open feud was maintained were fair prey. So the old men led the war parties and the young men slaughtered gaily enough and carried off a woman, wed or unwed. On some little island where the women of the village had walked in safety and the little girls danced with their grass skirts as flags, the unfortunate captive was raped by every man in the village, young and old. The men kept her in the boys' home; her particular captor collected tribute from the others; sometimes he even took her on a money making tour through friendly villages. The men dressed her in finery to further outrage the women, who disagreed with the spirits about the innocuousness of the whole proceeding. Everywhere the men went, they took their unhappy captive with them, afraid to leave her exposed to the vengeful hatred of the women. But the men did nothing to ameliorate her lot; they showed her neither kindness nor consideration. It is hard to describe vividly enough the exultant venom with which the respectable, virtuous married women of thirty-five and forty describe the misery of the prostitute's life. Upon her the men wreaked their hatred of women aroused by the frigidity of their wives and the economic exactions imposed by matrimony. Upon her single person the young men savagely expended all the pent-up energy of the youth which was denied the joys of courtship and flirtation. Worn and old in a year or two, or displaced by a new prostitute, she was permitted to go back to her home where she usually died soon after. Sometimes she died in captivity.

War, war dances, heartless revels with one unwilling mistress, occupied the energy of the young men before marriage in the old days. The years between puberty and twenty to twenty-four were occupied in learning no peaceful art, in forming no firmer bonds with their society. They did no work, except casually, as when a thatching bee followed by a feast or house raising involved the whole village. They were a group of arrogant, roistering blades, the terror of their own village girls, the scourge of neighbouring villages.

To-day this picture is entirely altered. War is forbidden. The capture of women is forbidden. The "house boy" is merely a small house where the young men of the village noisily kick their heels or hold parodies on the activities of their elders. Spears are used only to dance with, and quarrels with the bush people are settled in court. But the community has not had to devise some way of dealing with its youthful unemployed. The recruiting of the white man does that for them. Now all Manus boys go away to work—two years, five years, sometimes seven years—for the white man. This is the great adventure to which every boy looks forward. For it, he learns pidgin, he listens eagerly to the tales of returned work boys. Among themselves the small boys ape the habits of the work boys, forming partnerships for the division of spoils. Our group of fourteen-year-olds shared their weekly tobacco as the work boys, without a bank or means of saving money, share their monthly allowance. With a shilling or two shillings a month a boy can buy nothing important, so the boys form groups—each month a different boy receives the pool and with eight or ten shillings something really worth while can be bought: a flashlight, a knife, a camphor wood box. In that one far-away village, our small boys repeated this ritual, quite meaninglessly, with tobacco.

Different kinds of service, the relative advantages of

working for Englishmen, Chinamen, Malays, are discussed endlessly in the boys' house. The small boy has three possible ambitions: to be a "boats crew" on a schooner, a "police boy," or a "child's nurse." In the first capacity one sees the world, in the second one has great power and prestige, in the third one has that dearest of playthings, a baby, and also a possible chance to go to Sydney. When one comes home laden with the purchases from three years' earnings, the drums will sound, there will be dancing and merriment over much property. One can be lordly in the distribution of property to the elders who have a right to it because they have buried the family dead and paid for one's betrothal.

Through their work years it is impossible to follow the boys. Some are police boys and return to the village with increased respect for authority, knowledge of the white man's ways of government, respect for time and efficiency. These men become government appointees, active in future dealings with government officers, active in village affairs. Others work on an isolated plantation, eat and sleep with a group of their own people, return to the village little wiser than when they went away. The boys who have been on schooners in the Admiralties return with a smattering of other languages and some new friends in near-by villages who will be useful trade connections. Every work boy dreads returning alone to his village while his former playmates are away at work. From island to island messages are sent, "How much more time have you signed for?"—"A year," and the boy receiving the answers consents to sign on for one year only. So by careful planning a group of three or four usually "finish time" together and the drums beat for more than one pile of boxes and trade cloth.

The sex experience of boys away from home is as varied as their other experiences. Some go to Rabaul, where there are only a few native women who almost inevitably become prostitutes. Others isolated on plantations turn to homosexuality and finish their contracts in a passion of regret. All the affection, congeniality, mutual tolerance, sharing of wealth, which is absent in marriage, is given full play in these relationships. But they provide no pattern of personal relations which can be carried over into a Manus marriage, hedged about with precedent and tabu.

Many boys learn bits of magic, paying away part of their earnings for some formulas for causing and curing illness, winning a woman's charm, or extracting other people's property. So a smattering of alien experiences, foreign learning, and material objects, birds of paradise feathers and cassowary bones, baskets from Buka and pouches from the Ninigos, a knowledge of the properties of calomel, a deep dyed hatred of all Malays, a rosary and a half remembered pidgin English pater noster, a few stolen forks and spoons, worn camphor wood boxes with the initials of some white man burned in their lids, a torn photograph of a former master, are brought to the village by the returning work boys. For three years they have lived in a men's world, a world with its own social traditions, its pet economics, its feasts, its feuds, its legends. But these are not of the village, they belong to the polyglot, work boy culture, which has pidgin English as its speech, tobacco and shillings as its currency, a strong feeling of unalterable difference from the white man as a bond of union, homosexual friendships as its principal romance. Its legends are mainly of the white man's world and the sorcery of strange peoples, of the glass crystals which the Salamoa natives use to cause and cure disease. Or they tell of what happened to the Buka boy who stole a bottle of cognac, of the St. Mathias woman who died from a love spell put on her by an Aitape boy, of the weird habit of the natives of Dutch New Guinea who can only visit their wives by stealth, of the boy from Kieta who had a charm which would woo money paid away to a storekeeper out of the storekeeper's lock box and back to its native owner, of the master who beat a Manus boy and was found in his bed with his throat cut by the ghostly father of the injured boy.

It is a world where the boy is often lonely and homesick, overworked, hungry, sulky, shrinking and afraid; where he is as often well fed, gay, absorbed in new friendships and strange experiences. It is a world which has nothing in common with the life which he will lead on his return to the village; it is usually no better a preparation for it than were the old days of war and rape. Furthermore, the leaders in the village, the substantial older men who have the greatest economic power and therefore the greatest social power, did not go away to work. Their tales are of war, not of the white man's world. In deference to them, all pidgin English must be discarded except the few terms which even the women understand, like "work," "Sunday," "Christmas," "flash," "rice," "grease." In the world of the white man there was much evil magic afoot but at least his own Manus spirits were not concerned with his sex offences. He has suddenly returned to a world of which he has a fundamental dread, the details of which he never knew or has forgotten. The spirits whose oppressive chaperonage he has escaped for three years are found to take a lively interest in his surreptitious gift of tobacco to young Komatal who has grown so tall and desirable in his absence.

His return is celebrated by a ceremony which combines a family blessing and incantation with a feast of return. The blessing is called *tchani*, for the whole ceremony there is only the hybrid term, "*kan* (feast) —he—finished—time." Food is prepared and sent to other families, who have made similar feasts in the past, and the boy is ceremonially fed taro by his paternal grandfather or grandmother or aunt, while the following incantation is recited over him:

> "Eat thou my taro.
> Let the mouth be turned towards dogs' teeth,
> The mouth turn towards shell money.
> The shell money is not plentiful.
> Let the taro turn the mouth towards it,
> Towards plentifulness,
> Towards greatness.

The mouth be turned towards the little transactions,
Towards the giving of food.
Let it become the making of great economic transactions.
Let him overhaul and outstrip the others,
The brothers whom he is amongst;
Let him eat my taro,
May he become rich in dogs' teeth,
Attaining many,
Towards the attainment of much shell money."

He feeds him taro, a lump so large that the boy can hardly hold it in his mouth. Then, rolling another handful in his hand, he says, calling the names of the clan ancestors:

"Powaseu!
Saleyao!
Potik!
Tcholai!
Come you hither!
On top of the taro, yours and mine,
I bestow upon the son of Polou,
Upon the son of Ngamel.
He will monopolise the riches
Amongst all of his clan.
Let Manuwai become rich,
Let him walk within the house, virtuously.
He must not walk upon the centre board of the house floor,*
He must walk on the creaking slats,
He must wait below on the lower house platform,
He must call out for an invitation (to enter),
He must call out announcing his arrival to women
That they may stand up to receive him.

* Traditional phrase, i.e., he may not enter the house in a stealthy fashion, seeking to surreptitiously possess one of the women inmates. This is symbolic of any underhand dealings.

Afterwards he may climb up into the house.
Let him eat my taro.
He must do no evil.
May he grow to my stature!
I endow the taro with the power of war!
And I now fight no more.
I give this taro to my grandson!
Let him eat the taro.
I am the elder, thy father is the younger.
It passes to this boy.
I give him the taro for eating,
I give thee power.
He may go to war,
He shall not be afraid.
There may be twenty of them,
There may be thirty of them,
He shall terrify all of them.
He shall remain steadfast.
He shall stand erect.
They will behold him,
They will drop their spears,
They will drop their stone axes on the ground;
They will flee away.
Let him eat my taro.
I give him my taro and he eats of it.
Let him live, let him live long,
Until his eyes are blinded
As are mine *
Let him grow towards a ripe old age."

This incantation blesses him, as the parallel incantation blesses the adolescent girl, and gives him power to conform to the ethical code of his elders, industry

* The man who performed this ceremony in both cases where it was observed was blind. This is probably an individual touch.

leading to wealth, open and impeccable sex conduct, courage in war, health.

There are no tabus associated with this feast, nor are there important economic obligations. It is a family ceremony of blessing. The youth goes about as before, still unmarried, still free of economic or social duties, but with the shadow of his approaching marriage hanging over him.

XII

THE TRIUMPH OF THE ADULTS

THE way in which the jolly little tomboy has been transformed into a proper young girl has already been described. Begun much earlier, completed in the middle teens, it is not a very difficult task. But the subjection of the young men is more difficult. They have been allowed to grow up in much greater freedom than have the girls. The little boy who slapped his mother in the face, demanded pepper leaf from his father and angrily threw it back when his father gave him only half, who refused to rescue the dogs' teeth for his mother, who stuck out his tongue when he was told to stay at home and swam away under water, has grown to manhood with these traits of insubordination, uncooperativeness, lack of responsibility unmodified. He has spent all his years in an unreal world, a world organised by industries which he has not learned, held together by a fabric of economic relations of which he knows nothing, ruled by spirits whom he has ignored. Yet if this world is to continue, the young man must learn to take his part in it, to play the rôle which his ancestors have played. The adult world is confronted by an unassimilated group, a group which speaks its language with a vocabulary for play, which knows its

[204]

gods but gives them slight honour, which has a jolly contempt for wealth-getting activities.

Manus society does not meet this situation consciously or through group action. None the less subtle is the unconscious offensive which the culture has devised. To subject the young man it uses the sense of shame, well developed in the three-year-old, and only slightly elaborated since. The small children have been made ashamed of their bodies, ashamed of excretion, ashamed of their sex organs. The adult has been shocked, embarrassed, revolted, and the child has responded. Similar response to failure to keep the tabus of betrothal has grafted the later, more artificial convention on the former. The small boy also learns that he must not eat in the presence of his married sister's husband, or his older brother's fiancée. The onlooker, the brother-in-law, the sister-in-law to be, gives the same signs of confusion, uneasiness, embarrassment which his parents gave when he micturated in public. The act of eating before certain relatives joins the category of those things which are shameful. His embarrassment over his future marriage is also intense. A boy of fourteen will flee from the house, like a virgin surprised in her bath, if one attempts to show him a picture of his sister-in-law. He will scuttle away if he sees the conversation is even turning upon his fiancée's village. All of these things are of course equally true of girls. To the boys' tabus they add the ubiquitous tabu cloak and the shamed concealment of menstruation. But with girls there is no pause—the girl is ever more restricted, more self-conscious, more ashamed. It is a steady progression from the first day she wears a scrap of cloth over her head to the day she is married and sits in the bridal canoe, inert and heavily ornamented, with her head drooping almost to her knees.

But with the boys there is an interval. By thirteen or fourteen all these early lessons are learned and they are given no new ignominies to get by heart. As in the old days of war and rape, so in the more recent adventure of working for the white man, the standards of adult life are not pressed more firmly upon them. But the old embarrassments are there, grown almost automatic through the years.

Now comes the time when the young man must marry. The payments are ready. The father or brother, uncle or cousin, who is assuming the principal economic responsibility for his marriage is ready to make the final payment, ten thousand dogs' teeth, and some hundred fathoms of shell money. And in no way is the bridegroom ready. He has no house, no canoe, no fishing tackle. He has no money and no furniture. He knows nothing of the devious ways in which all these things are obtained. Yet he is to be presented with a wife. Not against his will, for he knows the lesser fate of those who marry late. He has been told for years that he is lucky to have a wife already arranged for. He knows that wives are scarce, that even on the spirit level there is a most undignified scramble for wives and the spirit of a dead woman is snapped up almost before it has left her body. He knows that men without wives are men without prestige, without houses of their own, without important parts in the gift exchange. He does not rebel at the idea of marriage, he cannot rebel in advance against his fiancée for he has never seen her. He knows there will be less fun after marriage. Wives are exacting, married men have to work and scarcely ever come to the boys' house; still—one must marry.

But as plan follows plan, he gets more nervous. So Manoi, the husband of Ngalen, listened to the plans made by his two uncles, his mother's brother and his mother's sister's husband. He preferred the latter's house; here he had always chosen to sleep when he didn't sleep in the boys' house. From his babyhood he has slept where he liked and screamed with rage if his preferences were opposed. But suddenly a new factor enters in. Says Ndrosal, the uncle whom he doesn't like, "You will live in the back of my house and fish for me. I am busy; your other uncle has already a nephew who fishes for him. You will bring your wife, the granddaughter of Kea, and you two will sleep in the back of the house." Embarrassment fills Manoi—never before have his future relations with his wife been referred to. He accepts the arrangement in sullen silence. After the wedding he finds his whole manner of life is altered. Not only must he feed his new wife, but also be at the beck and call of the uncles who have paid for her. He has done nothing to pay for his privileges. They have found him a woman— shameful thought—he must fish for them, go journeys

for them, go to market for them. He must lower his
voice when he talks to them. On the other hand his
uncles have not completed the marriage payment. So
he must go ashamedly before all his wife's male relatives. Not even to her father does he show his face.
His wife's family are making a big exchange. He is
expected to help them, but he cannot punt his canoe
in the procession for his father-in-law is there.

On all sides he must go humbly. He is poor, he has
no home; he is an ignoramus. His young wife who
submits so frigidly to his clumsy embrace knows more
than he, but she is sullen and uncooperative. He enters an era of social eclipse. He cannot raise his voice
in a quarrel, he who as a small boy has told the oldest
men in the village to hold their noise. Then he was
a gay and privileged child, now he is the least and most
despised of adults.

All about him he sees two types of older men, those
who have mastered the economic system, become independent of their financial backers, gone into the gift
exchange for themselves, and those who have slumped
and who are still dependent nonentities, tyrannised over
by their younger brothers, forced to fish nightly to keep
their families in food. Those who have succeeded have
done so by hard dealing, close-fisted methods, stinginess, saving, ruthlessness. If he would be like them,
he must give up the good-natured ways of his boyhood.
Sharing with one's friends does not go with being a
financial success. So as the independence of his youth
goes down before the shame of poverty, the generous

habits of his youth are suppressed in order that his independence may some day be regained.

Only the stupid and the lazy fail to make some bid for independence and these can no longer be friendly or generous because they are too poor and despised.

The village scene is accordingly strangely stratified —through the all-powerful, obstreperous babies, the noisy, self-sufficient, insubordinate crowd of children, the cowed young girls and the unregenerate undisciplined young men roistering their disregarding way through life. Above this group comes the group of young married people—meek, abashed, sulky, skulking about the back doors of their rich relations' houses. Not one young married man in the village had a home of his own. Only one had a canoe which it was safe to take out to sea. Their scornful impertinence is stilled, their ribald parodies of their culture stifled in anxious attempts to master it; their manner hushed and subdued.

Above the thirty-five-year-olds comes a divided group—the failures still weak and dependent, and the successes who dare again to indulge in the violence of childhood, who stamp and scream at their debtors, and give way to uncontrolled hysterical rage whenever crossed.

As they emerge from obscurity their wives emerge with them and join their furious invective to the clatter of tongues which troubles the waters daily. They have learned neither real control nor respect for others during their enforced retirement from vociferous social relations. They have learned only that riches are power and that it is purgatory not to be able to curse whom one pleases. They are as like their forebears as peas to peas. The jolly comradeship, the co-operation, the cheerful following a leader, the delight in group games, the easy interchange between the sexes—all the traits which make the children's group stand out so vividly from the adults'—are gone. If that childhood had never been, if every father had set about making his newborn son into a sober, anxious, calculating, bad tempered little businessman, he could hardly have succeeded more perfectly.

The society has won. It may have reared its children in a world of happy freedom, but it has stripped its young men even of self-respect. Had it begun earlier, its methods need have been less abrupt. The girl's subjection is more gradual, less painful. She is earlier mistress of her cultural tradition. But as young people, both she and her husband must lead submerged lives, galling to their pride. When men and women emerge from this cultural obscurity of early married life, they have lost all trace of their happy childhood attitudes, except a certain scepticism which makes them mildly pragmatic in their religious lives. This one good trait remains, the others have vanished because the society has no use for them, no institutionalised paths for their expression.

PART TWO

REFLECTIONS ON THE EDUCATIONAL
PROBLEMS OF TO-DAY IN THE LIGHT
OF MANUS EXPERIENCE

XIII

BEQUEATHING OUR TRADITION GRACIOUSLY

BECAUSE Manus society is so like our own in its
aims and values, we may compare its methods of education with ours, put current theories to the test of
Manus experience. American children are as a rule
very lightly disciplined, given little real respect for
their elders. This increasing lack of discipline has been
hailed by some enthusiasts as the type of what all education should be. There are theorists to-day who, proceeding upon the assumption that all children are naturally good, kind, intelligent, unselfish and discriminat-
ing, deprecate any discipline or direction from adults.
Still others base their disapproval of disciplinary measures upon the plea that all discipline inhibits the child,
blocks and mars his development. All of these educators base their theories on the belief that there is something called Human Nature which would blossom in
beauty were it not distorted by the limited points of

view of the adults. It is, however, a more tenable attitude to regard human nature as the rawest, most undifferentiated of raw material, which must be moulded
into shape by its society, which will have no form worthy
of recognition unless it is shaped and formed by cultural tradition. And the child will have as an adult
the imprint of his culture upon him whether his society
hands him the tradition with a shrug, throws it to him
like a bone to a dog, teaches him each item with care
and anxiety, or leads him towards manhood as if he
were on a sight-seeing tour. But which method his
society uses will have far-reaching results in the attitudes of the growing child, upon the way he phrases
the process of growing up, upon the resentment or enthusiasm with which he meets the inevitable social pressure from the adult world.

The Manus teach their children very young the things
which they consider most important—physical skill,
prudery and respect for property. They teach them
these things firmly, unrelentingly, often severely. But
they do not teach them respect for age or for knowledge; they enjoin upon them neither courtesy nor kindness to their elders. They do not teach them to work;
they regard it as quite natural if a child refuses to rescue
a lost necklace from the sea, or retrieve a drifting canoe.
When a new house is thatched the children clamber
over the scaffolding, shouting and useless. When they
catch fish they do not bring them home to their parents;
they eat them themselves. They are fond of young
children and enjoy teaching them, but refuse to take

any responsibility for them. They are taught to control their bodies but not their appetites, to have steady hands but careless tongues. It is impossible to dose them with medicine for all their lives they have spat out anything which they disliked. They have never learned to submit to any authority, to be influenced by any adult except their beloved but not too respected fathers. In their enforced servitude to their older brothers and uncles, they find neither satisfaction nor pride. They develop from overbearing, undisciplined children, into quarrelsome, overbearing adults who make the lagoon ring with their fits of rage.

It is not a pretty picture. Those things which the children learn young, which they are disciplined into accepting, they learn thoroughly and well. But they are never taught participation in adult life nor made to feel themselves an integral part of adult life. When participation is thrust upon them, they resent it as slavery. They are never taught to respect age or wisdom, so their response to their elders is one of furious inferiority. They have learned no humility while they were younger; they have little dignity when they are older. Manus elders have climbed to a place of authority upon the unwilling shoulders of resentful young men; they strut, but they have no peace there.

In many ways this picture is like our society to-day. Our children are given years of cultural non-participation in which they are permitted to live in a world of their own. They are allowed to say what they like, when they like, how they like, to ignore many of the conventions of their adults. Those who try to stem the tide are derided as "old fogies," "old fashioned," "hide bound" and flee in confusion before these magic words of exorcism. This state of discipline is due to very real causes in American society. In an immigrant country, the children are able to make a much better adjustment than have their parents. The rapid rate of invention and change in the material side of life has also made each generation of children relatively more proficient than their parents. So the last generation use the telephone more easily than their parents; the present generation are more at home in automobiles than are their fathers and mothers. When the grandparent generation has lived through the introduction of the telegraph, telephone, wireless, radio and telephotography, automobiles and aeroplanes, it is not surprising that control should slip through their amazed fingers into the more readily adaptable hands of children. While adults fumbled helplessly with daylight saving time, missed appointments and were late to dinner, children of six whose ideas of time had not yet become crystallised rapidly assimilated the idea that ten o'clock was not necessarily ten o'clock, but might be nine or eleven. In a country where the most favoured are the ones to take up the newest invention, and old things are in such disrepute that one encounters humourless signs, which advertise, "Antiques old and new" and "Have your wedding ring renovated," the world belongs to the new generation. They can learn the new techniques far more easily than can their more culturally set elders. So the young in America seize their material world, almost from birth, without any practice in humility, and their parade of power becomes a shallow jugglery with things, phrases, catchwords.

To this rapidly changing material world, we have added one other phenomenon which makes it easy for the veriest babe to outbid experience and training. This is the money standard. The result is a society very like Manus, an efficient, well-equipped, active society in which wealth is the only goal, and what a man has is substituted for what he is. Respect for the old has no logical place in such a scheme of values. In a world in which individuals are pigeon-holed among a multitude of possessions in which the very personality is defined in terms of clothes, it is the pigeon-holes which count, not the individuals. And our pigeonholes are very dull ones, houses, automobiles, clothes, all turned out wholesale. These define a man's position in the social scheme, and it takes nothing but money to buy the way from one cranny to the next. The people in one pigeonhole are too like the people in the next one. The variations which occur in this money defined culture are very slight and unimportant. Differences between social groups are like differences between apartments in the same building. Our ideas of individuality are like those of the woman living in apartment 18a in a large apartment house, who accused her poorer neighbour living in apartment 2a, of having "put the bed in the wrong place." Wealth is separable from age, from sex, from wit or beauty, from manners or morals. Once

it becomes valued as a way of life, there is no respect
for those things which must be learned, must be experienced to be understood.

It is idle to talk about disciplining children, about
inculcating a respect for authority which will give them
a sense of proportion, as if it were a matter which could
be settled by the purchase of a leather strap or its equiv-
alents. The difficulty is much more deeply rooted in
the very organisation of our society. Much has been
written about the disappearance of the craftsman and
his supercession by the machine which can be manned
by an eighteen-year-old boy with a week's training.
This is significant of the whole trend of modern American ideals. In the past there have been societies in
which the elders have been craftsmen in life, wise in its
requirements, loving in their use of precious materials.
The young men have felt they had something very
precious, which must be learned slowly, carefully, with
reverence. Their voices have been lowered in real respect and their children's voices were hushed also, not
merely muted sullenly as in Manus. But in Manus as
in America, life is not viewed as an art which is learned,
but in terms of things which can be acquired. Those
who have acquired them can command those who have
not. And in Manus and in America it is not with respect that youth views age. Youth grants the aged
neither greater wisdom nor greater prowess. They vote
them richer and therefore in the saddle.

We may tighten up here and there in America, force
our children to salute or courtesy, but we can expect

to have no real discipline and hence no real dignity until we shift our valuations from having to being. When the emphasis of a society is upon what people are—as individuals—even though it be only good hunters, clever swordsmen, or skilled horseback riders, much more so if it be as artists, scholars or statesmen, then discipline is in that people. The young are taught not only the rudiments of techniques and avoidances, how to handle a canoe or a telephone, judge the distance between houseposts or dodge an oncoming automobile, bargain over dogs' teeth or over preferred stocks, but are taught to value beauty of speech and gesture, the understanding of fine arts which can come only with age and experience. When the Samoan child said "o le ali'i" "the chief," he means some one who possesses certain qualities of leadership, of dignity or wisdom, for which he has been singled out above his fellows. But the Manus child who says: "He is a strong man for he has many dogs' teeth," the American child who says, "Gee, he's a rich guy," is speaking not of the man but of his possessions. They do not conceive the man as in any way better than themselves. They give his wealth envious admiration, to him they give only the lip service which is accorded one who accidentally and through no particular merit is in a strategic position. Hilaire Belloc has counted it a virtue that in America a rich man is never worshipped slavishly as he is in Europe. But a deeper probing reveals this as really symptomatic of a loss. In Europe rank and breeding and responsibility have for so long been the accompaniment of wealth, that the European who bows before the rich men, thinks that he is honouring those things. In America, where wealth has become disassociated from any standard of behaviour, youth looks, not at the possessor that he may admire, but at the wealth, that he may covet it.

We can never discipline our children into respecting us as the owners of things, we can only keep them in temporary subjugation by withholding those things from them. By lashing them, essentially undisciplined as they are, with the whip of economic inferiority, as the Manus do, we can make them conform. Ashamed of being poor they will work, day in and day out—as the Manus do—that they or at least their children may have the things which gave power to their elders and "betters." And we have as a result a dismal spectacle like "Middletown," with each economic class working desperately to push its children into the next class; a frantic driven climb through a series of pigeonholes which are essentially alike.

In such a picture there is little discipline and less dignity. The children take and take from the parents, of their effort, their health, their very life; take it as their due, accepting their parents' valuation that the child's rise to the next economic pigeonhole is the greatest good in life. Taking this tribute from the older generation, they do not respect the givers of the tribute. And yet the arrangements of life are such that the mature in years will always be in possession of those things which the society values, whether they be wealth or knowledge, printing presses or the engraver's art. We may thrust the very old from their seats, an occasional youth may climb to a place far beyond his age mates, but there still remains a vast adult body who are the possessors, while the majority of the young are the unpossessing. From the conflict between those who have mastered the culture and those who have yet to master it, there comes a kind of strain which seems so germane to the whole course of human development as to be inevitable. Only if a culture lacks intensity in every respect, as does Samoa, can this strain be eliminated. Where to the conflict between the old and the young is added the conflict between an old way and a new, as in a complex rapidly changing modern culture, the difficulties are greatly increased. It will not change this condition to relax all discipline, or to lower the age of marriage without parental consent. The age at which the conflict comes may be varied; the form which the conflict takes may be varied, but it will be present in some form whether the individual accepts his society with enthusiasm, with reluctance or only when coerced. All attempts to blink this fact fail as did the mother who abhorred the idea of status implied in the word *mother* and taught her child to call her "Alice," only to find the child referring to the other children's mothers as their "Alices." The parent-child situation is not so easily evaded.

But if it cannot be evaded, it can be met. We can so phrase the process of growing up that it will have graciousness and dignity. If we can teach our children admiration for their elders, concentrate their attention upon what their elders have that is worthy of praise, we can equip them to feel humility, that fortunate feeling in which the virtues of the other person are in the foreground and the self in the background. If we can give them no attitudes other than envy and negligence towards those who are in power we develop in them instead only a feeling of inferiority, the miserable emphasis not upon what others *are*, but upon what they, themselves, have not. Without admiration for their elders they can give them no homage; their attention is turned back upon themselves and they, the unpossessing, feel inferior.

In modern America, the shift in techniques, the changes in material culture, the great immigrant invasions whose descendants are inevitably better adjusted than were their parents, the emphasis upon the possession and control of a fluid undifferentiated material like money, have all undermined the respect for the aged as such. It would probably be impossible and equally undesirable to return to an attitude which bows to grey hairs and gives deference to parents no matter what their character or just deserts. Once the myth of the innate superiority of age is overthrown, no matter how irrelevant the agents of its downfall—in America these agents have been different language groups, the sudden growth of mechanical invention and the money dictated fluidity of class lines—it cannot easily be reinstated. It is because they do not realise this that parents and teachers who insist upon respect to-day are met with mocking eyes and shrugging shoulders. They insist upon respect given to status and the young people have tested the quality of status based upon the possession of wealth and found it wanting. If we wish to re-establish some sort of discipline which will make it possible for our young people to grow up less ungraciously, we must sacrifice the old insistence upon respect for *all* parents, *all* teachers, *all* guardians. We cannot deceive the perspicacity of present-day youth, but we can utilise it. The acumen which has been displayed in finding out some of its elders, may be turned to honouring others of them if only the elders will change their line of battle. The adult world to-day is like a long and straggling battle line, weekly defended by the advocates of an old fashioned respect for those in authority. The defenders of this line are too few, too scattered. Too many of those who would once have stood beside them have gone over completely to the young invaders, ad-mitting miserably that they have no bulwark worth de-fending. The remainder stretch their depleted ranks along too long a line, a line the defences of which are all known to the enemy. In defending all the bulwarks they lose the entire battle. It is time to admit the worthlessness of the present claims, to admit that neither age nor status nor authority are capable of com-manding real respect unless they are joined with def-inite qualities worthy of admiration. Then those who have deserted the battle line—in laziness, desperation, or real humility—can return to defend a modified **and** more exacting dogma of superiority.

In so doing, in rewriting the relationship between youth and age so that some of the aged will always outrank the finest youths, while admitting that many of the aged have earned no guerdon of respect, the elders will serve youth more than themselves. In offering them nothing they do them only injury. If children were moved by great internal drives which drove them into manufacturing a new heaven and a new earth, then the elders might benefit them by standing aside and letting the experiment have free play. But the children have no such creative gift. They have no stuff to build with except tradition. Left to themselves, deprived of their tradition or presented with no tradition which they can respect, they build an empty edifice without content. And come to maturity, they must make terms with the culture of their adults, live on the same premises, abide by the same values. It is no service to them to so rear them that they take over the adult life sullenly, with dull resentment. The perpetuation of the given culture is the inevitable fate of the majority of any society. We who cannot free them from that fate may at least give them such a phrasing of life that it may seem to them important and dignified. To treat our children as the Manus do, permit them to grow up as the lords of an empty creation, despising the adults who slave for them so devotedly, and then apply the whip of shame to make them fall in line with a course of life which they have never been taught to see as noble or dignified—this is giving a stone to those who have a right to good bread.

XIV

ALTHOUGH education can not alter the fact that the child will be in most important respects like the culture within which he is reared, methods of education may have far-reaching effects upon the development in the child of that sum total of temperament, outlook, habitual choice, which we call personality. Because the Manus have carried the development of personality to such extreme limits for a people bound within the narrow walls of a single tradition, the way in which each Manus baby is differentiated from each other Manus baby throws vivid light upon the problem. Within a homogeneous culture the problem of personality is seen stripped of all the trappings and superficial elaborations which a complex culture inevitably gives each individual born into its hybrid tradition. The result of these secondary elaborations we often take for personality differences when they are nothing of the sort. Let us compare for a moment the possible cultural variations permitted to a Manus adult male with those variations which are part of the individuality of every man in our society. Taking first the minor matters of appearance, a Manus man may wear his hair long and arranged in a knot, or short; he may wear earrings or not, similarly he may or may not wear a thin pearl shell

[223]

crescent or an incised bone in his nose. But in any case ears and nose will be pierced to receive these ornaments. His breech clout is of brown breadfruit bark, or of trade cloth. His jewelry is dogs' teeth, shell money and bead-work. The dogs' teeth may be strung with beads in between, they may be strung single or double; the shell money may have red beads in it, or red and black beads —very minor variations at best. Compare this with the variations implied in our range from the overalls of the working man through the important nuances described in the Theatre Programs as "What the well dressed man will wear." And when it is a question of possible tastes, beliefs, opinions, the contrast is overwhelming. The most aberrant man in Peri, and he is yet a young man, proclaimed his difference from his fellows as a boy by the unique act of hanging a charm on the back of a cousin whom he had seduced so that the spirits could not punish her. In later life, he used a vocabulary filled with obsolete words carefully collected from old men in different villages, and he laughed aloud at his sister's funeral. In all other respects he was very like his fellows, he married, his wife left him, he married again. He fished and traded for garden products, he engaged in economic exchanges, he observed the name tabus of his affinal relatives, as did all the other men in Peri. Another man in Peri was conspicuous on a different count; he had wept sincerely and lengthily for his wife when she died and he had kept her skull and occasionally talked to it. This made him a marked individual, unique in the experience of his kinsmen and neighbours. But in the bulk of his beliefs and practices he differed not at all from all the other men of the village.

Now let us consider a brief sample of the kinds of individuals which we find among ourselves. Among two men of the same general personality traits—i.e., both may be dominant, aggressive, originative, self-confident —one may believe in the Trinity and the Doctrine of Original Sin, the other be a convinced Agnostic; one may believe in free trade, state's rights, local option; the other in tariffs, big navies, national legislation on social questions; one may be interested in collecting prints of early New York, the other in collecting butterflies; one may have his house done in Queen Anne furniture, the other have a house with furniture assembled from half a dozen sources; one an ear trained to distinguish the most elaborate fugues, the other a knowledge of Picasso which enables him to date every Picasso painting; one a preference for Cabell, the other for Proust. And so one could go through the entire range of possible tastes and to complete the picture compare either of these men with a young clerk in a small city, whose only amusements are driving a Ford, going to the movies, reading the comic strips; whose house has been furnished in standard ugliness on the instalment plan and who is a Republican because his father was. Both antithetical tastes of the same kind, and the difference between complex and simple tastes, serve as a background against which the individual can stand out far more sharply than would ever be possible to any one in a simple culture. In Manus musical taste consists in being able to play a pan pipe or a nose flute, well or badly; artistic interest in carving or not carving perfectly traditional forms which have been developed by neighbouring peoples. But within this narrow range of cultural choices and possibilities there is as much difference in actual personality traits among Manus children as there is among American children, the recessive and the dominant, the calculating and the impetuous, the originative and the imitative types, can be seen quite clearly. And just because complex differences in tradition, training, reading, are not present to blur the picture, Manus is a good place to study the way in which these fundamental aspects of personality are developed in the young child.

This is a problem that has as much significance for us as it has for any primitive people. How are these special tendencies to make one kind of choice rather than another developed in the growing individual? A superficial survey of present day civilisations reveals the immediate relevance of the relationship between culture and temperament. The meditative person concerned with other world values is at a complete discount in America where even a parson must be a go-getter and the premium is always to the energetic. Conversely, the active-minded type which sees no fascination in thought and scoffs at philosophical perplexities would have been at a disadvantage in a society like that of ancient India. Among the Zuñi Indians the individual with undisguised initiative and greater drive than his fellows is in danger of being branded as a witch and hung up by his thumbs. The man who sought all his life for a vision and could not obtain one even by tearing his muscles from his back was helplessly handicapped among those fundamentalist Plains Indian tribes who had not yet adopted the device of buying and selling religious experience. Each society approximates in its chief emphasis to one of the many possible types of human behaviour.* Those individuals who show this type of personality will be its leaders and its saints. Those who have developed the dominant traits to a slighter extent will be its rank and file; those who have perversely seized upon some perfectly alien point of view, it will sometimes lock up in asylums, sometimes imprison as political agitators, burn as heretics, or possibly permit to live out a starveling existence as artists. The man who is said to have been "born at the right time" or "born for his age" is simply one whose personality is thus in tune with the dominant note of his society and who has also the requisite endowment of intellect. Societies are kept going, are elaborated and expanded by those whose spirit is akin to their own. They are undermined and superseded by the new faiths and new programmes worked out in pain and rebellion by those who find no spiritual home in the culture in which they were born. Upon the former group lies the burden of perpetuating their society and perhaps of giving it even more definite form. Upon

* For a theoretical development of this point of view, see Benedict, Ruth. "Psychological Types in the Culture of the South West." Proc. XXIII International Congress of Americanists.

the gifted among the misfits lies the burden of building new worlds. Obviously upon the balance of these three types depends part of the fortune of the culture. Without creating enthusiasts for the present régime or new forms of the same régime, a society or a section of social life will be leaderless, will sink into dulness and mediocrity. An example of this is to be found in American political life to-day which is neither led by the best type of American, that is, the personality type which best embodies American emphasis, nor given vigour and vitality by the presence of forceful individuals whose temperament makes them unsympathetic to correct American ideals. The fortunes of any society are influenced by the type of material its misfits feed upon, whether they build their philosophies of change from ideas sufficiently congruent with their culture so that real change can be brought about or whether they feed from sources so alien that they become mere ineffectual dreamers.

Any society, therefore, even if it be islanded from all contact with other cultures, is dependent at any moment upon the personality trends which the new born babies will eventually develop. In the case of the few really gifted individuals born into each generation, it will be of the utmost importance whether they have an enthusiasm for the continuation of present conditions or spend their lives in a restless driven search for something different. So the fate of any culture may be said to be dependent upon the calibre of its people, not in the sense that the intelligence of one people differs from another, but in the way in which its ideals appeal to the gifted in each generation, either stunning them into acquiescence or firing them with a violent zest for change.

Yet of the mechanisms by which one child becomes an enthusiast within the pattern, another responds with apathy, a third with positive aversion, we know very little. Perhaps the most fruitful attacks upon the problem have come from the psycho-analysts whose unwearied desire to subsume the whole of life under one rubric has led them to attempt the solution of problems which the orthodox psychologists have left strictly alone. One of their most useful conceptions is the idea of Identification, the way in which one individual identifies himself so strongly with another personality, either known, read about or imagined, that he makes the choices, the attitudes of that person his own. The psycho-analysts have used this concept to explain dozens of situations varying from identification with characters in a play or a book, to the process by which an identification with a parent of the wrong sex can produce inverted sex attitudes.

Among ourselves, the possibilities of variation through identification are many and contradictory. Either parent, the teacher, the favourite movie actor, the baseball player, a character in a book of play, a hero of history, a favourite playmate or God himself may be the point of focus. The asylums are filled with those who have carried these identifications beyond the borders of sanity and firmly believe themselves to be Na-

poleon or Jesus Christ, maltreated by a blind and hostile
world. And that this process in its more extreme forms
is not merely a phenomena of our own society is proved
by its occurrence in Samoa, where I found a man who
held firmly to the delusion that he was Tufele, the high
chief of the island, and demanded that he, a poor com-
moner, be addressed in the terms reserved for the highest chiefs. In its less pathological forms, the tendency
to identify is found in every fan, every ardent follower
of an individual leader, every one who seeks to reproduce, meticulously although in little, the behaviour of
some immensely admired person.

In Manus the child has no such range of choice.
Without important differences in rank, without religious
leaders, without great characters of history or myth, the
child has no gallery in any way comparable to that from
which our children can choose their models. Furthermore the culture and the willingness, perhaps one may
say tendency, of a child to pick a model has fitted closely
in Manus into the pattern of the father-son relationship. The reader will remember how close is the companionship between father and young son, how the child
follows his father through every phase of his daily routine, watches him as he schemes, quarrels, works,
lounges, entreats his ancestral spirits or harangues his
wife. We have seen how the children of older successful men can be distinguished from the children of
young or unsuccessful ones. And most significant of
all, we have seen how the correspondence between the
personality of father and adopted son is as great as that

between father and own son, and greater than that between a man and his blood son who has been adopted by a man of different temperament or status in the community. This evidence suggests that whatever the hereditary disposition—a factor which we at present have no means of measuring—it is greatly influenced by this close association with a mature personality. In the close fostering care of adult men for their children, the Manus have an excellent social mechanism by which personality traits may be perpetuated in the next generation.

Nor is this merely a way of preserving in the next generation the balance of the last between decisive and undecisive, aggressive and meek. If a strong man has five sons, they will be born to him at different stages of his career. The child of his youth will be of a milder temperament than the child of his assured maturity. This may be one of the reasons why primogeniture has so little practical effect in Manus, why younger brothers so often definitely dominate older ones. (A difference of intelligence is of course the alternative explanation in any particular case.) The proportion of each temperament may shift slightly from generation to generation, according to accidents of birth or adoption. Paleao, the aggressive, has only one son; Mutchin, his brother, mild, unaggressive, conservative, has four. Paleao has now adopted one of Mutchin's sons, but too late to appreciably alter the child's personality. Where only ten or fifteen men decide the fortunes of the community, three or four aggressive and initiating people more or less can make a great deal of difference.

It is interesting to compare these Manus methods, not only with our own, but also with those used by another South Sea Island people, the Samoans.* In Samoa, the idea of rank serves as a stimulus to children, but they receive little individual stimulus because men of importance never permit children to come near them. Children are shooed away from the presence of their elders and turned over to the care of immature children or old women. There is no guarantee that a strong man's son will have a personality in any way like his. But the idea of rank has some influence in forming the child's personality. If he is the son or the nephew of a chief, higher standards are enjoined upon him and he responds by making somewhat greater efforts than do his playmates. But "You are the son of chiefs" is an incentive to effort, not like our fatal emphasis upon the success of the father which frightens and stunts the development of the son. The effect upon the Samoan child's personality is relatively slight; small boys differ only slightly from one another, much less than Manus children. When they become young men, the chiefs take more interest in their possible successors and the young men have a chance for imitation after their characters are pretty well formed. But for sixteen or seventeen years the principal human determinant of a young Samoan's behaviour has been the standard of his age

* For a discussion of Samoan conditions, see "Coming of Age in Samoa."

group, not the personality of any adult. So strong is the tradition of conformity to the age standard, that the idea of rank and the late association with men of maturity and habits of command makes little headway against it. Samoan men are very much alike when compared with Manus men. The carefully fostered habits of moderated impersonal behaviour appropriate to status rather than to natural tendencies or shades of endowment, have fitted them far more into one mould.

In Manus the age group is of little importance among children. As individuals they respond to the distinctions among their fathers, the distinctions based immediately upon age, economic status and success, the last of which is dependent in some measure upon intelligence, but more upon aggressive initiative and energy. So in Manus we find three main types of personality, the aggressive, violent, overbearing type found in older rich men and in the children whom they are fostering and who have not yet reached marriageable age, the definitely assured but less articulately aggressive type found in young men who have not yet attained economic security but who were given a good start in childhood and the immature children of these men; and the mild unaggressive meek type—the older unsuccessful men who were presumably given a bad start or who have very little natural ability, and their children. The community is assured of having a certain number of successful men with drive and force in each generation. As in over half of the cases the successors of successful men are their own sons or at least blood relatives, this system creates a sort of aristocracy of personality which is certain of perpetuating itself. It produces strong individual differences between the men of even very small villages, and makes for a dynamic atmosphere absent in Samoa, even though personality there is bolstered up by chieftainship. This alert restless people are alive to the cultures with which they come in contact, quick to take advantage of the white man's ideas and use them to their own advantage. The Samoan use of white civilisation has been based, not upon the action of particular individuals but upon the flexibility of a pattern of life in which the individual counts for very little and there are no strong passions or heavy prices to be paid. In Manus on the other hand, there is much conflict, much friction between one type and another, and the development of much stronger feelings. The Samoan system is a very pleasant way of reducing the rough unseemly aspects of human nature to a pleasant innocuousness. The Manus is a device by which personality may be capitalised and used by the society.

In America we follow neither the one system nor the other. The degeneration of the father's rôle into that of a tired, often dreaded, nightly visitor has done much to make his son's happy identification with him impossible. When the child does attempt to identify with his father he usually has to seize upon the more conspicuous, more generic aspects of his father's character, his clothes, his physical strength, his deep voice, the very aspects which a small boy of five has the most difficulty in imitating successfully. As one small boy once told me dolefully, he could never be a big man like his father because he couldn't make a big noise when he blew his so much smaller nose. A father is the man who can lift one in his arms, who comes home at night, who is home on Sunday, who drives the car, who makes money, who has to shave every day, who has a bass voice. Such characteristics do not distinguish among any hundred of men in a given community. The child is forced to identify with a lay figure in trousers. He is not permitted the more intimate contact which would enable him to grasp his father as an individual, rather than as a member of a sex.

The conventions of our society are such that to an alarming extent bringing up children is regarded as women's work. Witness the overwhelming feminine interest in problems of education, hygiene, etc.—the almost complete neglect of such subjects by men. The boy is his mother's province until he is six or seven, and this produces difficulties of adjustment somewhat like those of Manus girls. Identification with members of the opposite sex is a precarious business in a heterosexual world. At six or seven the boy is handed over to other women. Mother, nurse, teacher, leader of play group, they pass in a long procession between him and any real contact with men. Their influence is a smoke screen through which the father's image filters distorted, magnified, unreal. And the child who responds strongly to a dominant father responds not positively and eagerly, as in Manus, but negatively with a feeling of inadequacy and inevitable failure. The

Manus would look with pity upon our long array of failures whose fathers were famous, often indeed of failures *because* their fathers were famous. Whether one places one's faith in inheritance of native ability or in the effect of early conditioning, a strong man's sons should be strong, every gain made by an individual should be conserved for the next generation, not dissipated nor paradoxically allowed to poison the lives of his unfortunate offspring. It is a very pitiable picture to see how, in contemporary life, without either the Manus training of young boys or the Samoan device of rank, the gains of men in one generation are so often unrepresented among their descendants.

The failure of children to identify with their fathers is intensified in this country by the rapidly shifting standards and the differences in outlook between parents and children. The evidence in "Middletown" * is confirmatory of this in showing the very few children who wished to follow their father's vocation. The child responds to a conception of his father as an unknown force hard to reckon with, as a recalcitrant bread winner who sometimes refuses to dispense the desired amount of pocket money, as a usually indifferent member of the household who suddenly exercises a veto supported by superior strength and economic superiority, as an old fogey whose ideas are mocked by the new generation. But the male child must, if he is to make any sort of happy adult adjustment, identify himself somewhat with his father or with some other grown

* P. 59.

man. No matter how close, how affectionate, how de-
serving of admiration and allegiance his mother may
be, she does not offer the male child a way of life. If
his allegiance to her is too close, it will stunt his emotional development; if he identifies himself with her it
is at the risk of becoming an invert, or at best of making
some fantastic and uncomfortable emotional adjustment. The heaviest prices which family life demands
from children are those which result from an antagonism to the father and an overdependence upon the
mother, for a boy child, and the opposite set for a girl.
Manus demands these prices of the little girl who identifies herself with her father at the expense of any attachment to her mother, and who makes the pitiable
discovery at seven at eight that she has made a mistake, that the ways of manhood are not for her.

We arrange things equally badly for the boy, a more
serious blunder when the bulk of cultural achievement
falls to the unhandicapped male. We muffle him in
feminine affection, and present his father to him as an
animated whip to enforce his mother's rôle of affectionate ruler. All through his most impressionable years
he associates with women whom he can not take as
models, interesting and admirable as they often are.
This being so, without being able to identify with the
only adults he knows, denied the stimulating companionship of men, he falls back on the age group—that
standardising levelling influence in which all personality
is subordinated to a group type. More and more in
this country the young people depend upon the applause

of their equals, scoffing at the judgments of those maturer than themselves, without thought or sense of responsibility for the younger ones. The whole finely tempered mechanism by which the gains of one generation are transmitted to the next is being lost. The grown men, completely uninterested in children, neither show any concern for the children themselves nor stimulate older boys into showing an interest. Each age group becomes a little self-satisfied coterie, revolving endlessly, dully about its own image.

That this age group system will work is shown by the conditions in Samoa. It is possible to let the age standard override every consideration of personality, individual gift and temperamental difference to substitute these meagre cross sections of human life for the complete picture which includes individuals ranging from those just born to those who are on the point of death. But this age standard is accepted at the expense of loss of individuality. It is the type of standard most easily diffused, most easily acquired, least productive of initiative or originality. Adult standards which have been differentiated by years of self-conscious intense living, can be passed on from father to son, from teacher to pupil, but hardly distributed wholesale through the movies, the radio, the daily press. An appeal which must strike an answering note in thousands of listeners or readers can seldom be intense enough to select out certain aspects of a child's temperament and give them form and coherence. Personal contact with mature individuals who are acutely concerned that the young people in whom they are interested shall develop personality and initiative is probably the only influence which can stem the flood of publicity directing "How the nineteen-year-old will feel" and "What the High School Senior will think."

So we have the disadvantages of both the Samoan and the Manus systems of education and we have the advantages of neither one. In Samoa the child owes no emotional allegiance to its father and mother. These personalities are merged in a large household group of fostering adults. The child unfettered by emotional ties finds sufficient satisfaction in the mild warmth which is the emotional tone of the age group. So the Samoan child suffers neither the reward nor the penalty of intimate family life. Manus children, on the other hand, are bound so closely by family ties that outside adjustments are not expected of them and may well be impossible to them. But in return the boy child receives the best that such a close association has to offer—a living sense of his father's personality.

American boys are not, like Samoan children, free from all demands for strong feeling, free to find contentment in the diluted amiability of the approving age group. Nor are they, like Manus children, rewarded by the close companionship with the father and the possibility of a happy identification with him. They are tied to a family group where the mother absorbs their affections and yet furnishes them with no usable model, where the mother makes too strong claims to let them be completely happy in the age group. The shadow

[239]

of the father falls just far enough across their young activities to spoil them.

Our girls often get a better time of it. When the differences between the points of view of mother and daughter are not too great owing to shifting social standards, the daughter can make a first identification with her mother which offers her a workable pattern of life. Antagonism to the father does not necessarily have the same blighting effect upon her that it has upon her brother. Very often she develops less of an antagonism to her father because he does not necessarily play an absentee Roman father to his daughters also. It may also be hazarded that possibly the daughter's emotional life is left freer than is her brother's; where their mother presents to the daughter a way of life she presents to the son only an emotional obstacle which he must overleap.

In the school as in the home, the girls are again more fortunate than their brothers. It is not without significance that interest in the arts and the considered use of leisure time and the development of the personality are all found almost exclusively among women in this country. It is not without significance that the English literature courses show a tendency to attract the superior women and the inferior men. The records of other countries do not show any special aptitude of women for the arts, in fact the exponents of the theory of feminine inferiority can find plenty of proof to the contrary. But in this country the arts are discredited as a male pursuit; and it may well be that one of the great causes of their low estate is that they are taught by the sex with whom the boy students can not possibly identify themselves.

No society can afford to so neglect the ways in which children make their choices and to deny to the sex which has the greatest freedom to make permanent contributions, the stimulus which can be given only in close personal association. The American boy's conceptions of manhood are diluted, standardised, undifferentiated. His choices are as generic as his vision. He chooses to make money, to be a success, he makes no more particularistic allegiances. The contrast between what we might make of our boys and what we do make of them is like the contrast between a series of beautiful objects made by individual loving craftsmen, and a series of objects all turned out by a machine. Whatever arguments may be advanced for the enrichment of life by the labour saving of the machine, can hardly be applied to human beings as well as to furniture. But those who argue that it is because this is a machine age that individuals are becoming standardised in this country may be overdrawing the analogy and seeing a complete explanation in what is only a partial one. The diluted personal contacts of the American boy may well be as important a handicap as the ubiquity of the machine.

Although there are a few trends away from this intensive femininity of education, more boys' schools with men teachers, more explicit statements from social workers and psychiatrists who plead for the child's need of a father, the bulk of our male children are still caught in the net. Our boys are condemned to approximate to a dull generic idea of *manhood*, rather than to a number of interesting, known *men.*

XV

IN the last chapter I have been discussing ways in which the personality of normal children is built up, the loss to the community when men who have been strong and effective fail to produce sons with similar drives. The identification with living people is a way of preserving the strong points in the culture, of assuring to the next generation strong captains in the causes for which they are enlisted at birth. Of equal, perhaps even greater importance, is the process by which those personalities are shaped who are destined to change their societies, to build new edifices of art or ideas, sometimes even to embody their aberrant dreams in new social and political forms. These temperamentally restive persons who stand in the vanguard of new causes or create new art forms, have not usually been given their drive by identification with some well understood person of their close acquaintance (though occasionally rebellion against a father or guardian may have directed their choices). Instead they have built up, in their need, fantastic and strange conceptions of life; they have drawn on hints from past periods and different civilisations, and from these curious combinations they have fashioned something new. Even the very gifted among these innovators have been dependent upon two

[243]

things, the socially defined lack in their own lives, and rich materials from which to build. Without the felt need, the imaginative potentialities will go unstimulated, without the material it will go unfed. It is therefore interesting to compare the possibilities for these imaginative creations which Manus and America offer their children.

By a socially defined need, I mean the presence in the society of a special pattern of human relationships which the child can learn about and which he can feel is wanting in his own case. These may be of different sorts, the society may teach the child that every one should have a father and mother, or a nurse or a French governess, or school teacher, or a sweetheart or a God. The dictated needs may be of the most diverse nature, but whatever they are, some children will respond to their presence by building up imaginative structures. The invisible playmate, the fabulous parent, the imagined love experience are all familiar enough to us. But what is not always clearly recognised is that none of these are basic human needs. A society which depends upon the manipulation of impersonal magic power will not teach its children the need for a personal god, nor for special religious experience; a society which does not recognise romantic love will produce no James Branch Cabells and conversely no Aldous Huxleys. The children of the poor will boast of no nonexistent French governesses, nor lament their nonexistence.

One of the most frequent blank spaces which may be

offered to a child for elaboration is that afforded by the death of a parent, occasionally by the real parent's failure to conform to the socially dictated standards of what a parent should be. This last happens when a child under the influence of literature, or of other children, finds his parent wanting and makes up myths about being an adopted child, or a child who was stolen as a baby. Child psychologists testify to the frequency of such fantasies in young children among ourselves. In Manus the child who is socially fatherless is almost unknown. The infant death rate is so high, and children are so loved and valued, that there are always eager candidates to adopt orphan children. There was just the one small boy, Bopau, in Peri, whose father was dead and who had found no substitute. He was the one child who claimed to talk with spirits, declaring that his father, Sori, had talked to him. But even he did not cling to his father's memory to the extent of refusing to admit a substitute, instead, it will be recalled, he eagerly welcomed Pataliyan's temporary adoption, and previously he had dogged the footsteps of his older cousin with wistful, hopeful attention. The social pressure in Manus to have a devoted father is stronger than among ourselves, but the habit of adoption and the small number of children makes the presence of fatherless children very rare.

Similar social pressure and one harder to satisfy is felt by fatherless children among ourselves. The most striking case which has come to my notice is that of a eugenic baby whose mother was demonstrating the right

of unmarried women to bear children. The little girl
had been told nothing about her father; she had never
seen him nor heard him mentioned. Yet as soon as
she went to kindergarten and heard the other children
talking about their fathers she began an endless stream
of imagining a father for herself. She would say: "Oh,
mother, why do I have to go to bed? My father never
makes me go to bed until it's midnight." "In my
father's house they stay up all night." "My father
gives me handfuls of money to spend as I like." This
instance shows very nicely the double rôle which such
imaginative pictures play, it compensated her for her
sense of difference from the other children, and it gave
her a device for criticising her mother and her mother's
régime. But in Manus, a dead or absent parent is compensated for by a new father, who fills the gap in a
solid realistic fashion and does not provide any such
lay figure to drape in imaginative trappings.

Another little girl of three was the daughter of
writers. In and out of her parents' home passed groups
of literary people; an only child, she was much with
adults and heard nothing but literary talk. In order
to take her place adequately in this exacting world, she
had to invent a whole troop of imaginary literary
friends, setting them over against her novel-writing
parents by proclaiming them poets, "uninterested in
prose." Her creations were of astonishing complexity
for a child of three. The day after her family arrived
in England, she had created an English critic named,
by a stroke of genius, "Mr. Stutts Watts"; on arriving

in France she immediately furnished herself with a group of French people with names eminently French in sound and with manners to match. Because she was such an unusually gifted child, she illustrates this filling-in process particularly well. Her social group demanded important literary friends; she supplied them where other children are supplying muscular little playmates or nurses in uniform. And the materials for her imaginative pictures were drawn from the brilliant talk which went on all about her.

Another little girl had only a brother when all her friends, all the characters in books which she read, seemed to have sisters. She accordingly made up a long tale of a twin sister who had been stolen at birth by robbers, and might eventually be recovered. For four years, the search for this twin sister occupied most of her day dreaming and sometimes extended into the exploration of deserted groves and tumble-down buildings which were thought to shelter the robber band and the sister, so desired as a companion and confidant.

In Manus, with rare exceptions, children have no such gaps in their social lives. There is no child without a playmate, and so there are no imaginary playmates; the spirit children are scorned. They are less vivid than real children; they were constructed to meet no need, to satisfy no lack. Mothers are less important and equally present. Nor does the group of children feel a lack of desirable adult patterns of social life; taught to ignore them, they feel no more need to construct an adult world in miniature, than do the children of the rich need to make up the patterns followed by the poor and despised. And the result is that neither individually nor in groups do they show any signs of building imaginative edifices. Their play, their conversation is quite barren. Yet this is not due to lack of imaginative ability. A little Manus boy who was in the employ of white people at the government station was overheard by his mistress giving an innocent visitor the most highly coloured account of an imagined trip to Sydney, a job on a Burns Philps boat, wonderful clothes and uniforms which he had been given by the people of Sydney for his remarkable cricket playing, and his final return to Manus because he disliked the Sydney climate. But this child had felt the need to be an important returned work boy; working on his only island, a few hours from his native village, he was very small fry indeed and he seized the first opportunity to convince at least one gullible visitor of his greater claims. The tales of other work boys, returned from visits to Sydney as white children's nurse boys, provided him with the necessary material.

It is not until Manus boys reach their teens that any need is felt. But after losing their fathers they do feel definitely bereaved, socially maimed, so to speak. And it is at this age that the only imaginative play takes place. The young men hold long mock séances in the boys' house. (They also give dramatic reconstructions of the adulteries which in a former golden age they would have been permitted to commit with impunity.) Upon the father in the spirit world the imag-

[248]

ination is permitted free range and here occurs what little fantasy there is in Manus life. Their myths are dull hand-me-downs, bits of the common stock of tradition of their race. Their everyday life is a matter-of-course, highly practical, realistic affair. Their social relations, so largely defined by economics, are equally realistic and unimaginative. Their bare, clear language, stripped of metaphor or analogy, provides them with no stimulus to creating poetry. Their dance is strictly conventionalised; it permits the innovator no interesting range. Only upon the unknown world of the spirits can their imaginations play. This play is slight enough. To the spirits they ascribe a strong and conscientious solicitude for the proper conduct of society, for the honourable behaviour of their descendants. The picture of the father as an upright, moral, sin-shunning, debt-paying person is given far greater intensity after the father has been translated. And this ascription of moral qualities to the spirit world is the principal source of moral behaviour in Manus. They idealise the remembered personalities and endow them with supernatural prowess to express their will. (I am not claiming the origin of Manus religion in the flights of fancy of any generation or group of men; but the peculiar form which Manus spiritualism has taken, its individualisation among related cults which have sprung from a common historical source, makes it reasonable to allow this margin to individual creativeness.)

In addition to the outstanding moral vigilance attributed to the spirits, the mortals engage in minor

flights of fancy. The spirits practise the levirate, that
is, a man may marry his brother's wife, or his father's
wife; there is also a tendency for the old men spirits
to capture all the available spirit maidens. Both of
these practices are found in full swing among the land
people, but are severely disapproved of by the Manus
living. Whether these are customs which the Manus
once practised and have since given up or are merely
forms of behaviour the possession of which they envy
their neighbours is immaterial—they are known forms
of forbidden behaviour which they in imagination permit to the dead. Similarly some people say that the
spirits do not have to observe the wearisome rules of
avoidance between in-laws which forms such a check
upon freedom of movement in Manus. In fact, in
the spirit world, a father can marry his son's dead wife.
(This was the alleged cause of one man's death. It was
reported by the medium that his dead wife objected
to his senile father as a spouse and killed her former
husband in order to rid herself of his father as a husband.) The absence of these tabus between in-laws
is known to the Manus to occur among the Matankor
people of the near-by island of Balowan, where engaged people may meet each other face to face and
chatter amiably and parents-in-law are present at the
public consummation of the marriage of their children.
So, members of the Manus community, irked by their
tabus, imagine their dead as unhampered by them.

Similarly the contact with the white man which
nearly always leaves the native worsted and often leaves

him humiliated, takes on a different colour in the spirit world. There is one large family group in Peri which has as guardian spirits the spirits of dead white men. As each new male member of the family grows to manhood, the original white spirit, a white man killed years ago on the island of Mbuke, is ordered to recruit another well-behaved, quiescent, anonymous white man who does the native's bidding with all of the white man's superior efficiency but without any of his arrogance. Members of other families also sometimes have white men's spirits. Still others have fabricated for their satisfaction white wives for their dead native guardians. The unsatisfactory contact with white culture is rewritten in the spirit world.

Women similarly compensate for their complete absence of claim upon their male children. Little boys who in life stuck out their tongues at their mothers, spat and pouted and sulked, or struck fiercely at their mothers' slightest attempts at discipline or constraint, become immediately they enter the world of the spirits, subservient, meek, tireless at errand running. And also, the spirits of dead women do not live in the houses of their blood kin, who claim their bodies and perform their burial rites, but with their spirit husbands. The marriage tie which is so weak and unsatisfactory on earth is given a place in heaven.

Compared with the amount of elaboration of unknown worlds permitted to us, these are slight indeed. They are entirely the work of adults, not of children. It is upon the Manus adult, not upon the Manus child that the culture presses in such a way as to stimulate his imagination. These slight imaginative attempts serve to illustrate how this blank space, this undetailed life of the dead, is used by the Manus for putting down borrowed or compensatory ideas. And it is reasonable to suppose that the continued ascription to the spirits of a puritanical and exacting morality is one of the most potent mechanisms by which the Manus cultural ideal has been built up. The neighbouring peoples whose culture resembles the Manus in so many respects, do not share this puritanism. Their dead care only about the proper performance of funeral ceremonies. So the Usiai maidens before their marriage to old and powerful men who could afford to buy young girls as their second or third wives, were given first a year of license and leisured dalliance in institutional houses for young people of both sexes. And from the light-laughtered island of Balowan, our boys brought back just one phrase in the Balowan language, "Come into the bush and lie with me." The neighbouring peoples who have heard of Christian teachings about sex call the Manus "all the same missionary" and laugh at their puritanism. The Manus see their puritanism as a new development. Their golden age, just before the memory of each oldest generation, was the time when the spirits felt less keenly on the subject. But, they explain, when men once began to die for adultery, their hearts were hardened after death, and they took care to punish the next offenders. And so, by projecting this very human desire for revenge upon the dead, the tradition of stern morality is stiffened and extended. Similarly the anxiety over unpaid debts and financial obligations which must be met, has been ascribed to the spirits, who thus become a force for the enforcement of commercial honesty. (And the high commercial standards of the Manus would compare favourably with those of almost any other known people in the world; there is a great deal of disagreement as to the amounts of debts, due to the absence of a system of records, but remarkably little attempt to evade or falsify economic obligations.) Upon the emptiness which is death, the Manus have written a new chapter which shapes their lives and makes them so different from their neighbours.

By a similar but infinitely more complex process are the dreams of civilised man sometimes engendered. Where the Manus can draw only upon the few differences between their culture and that of their neighbours or that of their new and little understood white conquerors, we can draw upon the history, the literature, the art of centuries. The Manus can endow his dead father and through him, the spirit world, with the intensification of qualities developed among the Manus themselves or with the daring and exotic customs of the Usiai and Balowan peoples. But the fatherless or motherless child among ourselves, the child disgruntled with its parents, the lonely child who desires a playmate, or the man who finds no human being who will fit into our culturally dictated patterns of romantic love, may reconstruct the unknown parent or lover from the lives of Napoleon or Christ, the Iliad or Shakespeare, the paintings of Michael Angelo and the operas of Wagner, or the poetry of Keats. He can have a father as beautiful as the Apollo Belvedere, a mother like Raphael's madonna or one of Leonardo's angels. His father may be given the heroism of William Tell or Robert the Bruce, the gentle asceticism of Saint Francis or the prowess of Cæsar or Alexander. Where the genius of generations has gone to creating an image of Christ, he may borrow it to fill in his father's face. And he may set this idealised figure in a world made up from reading Greek history, Irish epics, Arabic poetry, or Veddic legend. The most discrepant concepts, the most impossible dreams, the records of cultures that have been and the work of creative artists who have tried to escape from them, may all be jumbled together to fill in the place left vacant by a father or a mother; in adult years to fill the gap felt between the society in which he lives and the world which his imagination has engendered. When such dreams make the real world seem too unbearably drab in contrast they may lead to madness or suicide. They are always dangerous, but upon them can be built visions of such power as to startle or transfix the imagination of a people—if only the complex and shining vision be discovered by one who has the gift of the artist or of the leader of men.

Any social frame which calls for the fulfilment of certain requirements, whether they be those of a father and mother, companions, or lovers, will not always be able to meet the demands which it has created. There will be gaps in the lives of some, gaps which they will seek to fill in so that they may live in the sense of peaceful completion which their society has defined as the proper estate of man. The Manus have but slight material from which to rebuild the estate of their dead, the only serious gap which is offered them by a society which provides parents and playmates for all and has no idea of vivid friendship or romantic love. But we have the most diverse and varied materials for building new conceptions, and upon them, upon these pictures built by man which have the power to make him forever homesick for the land of his own dreaming, lies the burden of bringing important changes into our patterned existences.

If we generalise human relations too much, demand too little of them, we will lose the sense of gaps and deficiencies which set some children to dreaming. We may lose the valuable imaginative creations of those who must search the whole of history for materials to build up an absent father or an ideal love. For this is not an automatic matter, as some theorists believe. The child is not born wanting a father, he is taught his need by the social blessedness of others. No Samoan child, in a society where the parent-child relationship is diffused over dozens of adults, would dream of creating an ideal father; nor do the Samoans, finding such quiet satisfaction among their uncritical equals, build a heaven which reverberates on earth. Neither does the Manus child or adult build pictures of the ideal wife or mother, for his society does not suggest to him that it would be possible to find one. If we substitute for father-to-child, teacher-to-child relationships, only contacts with adults of the opposite sex and the applause of the age group, if we erect standards of casual relations between the sexes, relationships without strength or responsibility, we have no guarantee of so stimulating individuals to use imaginatively in new ways, the rich and diverse materials of our cultural inheritance.

Furthermore the Manus material suggests the need of giving children something upon which to exercise their imagination for it shows that they do not produce rich and beautiful results spontaneously, but only as a response to material provided them by the adult world.

With the automatic nature of this basic education taken for granted, and greater proficiency in teaching the three "r's," the schools are faced by increasing amounts of unfilled time. Just as we realise that it is not necessary to teach children the history of the American Revolution every year for five years, and that time spent in learning the conventional grade subjects can be enormously shortened by proper methods, we also realise that the time spent under school supervision is tending to need extension rather than curtailment. City life makes unsupervised play dangerous and virtually impossible. City apartments offer children no proper playgrounds. The increasing urbanisation of the country, the increasing number of families who live in apartments instead of houses and the greater employment of married women—these and numerous other factors are contributing to make the rôle of the school more important because of the ever larger number of hours of the child's life which must be spent under school supervision. Progressive schools are trying to fill these gaps left vacant by improved teaching of the old routine requirements with materials from other societies—Greece, Egypt, Mediæval Europe. The teaching of the necessary techniques is sandwiched into play activities centred about building a Greek house or making papyrus. Whatever popular objections to this type of education, it has recognised one important point, the need of content in the children's lives. It is in sharp contrast to such tendencies as those described in "Middletown," where content is being increasingly neglected in favour of instrumental courses which simply bind the children more firmly to life as it is lived in "Middletown." It is not enough to give children American culture as it is to-day and the details of its necessary techniques. American culture is too levelled; the conflict between alien groups bringing in contrasting and only partly understood European traditions, has neutralised the contribution of each. If art and literature and a richer, more creative culture is to flourish in America, we must have more content, content based, as all new ideas have always been based, upon the diverse experiments of older, more individualised cultures.

If the children's imaginations are to flourish, they must be given food. Although the exceptional child may create something of his own, the great majority of children will not even imagine bears under the bed unless the adult provides the bear. The long years during which children are confined in school can be crammed full of rich, provocative materials upon which their imaginations can feed. Those children who find life to their liking will be the better perpetuators of their own culture for their greater understanding of the riches of other societies. Those who find a need to build over some aspects of their lives, to fill in places which have been left vacant, can use this material to create visions which will leave their culture richer than it was when they received it from the hands of their forebears.

XVI

WE have seen how the Manus, like ourselves, give their children little to respect and so do not equip them to grow up graciously, how bringing up children to envy and despise their elders is doing those children scant service. We have seen how well the Manus develop personality in their children, especially in their boys, and how we neglect our boys and give them no intimate association with men whom they can take as models. And we have seen how infinitely richer we are in the traditional materials upon which the temperamentally restive, the specially gifted child may draw; realising at the same time that we are in danger of so attenuating and standardising human relationships that no one will feel a need to draw upon this rich material. All of these are special points, points upon which Manus has seemed to offer special illumination. But what of education as a whole? What does the Manus experiment suggest?

We have followed the Manus baby through its formative years to adulthood, seen its indifference towards adult life turn into attentive participation, its idle scoffing at the supernatural change into an anxious sounding of the wishes of the spirits, its easy-going generous communism turn into grasping individualistic acquisitiveness. The process of education is complete. The Manus baby, born into the world without motor habits, without speech, without any definite forms of behaviour, with neither beliefs nor enthusiasms, has become the Manus adult in every particular. No cultural item has slipped out of the stream of tradition which the elders transmit in this irregular unorganised fashion to their children, transmit by a method which seems to us so haphazard, so unpremeditated, so often definitely hostile to its ultimate ends.

And what is true of Manus education in this respect, is true of education in any untouched, homogeneous society. Whatever the method adopted, whether the young are disciplined, lectured, consciously taught, permitted to run wild or ever antagonised by the adult world—the result is the same. The little Manus becomes the big Manus, the little Indian, the big Indian. When it is a question of passing on the sum total of a simple tradition, the only conclusion which it is possible to draw from the diverse primitive material is that any method will do. The forces of imitation are so much more potent than any adult technique for exploiting them; the child's receptivity to its surroundings is so much more important than any methods of stimulation, that as long as every adult with whom he comes in contact is saturated with the tradition, he cannot escape a similar saturation.

Although this applies, of course, in its entirety, only to a homogeneous culture, it has nevertheless far-reaching consequences in educational theory, especially in the modification of the characteristic American faith in education as the universal panacea. All the pleasant optimism of those who believe that hope lies in the future, that the failures of one generation can be recouped in the next, are given the lie. The father who has not learned to read or write may send his son to school and see his son master this knowledge which his father lacked. A technique which is missing in one member of a generation but present in others, may be taught, of course, to the deficient one's son. Once a technique becomes part of the cultural tradition the proportions to which it is common property may vary from generation to generation. But the spectacular fashion in which sons of illiterate fathers have become literate, has been taken as the type of the whole educational process. (The theorists forget the thousands of years before the invention of writing.) Actually it is only the type of possibilities of transmitting known techniques—the type of education discussed in courses in the "Teaching of Elementary Arithmetic," or "Electrical Engineering." When education of this special and formal sort is considered, there are no analogies to be drawn from primitive society. Even if, as sometimes happens, a new technique may be imported into a tribe by a war captive or a foreign woman, and a whole generation learn from one individual, this process is of little comparative interest to us. The clumsy methods and minute rules of thumb by which such knowledge is imparted, has little in common with our self-conscious, highly specialised teaching methods.

GROWING UP IN NEW GUINEA

It must be clearly understood that when I speak of education I speak only of that process by which the growing individual is inducted into his cultural inheritance, not of those specific ways in which the complex techniques of modern life are imparted to children arranged in serried ranks within the schoolroom. As the schoolroom is one, and an important, general educational agency, it is involved in this discussion; as it teaches one method of penmanship in preference to a more fatiguing one, it is not. This strictly professionalised education is a modern development, the end result of the invention of writing and the division of labour, a problem in quantitative cultural transmission rather than of qualitative. The striking contrast between the small number of things which the primitive child must learn compared with the necessary educational attainments of the American child only serves, however, to point the moral that whereas there is such a great quantitative difference, the process is qualitatively very similar.

After all, the little American must learn to become the big American, just as the little Manus becomes the big Manus. The continuity of our cultural life depends upon the way in which children in any event receive the indelible imprint of their social tradition. Whether they are cuddled or beaten, bribed or wheedled into adult life—they have little choice except to become adults like their parents. But ours is not a homogeneous society. One community differs from another, one social class from another, the values of one occupational group are not the values of those who follow some different calling. Religious bodies with outlooks as profoundly different as Roman Catholicism and Christian Science, claim large numbers of adherents always ready to induct their own and other people's children into the special traditions of their particular group. The four children of common parents may take such divergent courses that at the age of fifty their premises may be mutually unintelligible and antagonistic. Does not the comparison between primitive and civilised society break down? Does not education cease to be an automatic process and become a vital question of what method is to be pursued?

Undoubtedly this objection is a just one. Within the general tradition there are numerous groups striving for precedence, striving to maintain or extend their proportionate allegiances in the next generation. Among these groups, methods of education do count, but only in relation to each other. Take a small town where there are three religious denominations. It would not matter whether Sunday School was a compulsory matter, with a whipping from father if one didn't learn one's lesson or squandered a penny of the collection money, or whether Sunday School was a delightful spot where rewards were handed out lavishly and refreshments served by each young teacher to the admiring scholars. It would not matter, as long as all three Sunday Schools used the same methods. Only when one Sunday School depends upon parental intimidation, a second uses rewards and a third employs co-educational parties as its bait, does the question of *method* become important. And at the same time the process under discussion has ceased to be education and become—propaganda.

So, if education be defined as the process by which the cultural tradition is transmitted to the next generation, or in exceptional cases to the members of another culture—as is the case when a primitive people is suddenly brought within the sway of the organised forces of civilisation—propaganda may be defined as methods by which one group within an existing tradition tries to increase the number of its adherents at the expense of other groups. Outside both these categories falls the conscious teaching of techniques, reading, writing, riveting, surveying, piano playing, soap making, etching.

America presents the spectacle of all three of these processes going on in great confusion. The general stream of the tradition—language, manners, attitudes towards property, towards the state, and towards religion—is being imparted effortlessly to the growing child, while the complex of minute and exacting techniques are being imparted to him arduously, through the schools. Here and there the propagandists range, Christian Scientists, Communists, vegetarians, antivivisectionists, single taxers, humanists, small compact groups in respect to religious or social philosophies, mere participators in the general American cultural stream in most other respects. And the rapid assimilation of thousands of immigrants' children through the medium of the public schools, has given to Americans a peculiar faith in education, a faith which a less hybrid society would hardly have developed. Because we have turned the children of Germans, Italians, Russians, Greeks, into Americans, we argue that we can turn our children into anything we wish. Also because we have seen one cult after another sweep through the country, we argue that anything can be accomplished by the right method, that with the right method, education can solve any difficulty, supply any deficiency, train inhabitants for any non-existing Utopia. Upon closer scrutiny we see that our faith in method is derived from our assimilation of immigrants, from the successful teaching of more and more complicated techniques to more and more people, or from the successful despoiling of one group's rôle of adherents by some other group of astute evangelists. In both of these departments method counts and counts hard. Efficient teaching can shorten the learning time and increase the proficiency of children in arithmetic or bookkeeping. A judicious distribution of lollypops, badges, uniforms, may swell the ranks of the Baptist Sunday School or the Young Communists. The parent who rigorously atones for his own bad grammar by tirelessly correcting his son may rear a son who speaks correctly. But he will speak no more correctly than those who have never heard poor English. By method it is possible to speed up the course of mastering existing techniques or increase the number of adherents of an existing faith. But both of these changes are quantitative not qualitative; they are essentially non-creative in character. Nor is the achievement of making Americans out of the children of foreign parents creating something new; we are simply passing on a developed tradition to them.

Those who believe in the changes which have been wrought by education point proudly to the diffusion of the theory of evolution. But this is a mere quantitative comment again. The gradual change in human thought which produced Darwin's type of thought instead of Thomas Aquinas' took place in the library and the laboratory, not in the school room. Mediæval schoolmen and their deductive approach had first to be ousted from the universities before the inductive method could be taught in the schools. And meanwhile whether induction or deduction was taught with a whip or a sweet smile or not consciously taught at all, made relatively little difference in the accuracy with which the mental habits of children conformed to the mental habits of their teachers and parents.

Those who would save the world by education rely a great deal upon the belief that there are many tendencies, latent capacities, present in childhood which have disappeared in the finished adult. Children's natural "love of art," "love of music," "generosity," "inventiveness" are invoked by the advocates of this path of salvation in working out educational schemes through which these child virtues may be elaborated and stabilised, as parts of the adult personality. There is a certain kind of truth in this assertion, but it is a negative not a positive truth. For instance, children's "love of music," with the probable exception of those rare cases which we helplessly label "geniuses," is more likely simply an unspoiled capacity to be taught music. Manus children under the age of five or six could hear a melody and attempt, clumsily, to reproduce it. But children above that age were to all intents and purposes what we would call tone deaf. In the same melody which the small child would sing with a fair degree of success, the older children and adults heard only a changing emphasis. They would repeat it with great stress upon the syllables denoting the high notes, but without any change in tone, and believe quite ingenuously that they were reproducing all that there was in the song. Only one Manus native could really sing melodies and he had been away at school continuously for six years.

So that if by "natural to children" we mean that a child will learn easily what an adult, culturally defined, and in many ways limited, will not learn except with the greatest difficulty, it is true that any capability upon which the society does not set a premium, will seem easier to teach to a child than to an adult. So our children seem more imaginative than adults because we put a premium upon practical behaviour which is strictly oriented to the world of sense experience. Manus children, on the other hand, seem more practical, more matter-of-fact than do the Manus adults who live in a world where unseen spirits direct many of their activities. An educational enthusiast working among Manus children would be struck with their "scientific potentialities" just as the enthusiast among ourselves is struck with our children's "imaginative potentialities." The observations in both cases would be true in relation to the adult culture. In the case of our children their imaginative tendencies nourished upon a rich language and varied and diverse literary tradition will be discounted in adult life, attenuated, suppressed, distorted by the demands for practical adjustment; while the Manus children's frank scepticism and preoccupation with what they can see and touch and hear will be overlaid by the canons of Manus supernaturalism. But the educator who expected that these potentialities which are not in accordance with the adult tradition could be made to flower and bear fruit in the face of a completely alien adult world, would be reckoning without the strength of tradition—tradition which will assert its rights in the face of the most cunning methodological assault in the world.

Let us take a Manus example of one of the things which we attempt to develop by special systems of education—drawing. Individual educators who feel that our culture is lamentably deficient in artistic interest or achievement, take groups of American school children, provide them with materials, give them leisure and encouragement and bid them draw. On the walls of the school room, in their books, the children see copies of the famous paintings of the European tradition. After their initial struggles with problems of perspective, they settle down to draw within the rules worked out by the concentrated attention of gifted adults in ages which valued painting and gave it high rewards. Setting aside the accidental good effects which are so frequent in the drawings of children, good effects based on freshness, naïveté and fortuitous but happy arrangements of lines, there will be found good work among the efforts of such a group of children. The teacher will point proudly to what can be done as soon as the artistic impulse is allowed to flower under favourable conditions.

In contrast, take the drawing which was done by my Manus children within a culture which had no tradition of drawing or painting. The children were given perfect freedom. I provided them with pencil and paper and smooth surfaces upon which to do their work. They were neither praised nor blamed; the very small children were sometimes encouraged but only in the most general terms. For months these children avidly covered sheet after sheet of paper, throwing themselves whole-souled into this new and amusing occupation. In their work most of the tendencies which we find highly developed in the arts of different people were present in the efforts of individuals, conventualisation, realism, attempted perspective, symbolism, arbitrary use of design units, distortion of the subject to fit the field, etc. But, and this is the decisive point, there was no work produced which could be called art. On the canoe prows, on the betel spatulas, on the rims of bowls were carvings of real beauty made by neighbouring tribes. But the children had no precedent for drawing, and their work shows this lack. Working without a guiding tradition their efforts are interesting but they lend no support to the theories of those who hope for great things when the potentialities of children are pitted against the adult world. And yet there is no reason to argue from any racial theory of ability that these people simply lacked an artistic gift, because the wood carving of their neighbours of the same race ranks with the finest work of its kind. Had every child been set to work with a penknife the results would in all probability have been far higher.

To return now to the group of child artists within an American experimental school: Under the stimulus of a good tradition, given leisure to draw, an opportunity to master the mechanics of the technique at an early age, and social recognition of success such as is accorded no artist in our adult national life, it may be possible to develop artists who will have to battle miserably with non-recognition in their own communities or flee to live as half aliens in Europe. Because of the accessibility of other traditions, traditions which have so much body and vitality that they can be transplanted from their own countries and set down among a group of school children, it is possible for us to bring children up in sympathy with a culture other than our own. This would be almost impossible among a primitive people. But the teacher who develops a child's sympathies with another tradition at the expense of the child's adherence to its own culture is not creating something new. She is simply diverting the stream of tradition so that the child drinks with complete unconsciousness from an alien source. The child is muffled in the

[270]

material trappings, the ideology, the standards of a different world until it comes to belong to that world rather than to the tradition of its own country. This child grown to manhood and looking about him with no recognition upon the culture in which he has no part will seem to point vividly the moral that education can accomplish anything.

But this is only partly true. Had the Manus children been shown the work of good artists, encouraged to admire and imitate this work, condemned for failure, praised for success, the work of children whose parents knew nothing of drawing or painting might show the discipline, the style, the conventions of an art—the art to which they had been exposed. Proficiency and interest in graphic art would not necessarily carry with it a complex of associated ideas which would make the artist socially acceptable in Manus. If his absorption in the execution of his work could be cultivated to the point where he refused to fish or trade, build canoes or houses, he would probably become a cultural misfit.

When we look about us among different civilisations and observe the vastly different styles of life to which the individual has been made to conform, to the development of which he has been made to contribute, we take new hope for humanity and its potentialities. But these potentialities are passive not active, helpless without a cultural milieu in which to grow. So Manus children are given opportunity to develop generous social feeling; they are given a chance to exercise it in their play world. But these generous communistic sentiments can not maintain themselves in the adult world which sets the price of survival at an individualistic selfish acquisitiveness. Men who as boys shared their only cigarette and halved their only *laplap*, will dun each other for a pot or a string of dogs' teeth.

So those who think they can make our society less militantly acquisitive by bringing children up in a world of share and share alike, bargain without their hosts. They can create such a world among a few children who are absolutely under their control, but they will have built up an attitude which will find no institutionalised path for adult expression. The child so trained might become a morbid misfit or an iconoclast, but he can not make terms with his society without relinquishing the childhood attitudes for which his society has no use.

The spectacular experiment in Russia had first to be stabilised among adults before it could be taught to children. No child is equipped to create the necessary bridge between a perfectly alien point of view, and his society. Such bridges can only be built slowly, patiently, by the exceptionally gifted. The cultivation in children of traits, attitudes, habits foreign to their cultures is not the way to make over the world. Every new religion, every new political doctrine, has had first to make its adult converts, to create a small nuclear culture within whose guiding walls its children will flourish. "Middletown" illustrates how art and literature and music, history and the classics are taught in the schools, but completely neglected in adult life by the

male members of the community. They are undoubtedly taught by teachers sadly lacking in real knowledge
or enthusiasm, but even given the best possible teachers,
the results of the teachings would not be able to hold out
against the contrasting pressure of "Middletown" life.
The little groups of painters and writers who cluster
forlornly together in out of the way spots in America
or gather in the cafés in Paris are earnest of this. Exposure to the ideas of other cultures has given them
an impetus towards the artist's life which they cannot
live out within their communities. And although the
production of gifted artists who must flee the tradition
which has but half nourished them, is better than the
production of no artists at all, it is but a sorry cultural
result when compared with what can be accomplished
within the walls of a rich and vital tradition.

So, although it is possible to induct a few children
into a cultural tradition to which they are not the lineal
heirs, this is not a process by which the children are
educated above their cultural background in its widest
sense. The tradition of Italian painting is exchanged
for the tradition of commercial success in Des Moines,
Iowa; the canons of German musical life substituted
for the canons of jazz. But the children have not developed a new thing; they have taken that which some
adult wished to give them out of his cultural richness.
Only by the contributions of adults are real changes
brought about; only then can the enlistment of the
next generation have important effects.

The truth of this conclusion has vivid illustration in

Manus, where although the society neglects so many of its educational problems until manhood, and permits rebellious youths to mock at its sanctities, or sulk at its commands, the youth has no resource in the end except conformity, because his culture has become, in spite of himself, woof and web of his being. The child will receive the general content of his culture no matter how it is transmitted to him; he will absorb the content in any event, but he is hopelessly dependent upon the quality of that content.

Our general neglect of content for method, our blind trust that all we need is a mechanical formula, is illustrated sharply in the kind of courses taught in teachers' training colleges as compared with courses in the Liberal Arts. The prospective teachers are taught how to teach everything under the sun, but they are taught very little about the art, literature, history, themselves. A slight, ill-comprehended body of material is transmitted from teacher to pupil in a most elaborate and unrewarding fashion. In the training colleges, the "value of teaching with dates," "the use of charts" takes the place of actually reading history. And thirty hours of pedagogy, courses in how to teach history or biology, are regarded by school boards as more valuable than academic distinction in these subjects. Prospective teachers, often coming from homes with a very slight cultural tradition, enter a college where they are given nothing to make up for their deficiencies. And yet we continue to depend upon the individual teacher to transmit the rich content of literary and scientific tradition which is available to us to-day. If we are to use these materials, if we are to have a richer culture, we must either abandon the dependence upon the individual teachers or give them a far better background during their years of training. If the teachers are to be the advance guard of civilisation they must first be given a genuine feeling for and understanding of that civilisation.

An alternative course is to relinquish our dependence upon the teachers and turn to other methods of diffusing cultural content. This method is symbolised by a recent educational plan of a large museum in an Eastern city. The museum sends out sets of slides to a series of city high schools. The children in each high school are then shepherded into the school auditoriums at a given hour, and a highly trained expert on the museum staff gives a radio talk which is illustrated by the slides. Even the signal for change of slides is given over the radio. Methods such as these, using the radio, the lantern, the motion picture and a far larger and more available supply of books, could be used to place great masses of good material before children. A comparatively small body of highly intelligent educators could direct the content prescribed and administered to millions of school children. Unlike the old text book, these new methods would teach themselves. The teachers would have to be little more than good disciplinarians and good record keepers. A dependence upon good material diffused mechanically, impersonally from remote but reliable centres is preferable to the present method in which a teacher who knows nothing of poetry herself is expected to interpret Shakespeare to her students. Such mechanical methods may be necessary to adopt as emergency measures, until we can revise the course of training in teachers' colleges and provide for our schools teachers who can combine knowledge of rich materials with personal leadership.

In either case, those who wish to alter our traditions and cherish the Utopian but perhaps not impossible hope that they can consciously do so, must first muster a large enough body of adults who with them wish to make the slight rearrangements of our traditional attitudes which present themselves to our culturally saturated minds. This is equally true of those who wish to import part of the developed tradition of other societies. They must, that is, create a coherent adult culture in miniature before they can hope to bring up children in the new tradition—even if they expect them to be brought up by radio. Such changes in adult attitudes come slowly, are more dependent upon specially gifted or wise individuals than upon wholesale educational schemes.

Besides encouraging a most unfounded optimism, this over-valuation of the educational process and under-valuation of the iron strength of the cultural walls within which any individual can operate, produces one other unfortunate result. It dooms every child born into American culture to victimisation by a hundred self-conscious evangelists who will not pause long enough to build a distinctive culture in which the growing child may develop coherently. One such group negates the efforts of another and the modern child is subjected to miseries which the Manus child never knows, reared as it is with unselfconscious finality into a Manus adult. Not until we realise that a poor culture will never become rich, though it be filtered through the expert methods of unnumbered pedagogues, and that a rich culture with no system of education at all will leave its children better off than a poor culture with the best system in the world, will we begin to solve our educational problems. Once we lose faith in the blanket formula of education, in the magic fashion in which education, using the passive capacities of children, is to create something out of nothing, we can turn our attention to the vital matter of developing individuals, who as adults, can gradually mould our old patterns into new and richer forms.

APPENDICES

I

THIS investigation was conducted upon the hypothesis that it is impossible to study original nature directly except in such very simple and undifferentiated terms as those studied in the basic experiments conducted by Watson. It is based upon the assumption that the original nature of the child is so subject to environmental influences that the only way to arrive at any conception of original nature is to study it as modified by different environmental conditions. The repetition of such observations will in time give us a far better basis of generalisation than can be obtained by the observation of individuals within the confining walls of one type of social environment. Observations may be made upon thousands of children within our culture; tested and re-tested within our society, they may hold good, but once taken beyond those bounds they will often be found to fail.

It is realised that in transferring an investigation from within our society where all the instruments of research, particularly language, are under perfect control, to a primitive society where controlled conditions are practically impossible and a new language has to be learned, certain sacrifices of methodological exactness are necessarily made. But it is felt that such disadvantages in method are more than compensated for by the advantages which result from a homogeneous culture. In our society we can study large numbers of cases of a known chronological age but we have constantly to make allowances for a cultural background so heterogeneous that no investigator can hope to control it. In a primitive society, the student has fewer cases, their chronological age, age of parents at their birth, order of birth, method of delivery, etc., are relatively unattainable. But the manners and morals, beliefs, avoidances, repugnances, enthusiasms, of their parents all conform very closely to the cultural norm. For studies of personality, social adjustment, etc., that is, for all those investigations where the social environment is the most important factor, research in primitive society is rich in its rewards. The religious beliefs, sex habits, methods of discipline, social aims, of those who constitute the child's family, can all be arrived at by an analysis of the culture itself. The individual within that culture does not differ importantly in these matters from others of his age or sex. For it must be remembered that in a culture like Manus, with only a sex division of labour between individuals (division of labour between localities does, of course, occur), without any priesthood with a great body of esoteric knowledge, without any method of keeping extensive records, the cultural tradition is simple enough to be almost entirely contained within the memory of an average adult member of the society. An investigator who enters such a society with ethnological training which makes it possible to refer the phenomena of Manus culture to convenient and well understood categories, and with the immense superiority over the native of being able to record in writing each aspect of the culture as it is learned, is in an excellent position for research in a comparatively short time. The fact that my husband was working on Manus ethnology made it possible to still further reduce this preliminary time period. A primitive culture is therefore less perplexing as social background than would be even the most isolated of rural villages in our society, for into these drift echoes and fragments from a hundred different kinds of complex cultural elaboration.

The study of human development in a primitive society has then these two advantages: contrast to our own social environment which brings out different aspects of human nature and often demonstrates that behaviour which occurs almost invariably in individuals within our own society is nevertheless due not to original nature but to social environment; and a homogeneous and simple social background, easily mastered, against which the development of the individual may be studied.

The anthropologist submits the findings of the psychologist who works within our society to the test of observation within other societies. He never seeks to invalidate the observations of the psychologist, but rather, in the light of wider social data, to test the interpretations which may be placed upon those observations. His is a special technique for the rapid analysis of primitive society. In order to acquire this technique, he has devoted a great deal of time to the study of different primitive societies and the analysis of the social forms which are most characteristic of them. He has studied non-Indo European languages so that his mind will adjust easily to linguistic categories which are alien to our own. He has studied phonetics so that he may be able to recognise and record types of sound difficult for our ears to distinguish and even more difficult for our organs of speech to pronounce, accustomed as they are to different phonetic patterns. He has studied diverse kinship systems and gained speed in handling kinship categories so that the Manus scheme, which results, for instance, in individuals of the same generation addressing each other by grandparent terms, is not a perplexing obstacle but falls readily into a clear and easily comprehended pattern of thought. In addition, he is willing to forsake the amenities of civilised life and subject himself for months at a time to the inconveniences and unpleasantness of life among a people whose manners, methods of sanitation, and ways of thought, are completely alien to him. He is willing to learn their language, to immerse himself in their manners, get their culture sufficiently by heart to feel their repugnances and sympathise with their triumphs. In Manus, for instance, it was necessary to learn a very real horror of the meeting of two tabu relatives, to guard one's tongue against ever uttering a tabu word and feel embarrassed contrition if one had made a slip; to learn to greet every news of illness or misfortune with the question of what spirit was involved. Such investigations as these involve a fairly drastic rearrangement of thought and daily habit. The willingness to make them, and the knowledge of the special techniques necessary to ethnological research, are the equipment which the ethnologist brings to the solution of psychological problems. He says to the psychologist who has made long and careful investigation within our society, from which he may or may not have drawn conclusions which he regards as final, "Let me take your results and submit them to a new test. You have made such and such generalisation about the thought content of young children, the relationship between mental and physical development, the connection between a certain type of family life and the possibility of happy marital adjustment, the factors which go to the formation of personality, etc. These results I find significant and important. Let me therefore submit them to the test of a different social environment, and in the light of such observation, on the basis of our combined research, on the basis of your initial definition of the problems and observations within our society, and my check observations in a different society, come to conclusions which will successfully withstand the accusation that the effect of social environment has not been properly allowed for. It will then be possible for you to divide your observations upon individuals within our culture into two parts: data upon the behaviour of human beings modified by present-day culture, which will be of the utmost importance in handling educational and psychiatric problems of individuals with the same cultural background, and second: theories of the original nature, the potentialities of man, based upon your observations and mine."

To the psychologists who are genuinely interested in the solution of fundamental theoretical problems

such an offer cannot but make an appeal. The psychiatrist, the social worker, the educator, whose concern is
with the immediate adjustment of individuals, may possibly say, with justice, "I accept your evidence that
many of the phenomena of human nature in our society which we treat as biologically determined, are
really socially determined. Theoretically, I think you
are right. Actually, I have five cases of maladjustment
which I must deal with to-day. The bulk of accumulated data upon the kind of behaviour of which these
cases are a sample, even though it is based upon individuals in our society, in fact just because it is so local in
time or space, is just what I need. The first case I
have is a case of exhibitionism. It is very interesting to
know that exhibitionism could hardly develop in Samoa,
where our habitual tabus are not observed. But meanwhile John is an exhibitionist and must be dealt with
in the light of other case material on exhibitionistic children in our society." With the comment of such hard
pressed practical workers, one must have the greatest
sympathy. But the same thing does not apply to those
who stand behind these workers, those who evolve
theories of human nature upon which educational
schemes and schools of psychology are built up.

It is most important that the psychologist should be
fully aware of the possibilities of research in other cultures, that he should be in intimate contact with modern
ethnological research. For ethnology is in a peculiar
position.

In many sciences the neglect of a field of research
by one generation of investigators is not ultimately important. The research neglected by one generation may

be taken up with equal and perhaps greater advantage by the next. This is the case, for instance, with experiments in animal psychology, on white rats reared in captivity. Presumably the supply of available rats will be as great in the next generation as it is now; the rapid rate of multiplication of the rats will make them equally good subjects for experiment. But if the animal psychologist were to find that experiments upon primates in a wild state were very valuable at the same time that he found that progressive invasion by civilisation of the wild parts of the world was diminishing their number and threatening to extinguish these primates altogether, he would have great cause for alarm, cause for urging other psychologists and scientific institutions to undertake the study of primates in the wild state before it was too late. And even so, his predicament would not be as serious as that of social psychology, for from one pair of wild apes the numbers of wild apes might be again recruited.

But in social psychology this is not the case. Because we must study, not only human beings, but human beings as modified by environment, a variety of check social environments is of the greatest importance. With the rapid diffusion of Western civilisation over the surface of the earth, societies are coming to conform more and more closely to the same cultural type, or if they are too divergent from the reigning type, to die out altogether. Good test cases are being eliminated week by week, as Western civilisation with its Christian ideology and industrial system penetrates Japan and China, and into the hitherto railless interior of Afghanistan, or on the other hand, as the last remaining Moriori or Lord How Islander dies, the only remnants of one-time living cultures which could not withstand the shock of white contact. It is of course idle to expect that the mores of the whole human race will become so standardised that differences between local groups will not always exist, but it may be that with improved methods of transportation and communication, comparatively isolated human societies will never again occur. No one small group of people may ever again be permitted to develop a unique culture, with little or no outside contact, over a period of hundreds of years, as has been the case in the past. No continent will be permitted to solve its own environmental adjustment problems, without outside influence, as the American aboriginals solved the problem of the cultivation of maize. The cumulative nature of our material tradition is such that we may well be coming to the end of an era which will never be repeated. Meanwhile, in New Guinea, Indonesia, Africa, South America, and parts of Asia, there are still in existence groups which can be used as invaluable checks upon all scientific attempts to understand human nature. The social psychologist of five hundred years from now will have to say: "If we could submit this conclusion to the test of investigating people brought up within a completely different social framework, we might get different results. That, however, is now impossible. There are no such societies where the problem could be studied; we cannot, if we would, create test societies and produce these necessary conditions of contrast experimentally. Our hands are tied." But we are in no sense so handicapped. The different contrasting societies are there ready for study. There are an increasing number of ethnologists with the necessary techniques for investigating them. Upon the co-operation of psychologist and ethnologist, the success of any such venture depends. If the training of the ethnologist is to be utilised to the full, he should spend most of his time, at least during his early years, in the field collecting as fast as possible this rapidly vanishing, priceless evidence of human adaptability and potentialities. Upon the psychologist in the laboratory and in the library develops the posing of problems to which the ethnologist's contribution will be important.

The student of human society to-day looks back hopelessly upon the beginnings of culture, realising that such problems as the origin of language can never be solved, that one guess is as good as another and that they must all remain in the realm of speculation. To the curious minded this is felt as a definite handicap, but hardly a point upon which our scientific progenitors of the stone age need our forgiveness. It is an incontrovertible assumption that they could not record these important and interesting experiments in speech which differentiated early man from his less accomplished ancestors. But we have no such alibi to offer. There are now in existence social experiments which we have only to study and to preserve. There are now in existence laboratories for research such as future ages will not have. Only by the co-operative effort of psychologist, psychiatrist, geneticist, can the problems be posed for which these societies offer laboratory methods of solution. Without the stimulation of the psychologist, the work of the ethnologist is far less valuable than it might otherwise have been. If the psychologist will take account of ethnological data, if he will familiarise himself sufficiently with ethnological material so as to realise its potentialities, if he will formulate his theories with regard for the influence of cultural environment, the ethnologist's task will be immensely simplified. He does not wish to confine himself to the negative activity of exploding theories which have been framed within one society and collapse when submitted to a check, nor has he the time nor the training to retire into the library and the laboratory and frame new psychological theories for himself. This, moreover, he cannot do without disloyalty to his own science. His first obligation is to use his training to record data of primitive society before these societies disappear. Field work is arduous and exacting. The ethnologist should do his field work in his youth and his theorising after his fitness for active work is diminished. Meanwhile the psychologist should offer suggestions for research. Many field trips which are now only historical investigations, of extreme value in adding to our knowledge of human society and the lengths to which it can influence human behaviour, are only half as valuable as they might have been if definite psychological problems could be attacked simultaneously.

I present this study as a sample of the kind of conditions which exist in primitive society and a suggestion of their bearing upon problems of education and personality development. I am far more anxious that the fertile thinkers in other fields should examine this material in the light of possible problems which data of this kind could solve, than that they should agree with my particular conclusions. Social psychology is still in its infancy. It is of the greatest importance that every available approach, especially those approaches which are only temporarily available, should be utilised to the fullest extent.

Background of This Study

This investigation of Melanesian children was undertaken to solve a special problem which is but lightly touched upon in this book: i.e., the relationship between spontaneous animism and thinking characteristic of mentally immature persons, especially children under five or six. The results of this research were negative, that is, evidence was found to support the view that animism is not a spontaneous aspect of child thinking nor does it spring from any type of thought characteristic of immature mental development; its presence or absence in the thought of children is dependent upon cultural factors, language, folk lore, adult attitudes, etc., and these cultural factors have their origin in the thought of individual adults, not in the misconceptions of children. These results will be presented with full discussion in another place.

Melanesia was chosen for this study because it is an area which contains many relatively unspoiled primitive groups and has been conspicuous in ethnological discussions as a region filled with the phenomena usually subsumed under the head of "Animism." The choice of a local area was made on the basis of what regions were relatively unknown, thus narrowing it down to the region of the Bismarck Archipelago, later narrowed to the Admiralties as the part of that territory about which we had the least information. The Manus tribe were chosen for a multitude of chance reasons, because a district officer recommended them as easy to deal with, because a missionary had published some texts in the language, and because we were able to get a school boy in Rabaul to act as interpreter at the beginning. Where nothing was known of any of the many diverse tribal groups in the Admiralties, the choice was at best a blind one. I document this matter because the peculiar relevancy of Manus attitudes and the Manus language to my results is the more striking. I did not choose this culture because of its attitudes towards children, because of its bare non-metaphorical language, because of the kind of results which I attained. I simply chose a Melanesian culture in a primitive state in which I could study the education and mental development of young children.

The method followed was primarily one of observation of the children under normal conditions of play, in their home, with their parents. For the study of the special problem, I collected the children's spontaneous drawings, asked them to interpret ink blots, collected interpretations of events and posed problem questions which would throw light upon their animistic conceptions. The children had never held a pencil before; I began by giving the fourteen-year-olds pencils and paper and suggesting that they draw, leaving choice of subject to them. The next day the next younger group were provided with drawing materials and this went on until the three-year-olds were enlisted. I felt that this was the closest approximation to normal methods of learning which I could make without permitting the adults to draw, which would have changed the terms of the investigation. The drawings were preserved with name, date, and interpretations when there were any. Their detailed analysis is a problem for future work.

This study has also as a background a detailed knowledge of the culture, of the social organisation, the economic system, the religious beliefs and practices. All current events in the village were followed with careful attention to their cultural significance and the rôle which they played in the lives of the children. The relationship between parents and children was noted and recorded in the light of detailed knowledge of the paternity and history of the child and the social status and personality of the parent. In each case, the child was studied with his social background, that of his own home and kin being known in detail, that of his culture being known also. This may be said to be a study in which the total situation approach is arrived at in the sense that a simple culture, a population of two hundred and ten people formed a background which could be controlled as a larger community in a complex civilisation could never be.

The native language was used throughout, although I was of course also familiar with pidgin English and so able to follow the conversation and play of the boys in both tongues. With the women and girl children, and with the very little ones, all communication was in the native language. Records of conversations, interpretations, etc., were all taken down in the Manus language. Translations when necessary were checked through our school boy interpreter, who understood a good deal of English and spoke perfect pidgin, and cross-checked between my husband and myself.

This book presents the aspects of my study which I feel bear directly upon educational problems. A description of the educational methods pursued consistently by an entire people and the results in adult personality should be of use to educators who must formulate theories of the inherent potentialities of human beings and the way in which these potentialities may best be developed by society through education.

I should like to add an explanatory note about the terminology which I have used. I have avoided as much as possible the use of technical terms. This is not because I do not realise that a science may have much to gain by the use of special and exact terminology. But I do not feel that there is any one terminology among the many in use by different psychological schools which has established itself sufficiently so that one may predict its survival at the expense of all the others. In the meanwhile such a study as this has a certain finality. In a few years the village of Peri will be invaded by missionaries; schools will be introduced; it will no longer be a primitive culture. It therefore seems advisable to couch this description in the language which has been developed outside the realm of controversy—in the field of the novelist—in order that it may be intelligible when some of the present dialectic points and their terminological disputes have been outmoded. Such a course has the additional advantage of making the material more accessible to students from other fields.

II

A COMPLETE ethnology of the Manus culture is being written by Mr. Fortune. Those who wish to place the observations in this book in a more detailed cultural setting will be able to do so by referring to his monograph. I shall only give here a brief summary discussion in order to make the material in this book more immediately intelligible to the Oceanic student.

The Admiralty Islands include about forty islands near the Bismarck Archipelago, north of New Guinea. They lie between 1° and 3° S. and 146° and 148° E. The Great Admiralty which forms the centre of the archipelago is about sixty miles long. All the islands of the archipelago, taken together, have an estimated area of about six hundred square miles. The population is estimated at about thirty thousand. The inhabitants are divided for convenience of classification into three main groups: the Manus, or sea-dwelling people, the Usiai, who inhabit the Great Admiralty, and the Matankor peoples who live on the small islands and build their houses on land but make some use of canoes. The Manus people are the only homogeneous group among these three; both Usiai and Matankor peoples include tribes speaking many mutually unintelligible dialects and showing great divergences in custom. This blanket classification is one which the Manus

[293]

people make; as the most enterprising group in the archipelago they have imposed their terminology upon the white man.

The Manus build their houses on piles, in the lagoons near the Great Admiralty or in the lee of small islands. Their some two thousand people are divided among eleven villages: Papitalai on the North Coast, Pamatchau, Mbunei, Tchalalo, Pere (Peri for purposes of this study as the latter spelling is misleading to those not familiar with Oceanic languages), Patusi and Loitcha, in the lagoons along the South Coast, and settlements near the islands of Mbuke, Taui, Mok, and Rambutchon, all islands off the South Coast. The language spoken is divided into two dialects, one in which the l sound is used exclusive of the r, the other which uses both l and r. (The latter is spoken in Peri.) This is a mere phonetic shift and the two dialects are mutually intelligible. The villages which speak a common dialect have, however, a vague feeling of unity as over against those which speak the other dialect. There are no political connections between any of the Manus villages, although Government has recently placed a Mbunei man of outstanding leadership in nominal charge of the relations of all these villages to the Administration. The different villages met as units in two ways—in very rare inter-village feasts, only one or two of which were held in a generation, and in occasional warfare. In some cases women of one Manus village were carried off by another Manus village as prostitutes. But the usual form of inter-village relationship was neither the large feast, which, with its ritual of challenge and competitive display, partook somewhat of the nature of war, nor war itself, but rather a network of interrelations between individuals and families in the different villages. There was much intervillage marriage and each new marriage contract set up a host of economic and social obligations between the affinal relatives involved.

The Manus peoples, with the exception of the people of Mbuke who are too far away from the main island, live by fishing and trading their fish for the garden products of their Usiai or Matankor neighbours. Daily markets are held for the exchange of foodstuffs and the purchase of other necessities such as bark for cord, baskets, spears, etc. Each local group among the non-Manus peoples specialises in some particular manufacture which is traded to the nearest Manus village for fish, or pots in the case of Mbuke, and then carried far and wide to other Manus villages and their neighbours, by Manus canoes. The large, single outrigger canoes, which carry two lug sails and a snug little house, distribute the material culture far and wide. The Manus people control the trade of the South Coast. Except for the Mbuke people who make pots, they make nothing beyond houses and canoes for their own use, cord for their own beadwork, and part of their fishing apparatus. Their finer fish nets, however, are made in Lou and other more distant Matankor settlements. They depend upon the daily markets and the less regular overseas trade for everything else which they use. With the Usiai they trade for sago, yams, taro, taro leaves, betel nut, pepper leaves, lime gourds, lime spatulas, paraminium nut used as gumming material, bark for rope and string making, paraminium nut-covered baskets, oil strainers, carrying bags, etc. From their own people of Mbuke they get pots. From the people of Balowan and Lou their Manus neighbours get yams ("mammies"), carved bowls, and other fine woodwork, fish nets, lime gourds, oil containers, spears, and tools of obsidian. From Rambutchon and Nauna they get carved beds, from Pak war charms of carved heads and frigate bird feathers, from all of the islands coconuts and coconut oil. Peri is the largest of the villages near the mainland; the inhabitants have the additional advantage of having sago swamps of their own, obtained from the Usiai by marriage and conquest, so they are less immediately dependent upon the local market than most of the other Manus peoples. The shell money used by all the Admiralty Island peoples consists of strings of shallow white shell disks, resembling the shell necklaces in use among the Southwest Indians to-day. It is made by the Matankor people of Ponam on the North Coast and traded all over the island. The North Coast Matankor also have a monopoly of dugong fishing and excellent turtle fishing. In the old days, wars used to be fought between them and the Manus because the Manus poached on their fishing rights. The North Coast has its own pottery centre at the island of Hus, where a white pottery is made, while the South Coast depends upon the black ware made on the island of Mbuke.

While the Manus practically control the trade of the South Coast, they have rivals on the North Coast who build good canoes and are excellent fishermen. In their own part of the Admiralties, however, they are the middlemen; they control the fishing, the traffic on the seas, and they are the carriers between Usiai and the island Matankor. Although a few individuals have learned to carve from some relative in another tribe, the Manus as a group produce no single item of art except beadwork nor, with the exception of Mbuke pots, any articles for export. Neither are they collectors; although their shelves are loaded with a greater variety of articles than any Usiai or Matankor house can boast, these are all there for purposes of trade. They will sell the most beautiful Balowan bowl, the finest bit of Usiai carving, with alacrity. After they have sold all the fine work which they have bought from their neighbours they will offer a white man the bones of their dead, or the beaded hair of the dead, for a price.

Although money is perfectly understood, and the shell money and dogs' teeth are in constant use, barter is frequently resorted to both in the daily markets and in the overseas trade. It is used primarily to compel the production or sale of the kind of article desired. So a canoe from Mok will load up with coconuts from the trees of the Matankor peoples on the near-by islands and sail into Peri, demanding sago and refusing to take either money or any other valuable in exchange. The burden of turning money into sago is thus shifted to the Peri people; the Mok people who have made the voyage simply wait until their demands are met. Or the people of Balowan who furnish mud hen eggs to the South Coast trade will give three eggs for two dogs' teeth, but ten eggs for a bundle of sago which can be bought for two dogs' teeth on the mainland.

With this traffic in material objects which results in

the distribution of the products of all the different localities all over the archipelago goes also a traffic in charms; charms to produce or cure disease, charms to make one's debtors anxious to discharge their debts, charms to induce one's relatives to contribute generously to some undertaking, charms to make a husband come home on time for meals or think lightly of his other wife. (Polygamy is unusual, but does occur.) These are traded from people to people and seem to be the more valued the more times they have changed hands— for a profit. Aspirant mediums from one village will go to a famous medium of another village to be trained. The canoes which are carrying people and trade articles and charms, gossip of births and of deaths, tales of the latest séance, are constantly coming and going from one Manus village to another.

Occasionally one of the loosely organised paternal clans splits in half and the disgruntled section moves to another village. When this occurs a nominal relationship is kept up between the members in the two villages; the kinship is claimed if it is desirable in arranging a marriage, etc. But the rule is for the clans to be confined to one village. The clans are small, a few have as many as ten adult members, others only two or three. If they become reduced to as few as two adult male members, however, the clan is either merged into another small clan or vanish entirely in a large one. So in Peri at the present time, Malean is the only survival of the clan of Kapet, and he has been adopted by Ndrosal and will probably always function as a member of Peri. Pokanas and Poli are the only two surviving members of Lopwer, and Kea is the only male member of Kamtatchau; all three of these men act with the small clan of Kalō and people are beginning to speak of them as belonging to Kalō. Where the clan names could be explained at all in Peri they were found to be taken from various types of fishing apparatus which the members of that clan had the hereditary right to make. Theoretically the members of a clan build their houses close together, but the custom of moving a house after a death breaks into this localisation (this can be seen on the map).

The whole attitude towards clan membership and towards kinship is very loose in Manus. Kinship is counted bilaterally, but a child usually belongs to his father's clan, unless, as is often the case, he is adopted by his mother's own or clan brother. The children of two sisters call each other by the same term as do the children of two brothers, adding, if it is necessary to be explicit, "of a different house." House is regarded as the equivalent of "father's line" and "place" is regarded as the equivalent of "Father's clan." This well reflects the feeling that the important point is residence. Difference in age is reflected in the kinship system: older siblings are classed with the parent generation, younger siblings with the child generation. The whole kinship system is organised around the relationship of brother and sister relationships between their descendants. The father's sister and her descendants in the female line are joking relatives and have the power of cursing or blessing the descendants of the brother. Male cross cousins are regarded as potential business partners through the preferential marriage of their children. Although the system is rigid, every fiction is permitted in order to fit an individual into the proper category to arrange or contract a marriage. So a man may be conceived as being sister's son to the clan of his father's second wife or his older brother's wife, and thereby having a right to return there to that clan to demand a wife for his son. Only first marriages are arranged in terms of the kinship system and these are the marriages which, having the least regard to the persons concerned, have the least duration. Discrepancies in intelligence are the commonest reasons for the disruption of a marriage, especially by the man's kin. Occasionally, however, they will influence a man to divorce a stupid wife, if he himself is stupid, so that he may marry an intelligent one, in order that she may advise him and enable him to play some rôle in the community. It is worth noting also that the richest and most influential men in the community have all been married for a long time to the same wife. There are various interpretations to put upon this. One may argue that they have stayed married because they were of equal high intelligence and that the high intelligence and drive has produced their success. (This would be borne out by the fact that there are occasional men who have been married a long time and had many children by one wife, but who are stupid and timid and play no rôle in the community.) Or it may suggest that constant change of marriage partners is a terrific economic drain on a man. A marriage which ends in a death is then decently liquidated in the death exchanges, but marriages ending in divorce leave a great many loose ends and result in a good deal of loss to the individuals who have contributed to the affinal exchanges. A man who is frequently divorced becomes a bad investment and people prefer to put their property into the exchanges centring about marriages which have proved stable.

There are faint echoes of rank in the privileges claimed by certain families who are called *lapan* in contradistinction to other families which are called *lau*. Both classes may occur within one clan. The privileges of the *lapan* are largely ornamental: the right to hang shells on his house, his canoe and his belt; the right to string one hundred dogs' teeth instead of fifty on a string, the right to build his house near to one of the little islets, and most importantly the right to boast of his *lapan*ship and insult the *lau* in the course of quarrels. From one *lapan* family in each village, a war leader, known as the *luluai* is chosen; he is the man of most prestige within that family. He also represented the village in the occasional inter-village feasts. Aside from these functions and the prestige of his title, he had no power to control the members of his village or to demand anything from them. The village unit is a loose democracy, characterised ably by one informant in pidgin as a place where "altogether boy, he talk." It is an aggregate of loosely organised paternal exogamous clans, all bound together by mutual economic obligations incurred through marriages between their members, obligations which are enforced by the spirits of the dead acting through the mediums. A single puberty ceremonial may agitate all the inhabitants of a village, but each one is acting as the member of a family or a clan, not as a member of the village.

III

A GOVERNMENT station was established in the Admiralties in 1912. Since that date the archipelago has been under government control, taxes have been collected, war, head hunting, capturing foreign women for purposes of prostitution, the maintenance of a public prostitute in the men's house, are all banned by law and offenders subject to punishment by imprisonment. Government officers make patrols several times a year, sometimes for purposes of medical inspection, once a year for tax collecting, and at other times. Civil cases are heard during patrols. A native is furthermore permitted to take complaints either criminal or civil to the district officer at any time.

Administration is represented in the native villages by appointed officers, a *kukerai* (or executive), a *tultul*, interpreter and assistant to the executive in dealing with government, and a doctor boy. The village of Peri was divided into two administrative units, owing to civil strife which arose some ten years ago because the young men of one section carried off an Usiai woman who was related by marriage to the *kukerai* of the village. Separate administrative units were subsequently formed so that Peri has two *kukerais*, two *tultuls*, and two doctor boys. These native officials are presented with policemen hats and exempted from the ten shilling tax. As men of personality are usually chosen, the government appointment increases their influence in the village. But village life is not appreciably altered through this agency, although if they are clever politicians they can often turn their positions to their own advantage. Native theories of disease and its cure are as heartily subscribed to by the doctor boys as by any one else in the community. The wearers of hats have simply added a few touches of elaboration to the social scene. When a "boy he got hat" dies, all other wearers of hats mourn for him by observing some tabu, such as a pledge not to smoke Capstan tobacco until after his final death feast is made by his relatives. Important *kukerais* give feasts known as *kan pati yap*, the "feast belonging to the foreigner," at which tables are made from planks spread out on logs, pieces of calico are spread as tablecloths and whatever enamelware or cutlery the village possesses is called into service; the feast is principally of rice and "bullamoocow" (bully beef). These feasts are however a rare occurrence and represent the final ceremonial effort of the natives to represent symbolically the connection between native officials and the august administration of the white man. The tendency of New Guinea natives to symbolise white culture by tablecloths and flowers on the tables, which has been remarked in Papua also, is the result of the frequent contact of bush natives with civilised domestic arrangements in their capacity of house boys.

The elaboration of the positions of boys with hats, their tendency to regard themselves as a fraternity with mutual interests and ambitions, their pride in their hats and desire to surround them with an aura of political piety and ritual are all fertile soil upon which administrative effort can work. The Manus have the idea of rank, of hereditary leadership in war, of blood carrying certain prerogatives of dress and privilege. Unfortunately this tradition of rank has nothing to do with ordinary everyday government in the village. As a result village life is anarchic, held together only by the stream of economic exchanges which bind all the families loosely together. This system is not suited to any sort of communal undertaking. But the idea of officialdom, instituted by the government, therefore falls on good land. The old ideas of rank and war leadership, the respect accorded certain families, can easily be mobilised under this new system, and a more coherent and efficient system of local government encouraged with very little disruption of the native life.

In speeches on important occasions prominent natives refer solemnly to the passing of warfare, the present peace and prosperity of the country since the "hat" descended upon them. Traders to the core, the Manus people have welcomed the government régime which made intertribal trade safer and more frequent; litigious and legalistic of mind, they delight in the opportunity to take disputes to the district officer's court. The endless circumlocutions of pidgin English combined with the exceedingly complex nature of native economic affairs often leads, however, to unfortunate misunderstandings in court. A dispute will be taken to the district officer's about a pig for which one man claims he has never received compensation. This said pig, which A paid to B as part of a marriage exchange, has since changed hands some thirty times, each party in the exchange passing on the obligation rather than eat the pig and have to replace him in the currency system. For until a pig is eaten he is virtually currency. The defendant B tries to explain that he is waiting for the value of the pig to be returned to him along this chain of thirty creditors, all of whom have had transitory possession of the pig. "Now me sell 'em along one fellow man, he man belong one fellow sister belong me fellow. All right. This fellow man he sell him along one fellow man, he belong Patusi, he like marry him one fellow pickaninny mary * belong 'em. He no pickaninny true belong 'em that's all he help 'em papa belong this fellow mary. All right. Now this fellow pig he go along this fellow man. This fellow man he no kaikai pig, he sell 'em along one fellow man, he sister belong mary belong 'em. All right. This fellow man he got one fellow brother, liklik brother belong 'em, he work along one fellow station belong Malay. Close up now he like finish 'em time belong 'em. Suppose he finish 'em time now he catch 'em plenty fellow money, 3 fellow pound, he bring 'em along this big fellow brother belong 'em, one time along plenty fellow altogether something. Now this fellow sister belong mary belong man belong pickaninny mary belong sister belong mary belong me he no—" † At this point

* "Mary" means any native woman.

† This being translated is: "Now I gave the pig to a man, a man who is my sister's husband. This man gave the pig to a man in Patusi who was planning to marry a daughter of his. She was not his own daughter, but he had inherited her father's position. This pig was accordingly given to this man. This man did not eat the pig but gave him to the brother of his wife." ("Sister" in pidgin means sibling of the opposite sex; "Brother," sibling of the same sex. This distinction which we do not make is felt by the native as essential and he has distorted our kinship terminology to preserve it.) "Now this man has a brother, a younger brother, who is working on

many a harassed district officer is likely to break in
with, "Mâskie, brother belong mary belong brother belong mary, this fellow pig be belong whose that?" If
the conception of pigs as currency which changes hands
in the same way as does a bank note were more vivid
to officials they would not feel such righteous resentment over the unlimited peregrinations of mere pigs.
Similarly, cases are taken to court where a man has
paid a large betrothal fee, and now that the marriage
arrangements have been for some reason upset, wishes
to recover his fee. In the normal course of events this
debt would have been liquidated by the bride's family
over a number of years, the dogs' teeth and shell money
in the bride price being scrupulously returned in terms
of pigs, oil, and sago. The disappointed bridegroom,
however, wants no slow return with which he is powerless to initiate negotiations for a new wife, but his original payment back. The district officer, if new to the
territory and untrained in anthropology, attempting to
follow this payment through its subsequent trips to
Mok, Rambutchon, back to Peri, etc., is likely to ex-
claim, "You fellow throw away plenty too much money
along mary. This fellow fashion he no good. More
better you catch him mary straight all the same fashion
belong white man." * Here again a more detailed

a plantation which belongs to a Malay. Soon he will finish his time
of indenture. When he finishes his time, he will receive a lot of
money, he will receive three pounds, together with many other
things. Now this brother of the wife of the fiancé of the daughter
of the brother of my wife, he—"

* "You people pay too much for your wives. This is a bad way to
do. It would be better if you simply got married the way the white
men do."

knowledge of native custom would show that there is no wife purchase, that in every item of bride price fixed valuables are matched by dowry payments of food, and that upon this constant interchange of valuables the whole structure of Manus intra- and inter-village relations is built. Under the stimulus of these constant showy exchanges, food is raised, pigs are purchased, pots and grass skirts are made in large quantities, ensuring the people a high standard of living and a firm economic basis for their lives. Interference with this system would have the most serious effects in disintegrating and demoralising the native life. Perhaps, however, the highest boon that formal education could bring to Manus culture in its present form, is the knowledge of arithmetic and facility in keeping accounts. Records of each exchange which would take financial matters out of the sphere of dispute would do much to smooth out the present irritability and quarrelsomeness of village life. At present, only the contested cases are recorded by government; if every case could in some way be recorded by the natives there would be far fewer court cases. For the Manus are exceptionally honest people ridden by an anxiety neurosis on the question of debt. We found it a far more efficient way of ensuring a steady supply of fish to advance tobacco against future catches rather than simply announce our willingness to pay for fish. The natives paid back the advances; sometimes when fishing was poor they would bring the few shillings in their small hoards and tender them in payment, unwilling to have the debt longer upon their consciences. If this anxiety to be out of debt could be coupled with an efficient method of recording debts, a most excellent economic system would be the result.

To the native currency of shell money and dogs' teeth, English money and tobacco have been added as subsidiary currency. That is, their value in terms of the old money and of goods is fully understood; money is used to pay small ceremonial debts, as for the performance of some small magical service, and also in the ordinary trading relations between people of different tribes. Tobacco has been given a more defined place in the ceremonial currency. It has become a definite part of the mourning ritual; at the feast ending mourning, each mourner who has slept in the house of death is paid in tobacco. (These feasts were the ones for which the natives desired to borrow tobacco from us. Foresighted as they are, preparing for big economic events sometimes months in advance, they cannot foresee death, nor easily collect the tobacco necessary for this ceremony which follows close on the heels of the death itself.) Those who assist at a house building are also now paid with a stick of tobacco in addition to the betel nut and pepper leaves which are placed on their bowls of food. Tobacco seems to have a tendency to displace betel nut on ceremonial occasions and to be used in the same way as individual dogs' teeth in small transactions. Shillings, on the other hand, seem to replace strings of shell money when made in ceremonial payments. Neither tobacco nor money have yet gained any importance in the large affinal exchanges when thousands of dogs' teeth change hands on one occasion. Money smaller than a shilling the natives have no use for. The tiny sixpences slip too easily through their fingers. But the native contempt for small change leads to their paying higher prices than would otherwise be necessary. Articles priced at 1/6 to a white man are sold to a native for a flat 2/. Money is obtained through the sale of thatch and sago to traders, through occasional sales of tortoise shell and pearl shell used in button manufacture. Returned work boys also sometimes bring money as well as goods with them. This is partly expended in trade with the distant stores —all five or six hours away by canoe—and partly saved for the tax—ten shillings for each able-bodied man, except officials who are exempted from the tax. Contrary to the attitude present in many native communities, the Manus do not resent the tax, but boast of the amount of taxes which they pay each year, pointing to their tax record as successful business men may do among ourselves as a sign of wealth and prosperity. To a group as wealthy as the Manus the tax is not a hardship; they reap a full return in the freedom from war which the presence of the government ensures them. Upon the poorer Usiai the tax sometimes falls more heavily and many of them have to work it out as a sort of corvée labour.

The two most important ways in which their material culture has been altered by white contact has been through the introduction of steel and cloth. Knives, adzes shod with iron, augers, saws, have completely replaced the older, clumsier tools of stone, shell, and obsidian. This has been accomplished without injuring any basic industry. Houses and canoes are still built in the old styles. The delicate art of making tortoise shell filigree, worn on a round shell disk, has practically vanished. The introduction of knives has not encouraged the finer carving; the large bowls which were one of the most distinguishing marks of Admiralty art are no longer made, and most of the smaller bowls are made less skilfully. Although a few agate and enamel dishes have crept into the villages, these have not to any extent displaced the large black earthenware pots used to hold oil and water, nor the shallow pots used for cooking. The formal use of pots in the marriage exchanges is probably a strong factor in encouraging their continued manufacture. Bark cloth has practically disappeared among the Manus, although the land people, richer in bark and poorer in purse, still retain it for daily and ceremonial use. The bark cloth was always of a poor quality, breadfruit bark beaten out on the severed bit of log. It withstood the water badly and cloth was therefore the more welcome to the sea-dwelling people. So the man's G-string of bark cloth is now replaced either by a G-string of cloth or a full loin cloth, known in pidgin as a *laplap*. The women retain their curly grass skirts, but have substituted cloth cloaks for their old clumsy tabu garment, a rain mat, merely a stiff square mat, folded down the centre and sewed together on the narrow edge, forming a sort of stiff peaked head and back covering. (These are still used as rain capes, which has mercifully prevented the introductions of umbrellas to distort the appearance of native ceremonies.) The calico cloak is simply two lengths of cloth, sewed together along the edge, and tied in a bunch at one end so as to fit the woman's head. The sewing is of the crudest sort and the material is usually not hemmed. A few immersions in the water turn the vivid reds and purples into drab dull colours, so that it is only on feast days that foreign colours relieve the brown monotony of the village scene. Blankets, of which each house has one or two, are also used by women as tabu robes.

Mirrors, knives, forks, and steel combs have drifted into the village and been seized upon as part of the bridal costume. They are never used, but they are stuck in the bride's armbands, or held in her arms on ceremonial occasions. Camphorwood boxes have been a boon to a people as interested in the care of property as the Manus are; now on many a naked breast dangles, suspended from the beaded headbands of the dead, a bunch of heavy iron keys. The locks are made so that it is necessary to give the key several revolutions and each revolution plays a little tune which betrays a thief. Boxes and axes are part of the conventional goods which returned work boys bring back to the village. Some boys also bring lanterns, soon hung up and disused for lack of kerosene—although usually one house in the village will have some kerosene—or flash lights which lie about unused after the first battery has burned out. Broken watches are sometimes flourished as ornament.

Perhaps the greatest real change, one which is more than the mere substitution of metal for stone, or cloth for bark cloth, has been brought about by the introduction of beads. The Manus possessed a tradition of tying their shell money disks together with a fine cord manufactured from bark. In this way whole aprons of shell money were made, and the edges of armbands and anklets were ornamented with shell money and red and black seeds. Trade beads found a technique ready for them, and among the Manus, to a less extent among other peoples of the Admiralties who had already absorbing handicrafts of their own, beadwork has been taken up with great enthusiasm. All the old decorative positions once held by the shell money and seeds have been taken over by beads, and many new ornaments devised. The hair of the dead is sewed into the back of a flat beaded bag, worn suspended from the shoulder of the widow. The widow's mourning hat, the bark cloth worn by the dead, armlets for holding the breastbone flaps which are also beaded, all come in for elaborate decoration. The patterns are geometric, nonsymbolic, and either directly derived from European patterns imported by traders or taken from textiles. While new, they make slight claim to any artistic distinction; after the salt water has faded and mellowed the colours, they are quite attractive and lend a very festive appearance to a village gathering. The use of beads has centred about the elaboration of the mourning costume, the ornamentation of the bride, and incidentally the groom, and the complication of the currency system. Bead belts, which are simply a number of strands of beads joined together at intervals with beads of another colour, have become a regular item in the exchanges between affinal relatives. They are a minor item, not commanding a return in pigs and oil, as do dogs' teeth and shell money, but commanding only raw sago or cooked food. This new feature of the affinal system illustrates neatly the indirect influence of foreign trade upon Manus internal economics. The Manus buy beads and make new belts which are given away in the affinal exchanges, swelling the amount which the man's side proudly contributes. To meet these bead belts, more sago must be manufactured. This extra sago is bought up by a trader who comes through the district every month or so. With part of the money which they receive for the sago, the Manus buy more beads, which are worked into belts, introduced into the exchange system, and still further increase the supply of sago worked. So without actually altering the standard of living, these trade conditions do alter the size and splendour of the display which any family can make at a ceremony.

During the German administration, dogs' teeth from China and Turkey were introduced in great quantities, inflating the currency possibly eight hundred or nine hundred percent. To some extent, this inflation resulted in increased prices for commodities; in other cases the old price was retained in the affinal exchanges which results in disparities between the two contracting parties; in others it has merely increased the amount of wealth which changes hands. Where a man once paid one thousand dogs' teeth to his son's wife's father, now he can pay ten thousand. The greater number of boys working for white men and the consequently greater amount of money with which to purchase pigs from the white man, has of course also raised the number of pigs in the community so that the women's side can meet these large payments of dogs' teeth.

Where the white culture has made a really important alteration in the native mode of life is in the prohibition of war and war-captives. This abolition of the customary interests of the young unmarried men in a society which permitted no love making for its young

girls or its married women, might have had serious consequences had not the abolition of war coincided with
the growth of recruiting. The young men are taken
out of the village during these years when the community has no way of dealing with them. They become an economic asset instead of a military one of
doubtful value. In some native societies where there
are rare treasures of magic lore and esoteric knowledge
to be handed down from the elders to the young men,
this removal of all the young men from the village is
a serious matter. The young men come back after their
fathers are dead and find themselves forever cheated
of their birthright. Although the matter was not investigated extensively, there seems reason to believe
that this is the case among the agricultural and more
magically dependent Usiai, of the Great Admiralty.
An agricultural people also sometimes suffers through
the diminution in the store of seeds while the young
men are away instead of at home working their gardens.
Also all communities which rely upon an early induction of their young boys into the ceremonial and industrial life of the group, suffer when the boys are suddenly reft away from their normal educational routine.
When this disturbance of the customary education pattern is coincident with missionary attempts to disrupt the
native culture, the two factors work together to produce
social disorganisation and maladjustment. Fortunately
in Manus among the Manus sea peoples none of these
lamentable results follow the present system of recruiting. By the time the boys go away to work they have
received all the training which the community ever gave
boys before; marriage, except upon matters of war and

prostitution, now erased from the social scene. They would only menace the existing moral and economic arrangements if they remained at home. As magical material which requires long and patient application to memorise is not part of the Manus system, Manus boys do not lose a magical inheritance and with it their power of agricultural or economic or social success as do boys who come from societies depending upon charm and ritual. The Manus boys return to their villages rich, and therefore in a position to command far more respect from their elders than if they remained at home. They begin paying off one of their debts at once, the debt which they owe to those who have made funeral payments for their fathers or other close relatives. Although the debt of marriage will hang about their necks for many years, nevertheless the present system by which a work boy's accumulated earnings are appropriated to a big initial payment to his creditors, is thoroughly in keeping with the Manus financial system. It also brings desirable foreign goods, such as new tools and cloth which have become a necessity, into the village.

If Oriental labour should ever be imported into the Mandated Territory with its probable displacement of the far less efficient Melanesian labour, so that Manus boys remained in the villages from puberty until marriage, some readjustment of native custom would be necessary. The present insistence upon absolute chastity for Manus women could not exist side by side with a government prohibition of prostitution and the present custom of late marriage. The re-introduction, even surreptitiously, of prostitution is improbable because

Manus respect for the virtue of their own women demands that the prostitute be a war captive, and war cannot be pursued without coming immediately to the attention of government. The alternatives will be either a marked lowering of the marriage age for both men and women, but especially for men, or the modification of the present exacting system of morals. The neighbouring Usiai, with whom the war prostitute was a less frequent phenomenon, solved the problem by a method of carefully supervised license in which young people were given a year of freedom with the mate or mates of their choice in a large house for both sexes which was maintained by some rich headman for his own daughter and others of her age group. There was always chaperonage in the house to see that no outrages were committed against the unwilling, and that behaviour was at all times decorous. This year also served as a sort of training school in manners and social attitudes. At the end of the year, the girls returned to their villages to marry older men who had finally completed the payments for them, and the young men married the widows of their deceased elder male relatives. Licensed freedom before marriage, combined with early marriages in which one partner was so much the senior as to play the leading rôle in matters requiring experience and wisdom, was the Usiai solution. It was a completely dignified and serious solution, well integrated in their whole pattern of social relationships. It is at present unfortunately interdicted. Representations of immorality made by the missionaries to government were responsible for its suspension at the same time that the Manus prostitution house, most unfortunately called by the same name, "house bomak," was forbidden.

The greatest effect which white culture has had upon the lives of the Manus people has been, as we have seen, in the realm of economic life. Religiously white culture has not yet touched the Manus people importantly except in the case of the natives of Papitalai and the very recent introduction of services by a catechist in Mbunei. Papitalai is on the North Coast, too far away to have any influence in the villages of the South Coast; the beginnings of mission work in Mbunei by a native catechist occurred while we were in Peri. A few boys have returned from work, nominal adherents of some religious faith, but too unversed in its ways to teach it to their people. A few scattered phrases, as "Jesus he like cook 'em you fellow," "Jesus will burn you" (in the flames of Hell)—give the natives a peculiar notion of what Christianity means. They know the two great missions in the north of the Territory, Roman Catholic (*Lotu Popi*) and the Methodist, *Tala-talas,* and have made definite choice between them upon two reported attitudes of the missions. For the *Tala-talas* they have no use, because they put a strong emphasis upon tithes and expose sinful church members to public censure and confession of faults. But the coming of the *Lotu Popi* they anticipate with approval because they exact no tithes. The Roman Catholics, having realised the magnitude of the task of converting the hundred diverse peoples of New Guinea, have settled down to a task which will last through several generations and established large and prosperous plantations, the Sacred Heart of Jesus, Ltd., etc., to sup-

port the brothers and sisters while they do their mission
work. Also they have heard of the auricular confession practised by Roman Catholics and think this will
afford them welcome relief from the present custom
by which every one's sins are proclaimed loudly to his
neighbours. They also believe that with the coming of
the Mission they will learn to read and write. The
Roman Catholic mission has purchased an island in Peri
so that it is reasonable to expect that the natives will
ultimately have the Mission among them which gossip
has made them believe to be the most desirable.

A few reflections of Christian contact also occur here
and there, as in the belief in the island of Mbuke that
the white man worships the sun because he always looks
up when he prays. But aside from such distortions of
accidental observations their religious life remains untouched except by the occasional comforting thought
that eventually when they have embraced the new faith,
they will be able to pitch their capricious spirits into
the sea. In the meantime the sway of the spirits is un-
disturbed.

The government regulation against keeping the
corpse for twenty days while it was washed daily in
the sea, has been enforced with very little difficulty because of the feuds between individuals and villages
which lead to any derelictions being reported. The
time for keeping the corpse has been shortened to three
days; the old requirement of killing a man to end
mourning, or at least taking a prisoner and using his
ransom in the funeral payments, has been abridged to
the requirement of killing a large turtle. The bodies
are exposed on the more remote little islands until the

bones have been washed clean, when the skull and certain other bones are recovered and installed in the ceremonial skull bowl. Mourning custom and economic arrangements have been somewhat rearranged, but in the old pattern, to meet these conditions.

To summarise, Manus contact with the white man has to date been a fairly fortunate one. War, headhunting, and prostitution have been eliminated. Recruiting has prevented these prohibitions creating new social problems, the recruiting period and its rewards have been fitted into the social economic scheme; trade with the white man has provided the natives with beads which have developed a new decorative art and furnished new incentives to the production of foodstuffs; the peaceful régime has produced more favourable conditions for inter-tribal trading. The Manus at the present time are a peaceful, industrious people, coping admirably with their environment, suffering only slightly from preventable diseases. Their ethical system is so combined with their supernatural beliefs as to receive great force and intensity from them. They are not taking any measures to reduce their numbers, being apparently ignorant of medicinal abortifacients (as they are ignorant of most herbal properties owing to their water life), and seldom resorting to mechanical methods. From the standpoint of government they are making a most satisfactory adjustment to the few demands which white contact makes upon them. (This is quite aside from the type of personality which is developed by their methods of education and their attitudes towards family life and marriage. These are subtler points which government will have no time to deal with.)

IV

OBSERVANCES CONNECTED WITH PREGNANCY, BIRTH, AND CARE OF INFANTS

IT is characteristic of Manus society where all the important ritual is cast in economic terms, that, although pregnancy, birth, puberty, etc., are marked by such conspicuous festivities, the individuals concerned are subject to very slight tabus. The kind of pre-natal tabu which depends upon imitative magic for its inspiration and forbids a woman to eat a paired banana for fear she will have twins, etc., is limited in Manus to the prohibition that a pregnant woman must not cut fish or wood with a knife or an axe for fear she will cut off one of the limbs of the child. All other malformations, blindness, deafness, club feet, etc., they attribute to the father's or mother's carelessly breaking one of the property-protecting tabus. These latter tabus are called *sorosol*. The owner of a tree will himself put a *sorosol* upon it if he owns one, if not he will pay some one else to do it. The *sorosol* carries a magically enforced penalty for transgression which takes various forms. A number of *sorosol* carry the penalty of causing a miscarriage or a stillbirth. Stillbirths are also sometimes attributed to the malevolent action of spirits of the dead. If a mother dies during childbirth and the infant dies soon after, the mother will be said to have "taken the child."

The nature of physical paternity is understood; the

child is believed to be a combination of semen and menstrual blood. The men believe that they cause menstruation in their wives and then, by making their wives conceive, cause the blood to clot. There is some obscure belief among the women that their fertility is dependent upon the spirits of their husband's houses. If the spirits wish descendants they will declare that the women shall become pregnant. They exercise this power in the same way that spirits control the supply of fish, that is, by working in co-operation with natural forces. A man expects only that his guardian spirit should drive the already existent fish into the near-by lagoon. Similarly, he believes vaguely that the spirits can facilitate the matter of conception, but he does not think the spirits could make an unmarried girl pregnant without the intermediary of intercourse. Intercourse is not forbidden during menstruation nor during pregnancy. It is forbidden for thirty days after birth, but as the wife is not allowed to even see her husband during this period, this prohibition follows naturally.

Women count ten moons to pregnancy, counting from the last menstruation. They keep little bundles of sticks as counters. The date is kept in mind by every one concerned because of the large economic preparations which have to be made. A few days before the expected birth, the "brother" of the woman divines or has divined the proper place for the delivery. In this case the "brother" is the male relative who is taking the financial responsibility for the economic exchanges with the husband. He may actually be the woman's father or cousin or uncle, etc. As every individual has to plan all his economic activities so that they dovetail, so that he gives sago and pots to-day and receives bead-work to-morrow, it does not always suit the same rel-ative to handle the exchanges surrounding a birth. Some women have had their feasts made by different relatives for each of four or five children; in other cases, two men will alternate the responsibility. The divination for the place of birth decides whether the husband shall move out of his abode and let his brother-in-law and his wife and family move in, or whether the pregnant woman shall be taken to the brother's house. This is supposed to depend upon the will of the spirits, actually it often conforms to the exigencies of the brother's immediate plans.

Only women who have borne children are present at the delivery. Men, young girls and children are ex-cluded. The feeling against the presence of a woman who has not had a child is so strong that I was unable to break it down. To fly in the face of such feeling would have prejudiced my work severely, so I did not see a birth in Manus and the following information comes from informants.

The woman is said to squat and support herself by a bamboo rope which is suspended from the ceiling. The cord is cut with a piece of bamboo. The cord is considered to be good and the afterbirth a bad and un-lucky object. The cord, *katchaumbotoi*, is cut into small pieces; one piece is wrapped, together with the afterbirth, *mbut*, in a small pandanus mat. The rest of the cord is smoked and preserved for good luck. No customs of disposal of the cord in order to influ-ence the future of the child were discovered. The mother is placed in a small log framed square on the

[322]

floor, with mats under her, a mat hung up to screen her from the rest of the house, and a fire right beside her. This is her personal fire and she has also personal cooking vessels in which only her food can be cooked. The little mat containing the afterbirth and bit of cord is stuck up on the wall back of her. Afterwards it is thrown away.

The child is washed and tended by the older women of both the mother's and father's kin. The mother is fed a mixture called *bulokol*, made of coconut milk and taro. The child is not fed until twenty or twenty-four hours after birth, when it is given milk by other nursing mothers and a bit of taro which its own mother has chewed fine. The mother doesn't suckle the baby herself until three or four days after birth. The other women suckle it in turn and are all rewarded for this service afterwards. If the mother is ill and cannot entirely nurse her baby for some time, then she is expected to return milk to these wet nurses' babies if she gets her health back.

Barrenness is believed to be accomplished by resort to the supernatural cursing power of a father's sister or a father's sister's daughter. This power to make the line of one's brother, or one's mother's brother, fail is essentially a curse, but a husband and wife who wish no more children may invoke it as a blessing. This paternal relative also ceremonially blesses the new mother and decrees that she shall have no more children until this one is old enough to walk and swim. A barren woman is called a *pilalokes*; the Manus group together women who have never had children and women who have not had any children for many years.

Such women are said to be *fastened up*. The menopause is described by a word which means "she can do nothing more." A married woman is said to be "finished." She will not grow any more.

Miscarriages, *ndranirol*, are treated as real births; the child is named and all the economic ceremonies are gone through. The women distinguish the time when they first feel life: "It has become a human being. Its soul is there."

Twins occur occasionally. They have never heard of triplets, and one woman on being told of one of our freak births of five, gasped out in the little pidgin which she knew (Manus was inadequate to the occasion): "Oh, you number One."

Children are fed taro from the beginning. The absense of coconuts in any great plenty is a serious handicap to feeding children. Sugar cane is also not plentiful. Papayas are regarded as good when they can be obtained, but taro is the mainstay. Sago is too heavy and fish is regarded as indigestible until a child is about three. They are given cigarettes and the outer skin of the betel nut from the time they are two and a half or three. A child is seldom weaned before this age unless the mother is pregnant again. If the second child dies, the older one often resumes suckling. Mothers, in order to wean their children, tie bundles of human hair to their breasts.

The death rate among little babies is enormous. Genealogies are at best an unreliable method, especially where the mother tends not to distinguish between miscarriages, stillbirths, and death a few days after birth. But in many cases the assertion that the child died before the thirty day feast was made is probably correct. This feast involves the return of the wife to her husband, or his return to her, and is a sufficiently marked and invariable event to afford some basis for dating. I give a sample of the births reported by the women in one end of Peri, whose reports I was able to re-check with other informants.

The genealogical evidence suggests that the highest mortality is within the first few months after birth, and between thirty and forty years of age. In both cases there is a high differential death rate for males. Among adults this can be accounted for by the greater exposure which the men have to undergo in all-night fishing and at sea. A certain number of the early deaths in the older genealogies were due to war.

Malarial fever is a constant drain upon the natives' health. In some cases this develops into cerebral malaria with resulting death; in other cases pneumonia sets in. The Manus have no conception of medicine. All curing is in supernatural terms, either by placating the spirits or by the recitation of set charms, usually by the person whose charm is believed responsible for the illness. Broken bones are treated by keeping the injured member in a natural position and by the application of heat. Heat is also applied to cuts, bruises, etc., and to girls at first menstruation and women after delivery.

I believe the high death rate among young children can be laid especially to insufficient and unwise feeding (the mother's milk is depleted after years of nursing older children), no sunlight, and no protection against changes of temperature. The houses with slat floors admit continual draughts, and a drop of a degree in temperature sets the whole community shivering. They have no adequate clothing for a change of weather. Little babies are also subject to bad sores. On the other hand, the children who survive the first year of life, seem to be fairly strong. There is relatively little illness among the children's group, with the exception of attacks of malaria and occasional tropical ulcers. The high infant death rate and the numerous deaths in middle life all serve to focus the attention of the anxiety-ridden Manus upon their sins. Each slight illness means confession and propitiatory payments, and hardly a night passes that the medium's whistle is not heard in some house where there is illness. Malaria is particularly well suited to stimulating recurrent anxiety over small sins; amends are made and the patient usually recovers, proving that the spirits' wrath is appeased.

V

DIAGRAM OF THE VILLAGE SHOWING HOUSE OWNERSHIP, CLAN MEMBERSHIP, RESIDENCE

Village Plan of Peri

6 7

13 14 15 16 17

4 5 8 9 10 11 12 18 19 20 21 22 23 24 25 26 27 28 29 30 31

32 33 34 35

42

40 41 39 38 37 36

43

1 2

3 A

B

C

House No.	House Owner	Clan	Head of Subsidiary Household	Clan	Relationship to House Owner
1.	Pomalat	M			
2.	Topas	M	Polau	M	Parallel cousin paternal line
3.	Pokanau	Po.			
4.	Luwil	M	Seot	P	Half brother by Peri father
5.	Tchaumutchin	M			
6.	Dropal	Po.			
7.	Ngandiliu	Lo.	Drauga	Pat.	Husband of wife's sib paternal aunt?
8.	Deserted				
9.	Maku	Pat.			
10.	Kampwen	Po.			
11.	Ngapo	Kt.			
12.	Selan	Po.			
13.	Ngamoto	Kt.	Pongi	Pat.	Husband of widow's daughter
14.	Pope	M	Nganidrai	Po.	Daughter's husband
15.	Pomele	Lo.			
16.	Kalowin	Po.			

House No.	House Owner	Clan	Head of Subsidiary Household	Clan	Relationship to House Owner
17.	Poiyo	M			
18.	Tunu	P			
19.	Bosai	M			
20.	Pomat	M			
21.	Pwisio	P			
22.	Paleao	P			
23.	Ngapotchalon (widow)	Kt.			
24.	Nane	Lo.			
25.	Banyalo	P.			
26.	Pondramet	M	Pomo	M	Daughter's husband
27.	Ndrosal	P	Sisi	Loitcha	Niece's husband
28.	Pokanas	Lp	Malean	Kp.	Adopted son. Member of an extinct sib
29.	Kea	Km.			
30.	Talikawa	P	Kala	Km	Distant maternal relative
31.	*House boy*				
32.	Tchanan	Kt.			
33.	Ngapolyon (widow)	Km.	Kaloi	Kt.	Son of widow

House No.	House Owner	Clan	Head of Subsidiary Household	Clan	Relationship to House Owner
34.	Kaiar play house				
35.	Sanau	Kt			
36.	Tuain	Ko.			
37.	Poli	Lp.			
38.	Ngamasue	Ko.			
39.	Ndrantche (widow)	Lo.			
40.	Kemai	Lo.	Polin	Rambutchon	Adopted son
41.	Talikai	P			
42.	Koroton	P	Tcholai	P	Son
43.	Ngamel	P			

A. Pontchal Islet—Barrack
Our Residence from two months

B. Peri Islet—our house
C. Peri Islet—No. 2

Abbreviations used for Clan names

M. Matchupal
P Peri
Po Pontchal
Lo Lo (offshoot of the sib of Tchalalo which had moved out
Ko Kalo   Lp Lopwer
Kt Kalat   Km Kamatachau   Patusi
Kp Kapet
Member of village of Patusi

[330]

Comment

In the residences of the younger men there is a distinct cleavage between the rich successful lines whose young men live with the father or adopted father or elder brother, and the members of the poorer families who live where they can. Among the poor or the irregularly married (e.g., Sisi, House 27, who had stolen his wife from another man and not yet paid for her properly. He had fallen out with his older brother over this match and so had no house to go to in his own village of Loitcha), there is often a tendency towards matrilocal residence, a system which makes the man's position very difficult as the mother-in-law tabu can never be obviated. In discussing the marriage system I have adhered to the conditions which are regarded as usual, for in these irregular and poorly financed marriages so many different factors enter in to complicate the picture.

VI

NEITHER boys nor girls can tell the exact clan affiliations of the owners of each house. They all recognize the houses of Kalat because they stand off by themselves and Kalat is used as a definite place name. Pontchal is also known to them, used to designate the part of the village where the houses of the members of the clan of Pontchal and Matchupal stand. Pontchal has been made an administrative unit by the government, with its own officials, and it is in this light that the children see it. They do not know who owns houses, nor do they know the clan affiliations of women. They do not know the guardian spirits of other houses than their own and sometimes, if their own houses have several guardians, they do not know their names.

The preceding map shows the village as a mature man or woman is able to describe it. It is impossible to show what rôle self-interest or attention plays in an adult's view of the village because the adult will report many things in which he is not interested. He views the clan locations and memberships in his village in much the same formal fashion as we think of states and their capitals.

Views of the Village *

Table showing the village of Peri as it appeared to Kawa, aged five (House 12); the way these same houses appeared to Ngasu, aged eleven (House 22), and some accompanying notes upon the households in question.

* The records of girls are given in both cases. It will be understood that boys give little of this type of comment; spending less time with the women they know less of what is going on.

House Number	Kawa's View. Kawa is the daughter of Selan, a member of the clan of Pontchal.	Comment	Way in which Ngasu, a girl aged eleven, sees the same part of the village. She is the daughter of Panau, who is dead. She and her sister, Salikon, have been adopted by Paleao, Panau's adopted father's adopted son. (See Chapters II and VI.)
4.	1. Father's sister lives here

2. Piwen lives here | 1. Refers to Molung, wife of Luwil. Molung was adopted by Ngandiliu, Kawa's father's older brother. She is really the daughter of Kali, an uncle who financed Ngandiliu's marriage. Selan, Kawa's father, calls her "sister," and Kawa calls her *patieien*, "father's sister."

2. Piwen is a small girl of three, Molung's adopted daughter. Molung's son Kalowin of nine Kawa doesn't mention. | House of Paleao's brother Luwil. Luwil's part of the house is in front. Kalowin and Piwen live there. Saot lives in back. "The wife of Luwil" and "the wife of Saot" run away from Paleau. They are his tabu relatives. |

| 3. Pwendrile lives here, I think | 3. Pwendrile is a baby boy of two, the son of Saot, Luwil's younger half brother, who lives with his wife in the back of House 4. Pwendrile is being adopted by Pokanas and his wife, Nyambula, who is the clan sister of Saot's father's first wife. Pwendrile spends much of his time with Nyambula, who will take him for good as soon as he is weaned. She cannot take him sooner, because she is a barren woman, not a recently bereaved mother who could suckle him at her own breast. Pwendrile is Saot's only child and he is very devoted to him, but Nyambula and Pokanas have helped to finance his marriage. They are rich and can early begin payments for Pwendrile's future wife. |

House Number	Kawa's View	Comment	Way in which Ngasu, a girl aged eleven, sees the same part of the village. (Cont.)
5.	1. Itong lives here 2. Ngaleap used to live here 3. Mutchin broke his wife's arm	1. Itong is a little girl of five. 2. Ngaleap is the daughter of the son of a clan brother of the father of Mutchin's adopted mother. When her father and mother died, he adopted her and she lived in his house. She was a jolly girl, much liked by the younger children. After she got into a scandal, however, another uncle took her to live with him, believing that Mutchin was too mild a mentor. 3. Mutchin broke his wife's arm because of a quarrel over a bowl of food which she wanted to send to a birth feast of her brother's wife, and he wanted to contribute to a feast for laying the house piles for a boy house for his half brother's	"Grandfather's" house. He's Paleao's brother. Yesa, Kapamalae, Pindropal, Itong, and Songan live there. Ngaleap broke her knee open swinging and Sain tells Popoli (Paleao's adopted son) that he will break his too if he never goes to bed.

The doctor boy of Pontchal lives there. His wife has a baby and Paleao made the feast for the birth. (See Chapter VII.)

adopted clan's young boys. He carried his point but the next day she failed to go and collect the dish in which the food was sent. She replied to him with unaccustomed venom when he told her that the bowl was being taken home as her own by the woman next door, so he broke her arm.

4. Pindropal is a little girl of seven, Mutchin's daughter.

(There are also in this house three boys, aged three, ten, and twelve, whom Kawa doesn't mention.)

4. Pindropal lives here

Knows nothing about this house

1.

House Number	Kawa's View	Comment	Way in which Ngasu, a girl aged eleven, sees the same part of the village. (Cont.)
3.	1. House to which mother ran away when father was cross at her because she had no tobacco	1. Selan's wife has no close relatives in Peri as she comes from the island of Taui. Pokanau, house owner of House 2, is a far distant cousin and in his house, Mateun, the wife of Selan and mother of Kawa, took refuge.	3. This is the house of the Kukerai of Pontchal. He and Paleao always fight.
	2. Masa has only one eye. So has Sori	2. Masa is the four year old daughter of Pokanau. One eye is only scar tissue from a bad attack of conjunctivitis. Sori is Masa's baby brother; he also has one bad eye. Kawa does not mention Pomitchon, aged six, Pokanau's oldest son.	
	3. Bopau sleeps there, I think	3. Bopau is the son of Pokanau's dead older brother, Sori. No one takes much interest in him, so although the home of Pokanau is	

6.	No comment	nominally his home, he wanders about and is seldom seen there. Bopau has a quiet reserved nature and Kawa likes him better than the noisy, self-assertive Pomitchon.	
7.	1. Grandfather's house	1. This is the house of Ngandiliu, Selan's older brother, whom he calls "father," and Kawa calls "grandfather." In the back of Ngandiliu's house lives his wife's maternal aunt and her aged husband. Kawa doesn't mention them.	1. House of "father's sister," Grandma lives there. (This is the wife of Ngandiliu, who is Paleao's sib sister and Komatel, the wife of Potik and foster mother of Paleao and Ngasu's own father, Panau.)
	2. Topal lives there	2. Topal, a little boy of seven, is really Kawa's own brother, who was adopted by the childless Ngandiliu at birth.	
8.	No one lives there	This house was abandoned after the death of its owner. His wife ran away and married again without	No one lives there. Sakaton's wife ran away.

House Number	Kawa's View	Comment	Way in which Ngasu, a girl aged eleven, sees the same part of the village. (Cont.)
		completing her mourning. All the relatives were distant ones; the house was old and falling to bits. Poiyo took refuge there for a while when the quarrels between his two wives made it impossible for him to keep them in one house. He was too poor to build a new house for his second wife.	
9.	1. Alupwa lives here	This is the house of old Maku who has had five wives and no children. His first four wives are all dead. His fifth wife, Melen, was married twice before. To her first husband she bore no children. She ran away from him and married Talikake of Matchupal, to whom she bore six daughters.	House where Poiyo's cross-wife lives. Alupwa lives there but she is always going away to visit in Mbunei.

One is married in Mbunei and has had six children; the two girls are dead and four boys living. One is married in Patusi and has borne two girls, one is living. Two of Melen's daughters died of the flu (from the spirits of the foreigners) and two live with her. Of these, the eldest, Kompon, is the heroine of two illicit affairs, had one illegitimate child by Selan, Kawa's father. This was before Selan was married. He fled to the north of the Admiralties after confessing his sin to Paleao. When Kompon's pregnancy became obvious, they dressed her as a bride and took her to the house of Ngandiliu, Selan's older brother, with whom he lived. Ngandiliu, advised of their coming, fled to the bush, first barring the house door.

House Number	Kawa's View	Comment	Way in which Ngasu, a girl aged eleven, sees the same part of the village. (Cont.)
		The baby was born and died soon after. Then Kompon got into an affair with Poiyo, who was already married, with several children. He married her under pressure, their child is Topal, who lives part of the time here with his mother, oftener with his father, although his father's other wife does not treat him well. Kompon has two other children, Kilipak, aged three, and a baby girl. She and Poiyo have quarreled so that she has left the deserted house of Sakaton (House 8) where they were living and moved back into the house of her mother's third husband, Maku. Her younger sister Lompan is	

disordered mentally, afraid of men, has never married.

1. Alupwa, of whom Kawa speaks, is a little girl of ten, the daughter of Melen's dead brother's dead son.

This is the house of Kampwen and his wife Ngaten. Kampwen had in his youth married Sasa of Patusi, who bore him four girls, all of whom died as infants, and then died herself. He then married Aluan of Mok, who died childless. Then he married Ngaten, who had been previously married to Talikotchi of Patusi. To him she had borne two children, a boy and girl, both of whom died as infants. She left him and married Kampwen, so she was his third wife, he her second husband. To Kampwen she bore

House where Kandra lives. Kandra is a "dumb" girl.

1. Kandra lives there. She is a bad girl

10.

House Number	Kawa's View	Comment	Way in which Ngasu, a girl aged eleven, sees the same part of the village. (Cont.)
	2. Manuai lives there	first a son who died as an infant. The death of this child she attributed, like the death of her two children by her first marriage, to the evil charms of her grandfather, who had never forgiven her for robbing his fish traps as a girl. (2) Then she bore Kampwen a son, Manuai, who was still living, a sickly child of three. 1. Kandra, the younger daughter of Poiyo's first wife by Pampai, the dead brother of Kampwen, has been adopted by Kampwen. She is a peevish, ill-tempered child, the butt of much teasing because she greets it with great fury. Her father died when she was about five. She does not like Kampwen,	

bullies and intimidates Ngaten with tantrums, and divides her time between the house of Kampwen and the home of her mother. Her marriage has already been arranged with a Patusi boy.

In this house there also lives an old woman named Kamwet, who has been married three times, to a Mantankor man in Lombrum, to whom she bore one daughter, who is dead; then to a Manus man in Papitalai to whom she bore no children, then to a brother of the second husband of the mother of Ngaten, the wife of Kampwen. With her she brought her sister's daughter Iamet, who is married to one of the chief men of the village, Talikai, but refuses to live in the house with his other wife. Talikai has sworn not to yield and

House Number	Kawa's View	Comment	Way in which Ngasu, a girl aged eleven, sees the same part of the village. (Cont.)
		build her another house, so she sulks and divides her time between this house, where her mother's sister, Kamwet, lives, and the house of her own mother, where her son lives with his grandmother.	
12.	My house. Father and Mother and Kiap live there. Mother is pregnant.	Selan is married to Mateun of Taui. Her mother belonged to the island of Mbuke so she has no close relatives in Peri and stays much to herself. In times of trouble she takes refuge in the house of Pokanau on the attenuated plea that Pokanau is *lom pen* (child through the distaff line) to some people in Patusi who are *lom pen* to Taui and whom she calls *polepol*, cross cousin. Selan had not married	Kawa lives there. Her mother is pregnant. Her father had a fight with the Luluai. Father heard the Luluai talking a charm before it was light.

anyone else but he had committed two sex offences, one with Kompon, the wife of Poiyo, and one with Main, the five times widowed sinner of the sib of Tchalalo. In Selan's own background his mother, Pwoke of Patusi, had married Popot of Taui, who was called lapan and had some special privileges, such as wearing dogs' teeth diagonally across the breast. Pwoke bore eight children, three sons who are still living, and five daughters all of whom are dead. Three died after marriage, one bore a male child which lived, one died pregnant, and one bore a male child which died. The oldest brother stayed in Taui. But when Popot died, Pwoke returned to Patusi with the two other sons, Ngandiliu and Selan, and mar-

House Number	Kawa's View	Comment	*Way in which Ngasu, a girl aged eleven, sees the same part of the village.* (Cont.)
		ried Kali of Tchalalo. To him she bore Molung (House 4). Kali financed Ngandiliu, who later adopted and financed his young half sister Molung. Selan was adopted by Tchokal of Tchalalo, who was no relation to him. Selan's guardian spirit is Topal, a foster brother who was also adopted by Tchokal. Now Selan acts as a medium with Topal as his control. Tchokal also left Selan the right to work his sago lands. But when Tchokal died, the financing of Selan's marriage was arranged by Ngandiliu, to whom he gave his oldest son, Topal. Next after Topal comes Kawa, oldest child in the household. Then	

House of "Father's" younger brother Tunu. Tunu is the brother of Luwil, too. The "wife of Tunu" is dying. The Usiai said she got a snake in her

there was a baby girl Ipwen, who choked to death as a small child. It is believed she was strangled by the spirit of a Taui man. (Selan's father and Mateun's mother both belong to Taui. This is the mother's version of the death. It is most frequent for the deaths of children to be attributed to the malice of the father's spirits, if the mother is talking.) Kiap, the baby, is about three and Mateun is expecting a baby in a few weeks. This is the house of Tunu, the son of Komatol and Potik and his wife Alupwa. They are the parents of Piwen (House 4), who was adopted by Luwil, Tunu's younger brother, whose wife, Molung, has just lost a child and could suckle Alupwa's child when she was too ill to do it herself. Alupwa has just borne a

House where Alupwa is going to die. Then there will be some tobacco.

18.

House Number	Kawa's View	Comment	Way in which Ngasu, a girl aged eleven, sees the same part of the village. (Cont.)
		child which is being cared for by her husband's mother who lives in the back of Ngandiliu's house. Alupwa is very ill from an infection following birth and all of her family's resources have been drained in an attempt to pay Usiai dreamers, Matankor practitioners and angered Manus spirits whom various mediums have designated. Alupwa has confessed every sin she ever committed including an accidental physical contact with Panau when a boat was upset. Panau has been dead two years. Pwasa, the nine-year-old sister of Alupwa, also lives here. She calls her older sister "mother," and her	belly from climbing a betel nut tree. Pwasa lives here. Pwasa went to sea with Talipotchalon and nearly drowned. They lost all their food. Pwasa cried.

No.	House	Description	Note
43.	House where Ponkob and Nauna live	old mother, Ndrantche, "grandmother." This is the house of Ngamel, an elder of Peri, who lives with his wife Ngatchumu. See Chapter II.	House where Ponkob and Nauna live. Nauna is going to marry Sapa who belongs to Kalo.
42.	House of the Luluai. He's fighting with father	The old blind Luluai of the village is making use of his superior magic and his blindness, which makes him immune from government imprisonment, to default on his debts. He and Selan have had a furious altercation over a pig, which Selan paid him, he ate, and never made the return payment for. The Luluai has threatened Selan with death and Selan has employed Pataliyan who has much strong magic to make him immune from the Luluai's magic.	House of the Luluai. He eats all his pigs and never pays his debts. He hasn't paid for Tcholai's marriage.

House Number	Kawa's View	Comment	Way in which Ngasu, a girl aged eleven, sees the same part of the village. (Cont.)
		With the Luluai lives his son Tcholai who was married early that his rapidly failing sight might see the match; Tcholai's wife who comes from Taui, and their two children, Salieyao of three and a baby boy. Tcholai goes about in much embarrassment because his father does not pay his debts and has not paid properly for Tcholai's wife. With the Luluai lives also Taliye, the daughter of the Luluai's dead wife, the sister of Main. Taliye is her father's guide wherever he goes. Her older sister, Ngakakes, has been adopted by Nyambula, the wife of Pokanas.	
40.	House of Po-	This is the house of Kemai and Isali. House of Pop-	

pitch. House of mourning

Popitch, the middle son of Nane, Kemai's father's father's brother's son's son, has died and the mourning is being conducted in the house of Nane's older "brother" whom he calls father. In all the seances surrounding Popitch's illness and death, Isali has been the medium, communicating with the spirit world through Tchaumilo who died because of Main's, Kemai's father's brother's daughter, intrigue with Selan, Kawa's father. In the house of Kemai lives Kisapwi, the daughter of Iamet by her third marriage. Kisapwi is fifteen, has been engaged and the negotiations broken off several times. Her father belonged to Tchalalo, the clan of Kemai, so Kemai has adopted her. Here also lives Lauwiyan, the daughter of

itch. The house of mourning. We went to sleep there and Isali held a seance and she said Tchaumilo said that father hit Popitch on the back of the neck with a hatchet. Then mother and Ngasu and I left. Isali said there was blood on our floor, but that wasn't Popitch's blood, it came from Nauna's foot when he cut it on a clam shell. Lauwiyan lives

House Number	Kawa's View	Comment	*Way in which Ngasu, a girl aged eleven, sees the same part of the village.* (Cont.)
		Kemai and Isali (see Chapter VIII) and Pomat (Chapter VI), the son of Isali's dead sister. Here also is Main, and Nane and his wife and their sons, Kutan, Posuman, Tchaumilo, and Mwe, who all moved in to mourn for Popitch, and here also lives Kalowin, the son of a Tchalalo mother. Before Popitch's death, Posuman, the son of Nane, had fallen ill and the spirits, speaking through Isali, had commanded Kalowin (who used to have mad fits when he used to go out to the reef and start building it up with stones after the fashion of the women who built up the little islets) to take Posuman back to Nane and	there. Noan made away with her. Now she has shaved her head. That's why Popitch died. Isali doesn't like Paleao. All the people who belong to Lo are no good.

go and live there himself with his wife, Tchomole, and their two small children, Selemon and Inong. Only old Kali, the father of Nane and Molung, the second husband of Selan's mother, was left in the house of Nane, where Popitch had died, where Nane's guardian spirit had betrayed the house in letting Popitch die, the house which was to be torn down and rebuilt near the old islet of Tchalalo, with Popitch as its guardian after his head had been dried and properly installed.

Many causes had been advanced for Popitch's death; one of them, that he had been struck down by Panau who was jealous of Nane because he was making his *metcha* (see Chapter III), was broached after his death by Isali in a seance

House Number	Kawa's View	Comment	Way in which Ngasu, a girl aged eleven, sees the same part of the village. (Cont.)
		in the house of mourning when she thought that the widow of Panau and Salikon and Ngasu were asleep.	

Ngasu's knowledge of houses of which Kawa knows nothing.

19. House of Bosai. This is our house, too. Bosai's wife comes from Mbuke.
20. House of the Tultul of Pontchal. He's not much. His wife is silly. Their baby (Pope) doesn't talk much. (See Chapter VI.)
21. House of Pwisio. He had a fight with his wife because Noan slept there and saw her with her grass skirt off.
13. Polam lives here. He is a funny boy who won't play with anyone. His mother is Talikai's other wife (see House 10). There is an old woman in that house who never goes out. (This is the mother of Iamet, the wife of Talikai.)
14. Tchokal lives here. He fights a lot and he is older than he looks. Noan lives here. He is a bad boy. He said he seduced Salikon (her sister) but he didn't. But he did seduce Lauwiyan. That's why she cut her hair.
15. Melin, Sain's sister, lives here. Her husband is called "Son of Lalinge."

(Lalinge is Paleao, Ngasu's adopted father.) Lalinge paid for Melin. Their house isn't strong. The floor might break through if too many people were there.

16. Kalowin lives here. He used to live in Nane's house, then he moved to Kemai's house after Popitch died, but this is his real house. Inong, his daughter, is going to marry Pokus. But she is too little to understand that yet.

17. Ponyarna, Poiyo's first wife, lives here. She fights with Kompon all the time. Kisapwi and Kandra are her children but Kandra lives in the house of Kampwen. Kandra is engaged to be married.

22. This is Paleao's house. This is where we live now. This was father's house before. Father's head is in the bowl up there. Popoli (Paleao's adopted son) is going to have his hair cut soon. Paleao has piles of cocoanuts piled up there in the back of the house for Salikon's *kekanbwot* (first menstruation) ceremony. This house has a strong floor. When the man from Mbunei died they moved the body in here because the floor of Melin's house isn't strong.

23. Sain's mother, Ngapotchalon, lives here. You mustn't say her name to Paleao. It's forbidden. She stays in the house all the time. Popoli is always going there crying for food. When Banyalo was sick he stayed because Popoli's guardian spirit said he should. Banyalo took his box there too. Paleao didn't want to build that house.

24. Nane's house. He's going to pull it down because Popitch died. He killed a turtle yesterday.

25. Paleao's brother's house. He has four children. He has a new baby. It's ?

nasty little house. They never play, they always ride about in their father's canoe.

26. Pondramet's house. His wife is very sick. Paleao says it's because she tried to tie a string around her belly. (Attempted abortion from which she died afterwards.)

27. Ndrosal's wife has sore eyes because Ndrosal threw lime in them because the baby cried. The baby always cries. Sisi and Pwondret live here. (See Chapters II and IX.) Paleao stole Pwondret for Sisi; Pwondret's husband had another wife, anyway.

28. This is Pokanas' house. Sometimes we live here. His wife knows a lot more than he does. She is a medium. She hasn't any children. Komatal is Pokanas' daughter. She is going to be married soon. She can't say Sain's name, because she is going to marry a boy in Kalat. Last week Pokanas beat Nyambula and she called Ndrosal, he's her brother, and he came and hit Pokanas' mother and then he and Pokanas wrestled and they both fell into the water. The Taui bride lives in the back of the house. She was cross to me because I peeked. She doesn't like me.

29. Kea's daughter Mentun is a thief. I only play with her sometimes. She picks up things from under people's houses. Kea's wife is crazy. She quarrels with everybody and thinks everybody is a liar.

30. Talikawa is the doctor boy of Peri. My father was the doctor boy of Peri. His new wife has just had a baby. He had two other wives but he chased them away. His little girl Molung has just come back from Mok.

31. This is the boys' house. We can go there if none of the youths are there.

When Sain's brother came back from Rabaul he brought piles of boxes and they danced all night.

32. This is Kalat. Sain belongs to Kalat. My brother (who is away at work) is going to marry the girl who has just menstruated. She is my sister-in-law. We can't say each other's names. Tamapwe lives here too. He is going to marry a girl in Pamatchau.

33. This house belongs to the widow of Polyon. When "the wife to be of my brother" had her menstruation feast, we all slept there every night and we took torches and sago around the village.

34. That little house is where all the children of Kalat played because they haven't any little islet.

35. Sanau lives here. His wife hasn't any children. She has breasts like a young girl.

36. This is Kalo. This house belongs to Tuain. He's my mother's brother. He's going to go and live in Kemai's house when Kemai goes to Tchalalo to fish.

37. This house belongs to Kalo too. My mother belongs to Kalo. So does Sain, but she belongs to Kalat too.

38. This is where Sapa lives. She is going to marry Nauna. She knows it so she can't come and play on our islet.

39. Kapeli's mother lives here. So does Kapeli.

VII

A SAMPLE LEGEND
THE STORY OF THE BIRD "NDRAME"

NDRAME married Kasomu.* He wanted to go
and work sago. He said, "Kasomu, a little sago towards the mouth, give it to me, that I may eat."
Kasomu said, "Ndrame, I have become ill." Ndrame
put the food in his mouth. He ate. He took sago
cutter, sago strainer, rope bag for sago. He went to
work sago. The sun went down. He came here to
the village. He said, "Kasomu, a little sago towards
the mouth, I will eat." Kasomu lied that she was ill.
She painted herself with ashes. Ndrame he put food
in his mouth. He ate. He went to work sago. Kasomu
stood up. She put on a good grass skirt. She took
her shoulder bag. She took lime, betel nut, pepper
leaf. She went to the mangrove swamp. She called
Karipo.† "Kailo fish never mind! Mwasi fish never
mind! Paitcha fish never mind! Ndrame has gone.
Come here, we two will stop together." Karipo he
came here. They two stopped together. They two together. They two together. Kasomu, she said: "This
is the time that Ndrame will be returning here to the
village. You fly away and I will go to the village."
She came here to the village. She bound fast her forehead. She bound fast her belly. She bound fast her

* Fresh water clam.
† A bird.

[360]

wrists. She painted herself with ashes. She sleeps in the men's house. Ndrame he came here. He said: "Kasomu, a little sago to the mouth, I will eat." Kasomu she said: "Ndrame, I have become ill. Who is it who wishes to work a little sago for the mouth, to be eaten?" Ndrame he put food in his mouth. He ate. He sleeps. At dawn he took sago cutter, he went to work sago. Kasomu breaks the rope away. She washed. She puts on a grass skirt. She takes shoulder basket, betel, pepper leaf, and lime. She goes down to the mangrove swamp. "Karipo, kailo fish never mind! Mwasi fish never mind. Paitcha fish never mind! Ndrame has gone away. Come here to me." They two stop. Ndrame, he returned here. He took his sago cutter. He took the shell of the hollowed-out sago palm. He came here to the village. He here looked for Kasomu. She was not there. He went down to the mangrove swamp. He saw down there Kasomu and Karipo they two together. He took a rope of mangrove. He struck Karipo on the neck. Karipo became long necked. He broke Kasomu. Now there are clams in plenty along the mangrove shore.

This is the type of myth which the Manus share with many other Melanesian peoples and to which they attach little importance. Such myths are not invoked in discussions of natural phenomena. The identity of the principal characters as birds and a clam is practically lost as it is customary for human beings to be so named. Children who have heard scraps of such stories tend to think of the characters as human beings who once lived. The monotonous reiteration of adultery in the tales does not interest the children. If the adults ever stimulated their interest by prefacing a tale with, "Do you know why the karipo has such a long neck?" or "Do you know why there are so many shells in the mangrove swamp?" and then told the tale to the children, the results in children's interest in tales would presumably be quite different.

VIII

210 people
  44 married couples
  87 children under or just at puberty
   9 young people past puberty, unmarried
  20 widows
   6 widowers

1.9 children per married couple
53 households
1.6 children per household
Of the 87 children, 24 or 26% are adopted

Sex ratio for people under 40, 100%
Sex ratio for entire population, 86.92
     (due to excess of aged widowed females)

RECORDS OF FIFTEEN PERI WOMEN *

					Children	
Woman	Order of Marriages	Births	Sex	Age of Death	Age now Alive	
Ngasaseu	1	0				
	2	1	f			
		2	m	Under 1 mo.		
		3	f		3	yrs.
		4	f		2	mos.

* These I have checked so extensively as to consider them reliable.

[363]

Woman	Order of Marriages	Births	Sex	Age of Death	Children Age now Alive	
Ilan	I	1	m		3	yrs.
		2	f		6	mos.
Pwailep	I	0				
Indalo	I	1	f	Under 1 mo.		
		2	m	Under 1 mo.		
		3	f	Under 1 mo.		
		4	m	Under 1 mo.		
	2	5	m	At birth		
		6	f	At birth		
		7	f		4	yrs.
		8	m		1	yr.
Indolo	I	1	m		12	yrs.
		2	m		10	yrs.
		3	f		7	yrs.
		4	f		5	yrs.
		5	m		5	yrs.
Ngalen	I	1	m	Under 1 mo.		
		2	m		3	yrs.
	2	3	m	Under 1 mo.		
		4	f	Under 1 mo.		
Mateun	I	1	m		7	yrs.
		2	f		5	yrs.
		3	f	At birth		
		4	m		2½	yrs.
		5	m			infant
Iamet	I	1	m	Stillbirth		
	2	1	m	Stillbirth		
		2	m	Under a yr.		
		3	m	Under a yr.		
		4	m	Under a yr.		
		5	m	Under a yr.		
		6	m	Under a yr.		
Melen	I	1	f	Under 1 mo.		

APPENDIX VIII

Woman	Order of Marriages	Births	Sex	Age of Death	Children Age now Alive	
		2	f		3	yrs.
Patali	1	1	f		8	yrs.
	2	2	m	Under 1 mo.		
		3	f		3	yrs.
Sain	1	1	f	1 month		
Main	1	1	f	1 month		
	2					
	3					
	4					
	5					
Ngakam	1	0				
	2	1	f		13	yrs.
		2	f		11	yrs.
		3	m	Under 1 mo.		
		4	f	Under 1 mo.		
		5	f	Under 1 mo.		
	3	6	f		6	yrs.
		7	m	Under 3 mo.		
		8	m		2½	yrs.
		9	f		3	mos.
Ngakume	1	1	m	Miscarriage		
	2	2	m	Under 3 mos.		
	3	3	m	Under 1 yr.		
		4	m		2½	yrs.
Ngatchumu	1	1	m	Under 3 mos.		
		2	m	Under 3 mos.		
		3	m	Under 3 mos.		
		4	m	Under 3 mos.		
		5	m	Under 3 mos.		
		6	m		8	yrs.
		7	f		5	yrs.
		8	m		3	yrs.
		9	f		1½	yr.

Analysis of These Results Shows

15 women still of childbearing age
30 marriages
65 births
34 died under three years old, 31 under 3 months
Of these births 40 were males, 25 died; 25 were females,
9 died
Result: 15 males, 16 females

Household Record Sheet

House Owner   clan   genealogy

Marriages   How disrupted

Children by each marriage

Present whereabouts of these children   If dead, cause of death

Relationship of first wife to himself

Who financed his marriage

Who is his guardian spirit

Can he divine

Has he sago lands or right to work sago anywhere

What birth exchanges has he financed

What marriages is he financing

Wife of House Owner   clan   genealogy

Marriages   How disrupted

Children by each marriage   If dead, age and cause of death

Relationship to first husband

Who financed her marriages

Who financed her birth feasts
Is she a medium
Who is her control
Has she any sago land or right to work sago

| Own children of this marriage | age | sex | betrothed | adopted elsewhere by whom |
| Adopted children | age | sex | betrothed | Relative from whom they were adopted |

Other people living in the household, age, sex, marital status relationship.
If father-in-law daughter-in-law situation, has tabu been removed?
If husband has thrown away his divining bone, why?
If wife has renounced her mediumship, why?

Child's Record Sheet

Name		Household number
Name of father	House no.	Clan
Name of mother	House no.	Clan
Adopted		
Betrothed		
Suckled	Date stopped	Food eaten

Chews   betel,   nut, pepper leaf   Smokes pipe cigarette
Wears clothing   Urinates in public   Dances
Swims   Swims under water   punts small canoe
                                           punts large canoe   paddles
Owns a canoe
Owns armlets   belt   beads
Catches small fish   Uses spear   bow
Households familiar
Geographical range of play
Parent preference
Chosen companions
Games played: 1   2   3   4

1. Shadow game. Depends upon guessing the identity of the shadow of a child who is purposely distorting it.
2. *Cockero.* A form of "drop the handkerchief" where the person who is "it" tags some player in the ring.
3. *Caleboosh.* A form of prisoners' base
4. *Muli ball.* A form of football played with a wild lime.
   (*2, 3, and 4 are almost certainly introduced games.*)

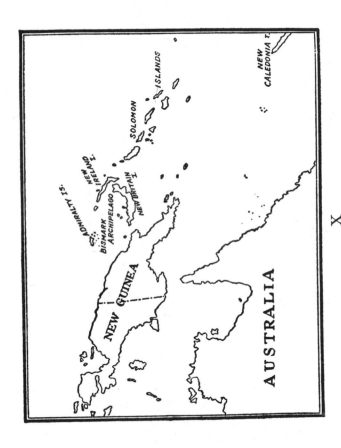

X

MAP SHOWING POSITION OF THE ADMIRALTY ISLANDS

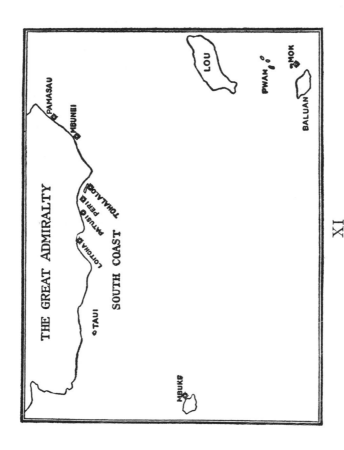

XI

MAP SHOWING POSITION OF THE MANUS VILLAGES

INDEX AND GLOSSARY

INDEX AND GLOSSARY

INDEX AND GLOSSARY

INDEX AND GLOSSARY

INDEX AND GLOSSARY

INDEX AND GLOSSARY